CULTURAL RIGHTS

Cultural Rights aims to combine sociology of culture and cultural studies approaches to provide an innovative interpretation of contemporary culture. It develops Walter Benjamin's arguments on the effects of mechanical reproduction to see what has happened to 'originality' and 'authenticity' in postmodern culture. One aspect of this culture is that reproduction and simulation have become limitless, so that distinguishing what is real from what is fabricated is a problem of daily life for everyone.

Celia Lury establishes a clear framework for studying these matters by comparing a regime of cultural rights ordered by copyright, authorship and originality with one defined by trademark, branding and simulation. This move is illustrated through concise and accessible histories of three major cultural technologies – print, broadcasting and information technology – and the presentation of research into the contemporary culture industry. The gendered dimensions of this transformation are explored by looking at the significance of the category of 'women' in the process of cultural reproduction. *Cultural Rights* will be of interest to students in the sociology of culture, cultural studies and women's studies.

Celia Lury lectures in Women's Studies and Cultural Studies in the sociology department of Lancaster University.

INTERNATIONAL LIBRARY OF SOCIOLOGY
Founded by Karl Mannheim

Editor: John Urry
University of Lancaster

CULTURAL RIGHTS

Technology, legality and personality

Celia Lury

London and New York

First published in 1993
by Routledge
11 New Fetter Lane, London EC4P 4EE

Simultaneously published in the USA and Canada
by Routledge
29 West 35th Street, New York, NY 10001

Typeset in Baskerville from the author's wordprocessing disks by
NWL Editorial Services, Langport, Somerset

Printed and bound in Great Britain by
Biddles Ltd, Guildford and King's Lynn

British Library Cataloguing in Publication Data
A catalogue record for this book is available from the British Library.

Library of Congress Cataloging in Publication Data
Lury, Celia.
Cultural Rights: technology, legality, and personality / Celia Lury
P.   cm.   – (The International Library of Sociology)
Includes bibliographical references and index.
1. Culture. 2. Intellectual property. 3. Copyright.
4. Trademarks. 5. Printing. 6. Broadcasting. 7. Information
technology.   I. Title.   II. Series.
HM101.L87   1993   92–37656
306 – dc 20   CIP

ISBN 0–415–03155–9
ISBN 0–415–09578–6 (pbk)

CONTENTS

Acknowledgements

Many friends and colleagues have contributed to the ideas and arguments expressed in this book. I would like to acknowledge the enthusiasm and encouragement of Nick Abercrombie, Lisa Adkins, Sarah Franklin, Liz Greenhalgh, Geoff Hurd, Scott Lash, Karen Lury, Janet Newman, Stephen Pope, Chris Rojek, Dan Shapiro and Jackie Stacey. I would especially like to thank John Urry for inviting me to contribute to the International Library in Sociology series, his sound editiorial advice and his patience in waiting for the appearance of this contribution.

1

INTRODUCTION

There has been much debate in recent years about the significance and impact of cultural studies (Hall, 1987; Turner, 1990; Franklin *et al.*, 1991; Grossberg *et al.*, 1992): its prospects, its potential relation to the academy and to politics are all uncertain. Whatever its future as a free-standing field of intellectual enquiry, however, there is little doubt that its emergence in Britain in the 1970s contributed to a radical rethinking of approaches to the study of culture in a range of disciplines. This book seeks to develop a conceptual framework within what might be called the sociology of culture, but a sociology which has been disturbed by the insights offered by cultural studies. It thus draws on both institutional analyses of the culture industry (DiMaggio, 1977; Coser *et al.*, 1982; Garnham, 1979; Wolff, 1990) and cultural studies (Hall and Jefferson, 1976; Johnson, 1983; CCCS, 1982a; CCCS, 1982b; Women's Studies Group, 1978).

This hybrid framework employs a number of terms which have been chosen to avoid a priori privileging of particular processes, including 'cultural value' which is used to refer to meaning or symbolic content. The model of value implied is not a representational one: value here is not intrinsically a derivative or metonymic property; it is not finite, determinate or distributable. Rather value is seen as a regulative medium of preference (Fekete, 1987); and the organisation of value is explicated as a function of the force field of value, a network of strategic evaluations, or a circulation process of a collective system of value relations and practices. Rather than seeking to develop a 'grand' theory of value then, as might have been the aim of some sociologies of culture, the intention here is to investigate some of the ways in which what Fekete calls the

1

medium of 'alternativity' has historically been realised in variable forms in social life.

Perhaps the most important term in this exploration is that of *reproduction* or, more specifically, the processes of cultural reproduction. It is a term which is used widely in cultural and social theory, and its everyday meanings are diverse, ranging from procreation through propagation and multiplication to making a copy, or simply a copy itself. Its significance for a sociology of culture has been lucidly captured by Raymond Williams, whose book *Culture* (1981) and other writings have been an inspiration for this work. In a chapter in *Culture*, Williams points out that reproduction is inherent in the very concept of culture. However, he also notes that while reproduction shows up the temporal dimension of culture, in the sense of continuity in the transmission of meaning, its use has not always been historical; furthermore, as a term it can obscure the processes of change, struggle and competition. However, it is in these two respects, most particularly, that the attention within cultural studies to the specificity of the processes of meaning making has been particularly illuminating.

Bearing these problems in mind, this introduction will provide a preliminary outline of the meanings of the term reproduction as it is used in this book. At an abstract level, it refers to the complex cycle of the production, distribution and reception of cultural works, that is, works (objects, performances or services) whose primary purpose is the making of meaning. However, it is the relations between these moments in a cycle or mode of reproduction which are of particular concern here (Johnson, 1983); the advantages of such an approach having been thrown into relief in the light of the recent pendulum swing from an emphasis on text to audience in cultural studies. Clearly, however, these relations are not fixed at an abstract level, but, rather, are historically specific: each moment in a cycle is both variously determined, and stands in various relations of determination to each other. Such modes of reproduction can be seen in terms of power, or as fields of forces, and the relations between each moment are subject to change.

The concept of reproduction can be used to analyse such changes in the cycle of production, distribution and reception in (at least) two inter-related senses. The first concerns the ways in which this cycle involves, literally, some form of reproduction or

2

copying as part of the moment of production. As Williams notes, reproduction in this sense operates along a continuum from the uniform, in the sense of the production of exact, accurate copies, to the generative, that is, the creation of intrinsically variable individual examples of a type. Walter Benjamin, in his well-known essay, 'The work of art in the age of mechanical reproduction' (1970), identified the significance of technologies of culture for changes in the functioning of this continuum within cultural practice through an investigation of the impact and implications of what he called mechanical (or technical) reproduction.

As Chapter 2 suggests, one of the strengths of Benjamin's analysis in this respect is that he does not take a narrow, technically determinist view of the role of technology, but rather explores the conditions in which a technology is realised as a cultural apparatus. This book takes up this approach, and extends the historical range of Benjamin's analysis through a consideration of not only mechanical, but also electronic and micro-electronic technologies of culture, and explores their implications for the regimes of copying which characterise particular modes of cultural reproduction. In each case, the aim is not only to explore a key moment in the historical emergence of a particular technology, but also to look at their characteristic modes of address, cultural forms and accessibility.

The introduction of these technologies of culture made possible the separation of cultural works from their context of production, resulting in a new mobility for cultural goods. This is seen to produce a decisive transformation in cultural reproduction, described in Chapter 2 as a shift from a mode of *repetition* to one of *replication*, terms which refer to different kinds of copying or reproduction in this first sense. It is argued that it is only with the emergence of the mode of replication that the asymmetry or divergence between cultural and social reproduction associated with the modernisation process arises (Williams, 1981; Lash, 1990).

Linked with this sense of reproduction as copying, the first section of the book (Chapters 2, 3 and 4) adopts a framework to explore the *rights of copying* existing in relation to cultural works. At the heart of the argument in this section is the view that the modern technologies of culture provided the potential for unlimited copying of cultural works, and that this potential has been regulated (that is, both realised and limited, or rather given a social shape) through specific regimes of rights of copying. While these regimes are codified in law, it is suggested that their operation is not solely juridically determined, but is, rather, the outcome of economic, political and cultural struggles between the participants in cycles of cultural reproduction. The two principal regimes associated with replication as a mode of cultural reproduction identified here are those of copyright and trademark; such regimes constitute cultural works as intellectual property, and define the terms under which such property may be copied and distributed for reception. As such, the analysis of such regimes of rights provides one means of investigating the distribution of power within cycles of cultural reproduction.

A further concern in the chapters in this first section is the analysis of the administration or regulation of cultural production; a particular concern is the regulation of innovation within cultural production, and the author function (Foucault, 1979), supported by copyright, is identified as a key mechanism in the recognition of innovation as originality. This example of the strategic manipulation of innovation in high culture formations is contrasted with the invention of novelty within the iterated or serial production which characterises popular culture. However, novelty itself is seen to be being gradually subsumed within a more general process of branding in contemporary culture, defined, in simple terms, as a set of techniques attempting to link image and perception. It is a term taken from the advertising industry; in this context, the function of the creation of a brand, as Baudrillard notes, is,

> to signal the product; its secondary function is to mobilise connotations of affect. . . . The psychological restructuration of the consumer is performed through a single word – Philips, Olida, General Motors – a word capable of summing up both the diversity of objects and a host of diffuse meanings. . . . In effect this is the only language in which the object speaks to us, the only one it has invented.
> (Baudrillard, 1988: 17)[1]

In relation to the culture industry, it is used here to refer to the creation of cultural works which signal or advertise themselves. This is seen to be achieved through the simulation of innovation or the strategic manipulation of exhibition value (Benjamin,

1970). Associated with the development of branding is the emergence of a new regime of rights associated with trademark law, in which the commercial operation of branding not only within but also outside the culture industry is protected.

The second major understanding of reproduction that is employed here refers to the ways in which the moment of the production of cultural works is, to the extent to which it can be seen in terms of the process of communication, inextricably tied to the moment of reception and an audience. The usefulness of the term reproduction is thus that it indicates the ways in which production is always oriented towards the moment of reception, and cannot be analysed in isolation from this moment in a cycle of production, distribution and reception. Modern technologies of culture can be seen to have had an enormous impact on reproduction in this sense too; they enable reception in multiple ways, across diverse spatial and temporal dimensions, and with various degrees and types of accessibility.

Perhaps the most significant innovation within technologies of culture from this point of view has been the development of techniques which make possible the separability of the cultural work from its context of production; such techniques instituted a radical split, or 'deep contradiction' in Williams' phrase, between production and reception, and made cultural works mobile, cutting them loose from the ties of convention and ritual. It must be stressed that this split, and the associated mobility of cultural works, does not render redundant the second understanding of reproduction advanced here; but it does indicate the complexity of the processes through which modern cultural production is organised for and in relation to reception and the audience.

As John Thompson (1990) argues, the institution of a fundamental break between production and reception of cultural works provided the focus for the specialised development of media as *productive* forces; cultural works came to be, literally, mediated by the technical media in which they were fixed and transmitted in a largely one-way flow of messages from the producer to the recipient. It is on this basis that the media have been seen to challenge, at a very fundamental level, the nature of the exchange between producers and audiences; indeed, it has been suggested that they fabricate communication by making impossible the reciprocity of speech and response which underpins its definition in ideal terms. Baudrillard writes,

5

To understand properly the term response, one must appreciate it in a meaning at once strong, symbolic, and primitive: power belongs to him [*sic*] who gives and to whom no return can be made. To give it and to do it in such a way that no return can be made, is to break exchange to one's own profit and to institute a monopoly: the social process is out of balance.

(Baudrillard, 1988: 208)

Thompson further argues that one consequence of this development is that the moments of production and distribution in modern modes of cultural reproduction are characterised by a distinctive form of indeterminacy, in that producers are deprived of a direct and continuous monitoring of audiences' responses. It is argued in the second section (Chapters 5, 6, 7 and 8) that one response made by producers to this indeterminacy has been the *internalisation* of some notion of the audience. This process of internalisation includes the invocation of particular audiences, with specific trainings and dispositions; the major types of internalisation discussed here will be the invocation of the audience as public, as market, and as consumers.

This process of internalisation is seen as one of the principal mechanisms which enable production personnel to reduce the indeterminacy stemming from the break between production and reception. As such, it is obviously particularly significant for the economic valorisation of cultural goods, since the commercial success of cultural production is crucially dependent upon the nature and extent of reception; as Jody Berland writes,

the profitable dissemination of entertainment commodities ... [relies] on the ability of producers to make reception – requiring more refined knowledge of audiences' situation and location as well as their taste and interpretive response – part of the productive apparatus.

(Berland, 1992: 40)

However, internalisation is also an issue for those concerned with political and social valorisation. This process should not, though, be seen as an external requirement on cultural production; although clearly socially organised, it is recognisable as a particular, historically specific, form of the more general process described above as cultural reproduction, that is, production organised for and in relation to reception. Moreover, this process of internalisation is by no means always or entirely successful; on the contrary, it is commonly unsuccessful: that is, the internalised audience does not often correspond with the actual recipients and their concrete activity. These activities are described here in terms of *reactivation*, another term taken from Benjamin, and referring to the diverse activities in which cultural works are put to use in their recipients' everyday life.

Nevertheless, it is argued that this process of internalisation has been one of the central mechanisms through which cultural reproduction has been linked to social reproduction. More particularly, it is suggested that the process of internalisation, consisting in the (implicit or explicit) adoption of a particular conception of the audience and an implied activity of reception, has contributed, directly, to the development of particular cultural forms, and, indirectly, to the formation, identity and influence of particular social groups defined through the implied activity of cultural reception. In this way, culture is considered as an aspect of the increasing governmentality of social life (Bennett, 1992). As was suggested earlier, it must be stressed that the process of internalisation does not operate in the abstract, but is historically variable, and the second section of the book is concerned with the ways in which this process of internalisation has operated in practice. For this reason, Chapters 5, 6 and 7 take as their focus the emergence of the distinctive internalisations of the audience associated with the development of three particular technologies of culture: print, broadcasting and communication.

The penultimate chapter, Chapter 8, is also concerned with the relations between cultural and social reproduction, and, in line with the immediately preceding chapters, presents an account of the ways in which the internalisation of specific conceptions of the audience has shaped the processes of cultural and social reproduction. More particularly, however, it is concerned with the gender differentiation which marks this process of internalisation, and seeks to establish the social and political implications of the gendered process of internalisation, defined as the differential inclusion and exclusion of male and female recipients. This chapter thus employs a conception of technology as a set of techniques to look at both how the processes of cultural production inform the changing constitution of the category of women, and the ways in which definitions of femininity shape the course of the development of cultural production.

The relations between producers and audiences, including this process of internalisation, can be analysed in terms of the framework of regimes of rights of copying introduced earlier. Such regimes provide one set of conditions structuring these relations within a cycle of reproduction. So, for example, the legal framework of copyright adjudicates between the need to secure the free circulation of ideas, a process which is commonly accepted to be integral to the functioning of the public sphere, and the commercial demand for monopoly rights in copying and the associated creation of markets in cultural commodities. Through this process of adjudication, copyright has helped to structure relations between producers and audiences in the modes of cultural reproduction associated with print, broadcasting and communication technologies. Regimes of rights can thus be considered in terms of both the possibilities and constraints that they offer cultural producers in the organisation of the process of internalisation, and the actual conditions that they offer for reactivation.

Conversely, the mobility of cultural goods made possible by modern cultural technologies and the associated indeterminacy of the relations between producers and audiences have, in turn, shaped the effectivity and distribution of rights of copying. In particular, it is argued in Chapters 4, 7 and 8 that recent developments in technologies of culture have increased this indeterminacy in ways which have contributed to a change in relations of authority between producers and audiences, specifically, a shift in authority from producers to the audience (Abercrombie, 1991). This shift is legally acknowledged in the previously noted movement from copyright to trademark as the principal legal principle through which rights in intellectual property are constituted in relation to audience practices, and is related to what is seen as an increasing, although not complete, convergence between cultural and social reproduction.

The central aim of the book is thus to explore the complexities of the process of cultural reproduction, that is, the cycle of production, distribution and reception of cultural works from a historical perspective. This process will be explored primarily through an analysis of what have been called regimes of rights, a term used to pinpoint the key sets of relations through which

8

cultural works are variably constituted as intellectual property. Struggles over the exploitation of such rights is seen as an integral aspect of such analysis if the problems of ahistoricism and a failure to recognise conflict are to be addressed.

NOTE

1 The movement by a number of major companies (including, for example, Guinness) to list product names as assets in their balance sheets can be seen as an attempt to claim ownership rights to the 'host of diffuse meanings' associated with the product. Not surprisingly, this move has been supported within the advertising industry on the grounds not only that 'there is a fantastic value to be had in the ownership of a successful brand', but also that 'like most other assets on a balance sheet, brands must be properly maintained' (Kirvan, *Campaign*, 3 March 1989: 39). What has been described as consumer terrorism, acts such as the addition of poison, razor blades or glass in food substances, drugs or other consumer goods, with the aim of damaging the manufacturer is only effective to the extent to which it is able to undermine such ownership rights through the use – or rather abuse – of public recognition developed through branding.

Part I

REGIMES OF RIGHTS

2

FROM REPETITION TO REPLICATION

Howard Becker starts his book on the constitution of art worlds (1982) with a quotation in which Anthony Trollope thanks the old groom whose duty it was to wake him every morning at ten to six with a cup of coffee since, the novelist suggests, he may owe more to him than to anyone else for his literary success. For Becker, the tale serves as an illustration of the fact that it is the co-ordination of the sometimes mundane activities of a number of people which leads to the production of art works. He remarks, 'Through their cooperation, the art work we eventually see or hear comes to be and continues to be. The work always shows signs of that cooperation' (Becker 1982: 1). Yet, as Becker also notes, being woken at 5.50am does not necessarily positively contribute to the quality of any work produced at that time: 'The way the work is produced bears no necessary relationship to its quality. Every way of producing art works for some people and not for others: every way of producing art produces work of every conceivable grade of quality' (1982: 2). In short, while the art or cultural work always 'shows signs', or bears the imprint, of the way it was produced, the organisation of that process has no direct relationship to the quality of what is produced; nor does it provide a guarantee of its popular appeal or its commercial success.

This paradox has provided particular problems for those concerned with the process of capital accumulation, since they have sought to organise cultural production in ways which will increase the likelihood of the works that are produced being of predictable grades of quality and guaranteed commercial successes. This chapter and the next two will consider the specific problems this need for predictability raises in the field of cultural

13

production, and, in particular, investigate how creative labour has been managed in the service of the production of cultural commodities. It will suggest that the development and implementation of modern technologies of culture (see below) have had significant effects on this process.

These three chapters will take up the concepts and terms of analysis provided by Walter Benjamin in his well-known essay on the changes in the aesthetic qualities of the cultural work associated with the rise of mass or mechanical reproduction (1970). In this essay, Benjamin argues for the significance of the reproducibility, or technical ease of copying, of a cultural work for an understanding of the terms of the realisation of cultural value, including the categories of aesthetic quality. However, some of the ambivalence which characterises Benjamin's analysis of the impact of the development of what were then still relatively new cultural technologies may be attributed to the fact that, at times, he fails to distinguish between the technical possibilities of reproducibility allowed by particular cultural means, and the inevitably selective realisation of those possibilities as they occur in particular social contexts.[1] The actual realisation of these possibilities will be explored here in terms of two major modes of cultural reproduction, repetition and replication.

These two modes of cultural reproduction will be differentiated not only in terms of the different ways in which techniques of copying shape production, but also in terms of the different relations between producers and the audience. The importance attached to this second understanding of reproduction derives from the view that (actual or anticipated) reception is an integral part of cultural form and creative intention; that is, the expectation of having recipients is a structural element of the notion of a cultural work. From this perspective, reception has always been a concern for cultural producers; in this sense, reception is not external to the process of cultural production, but is rather always an integral aspect of its organisation. However, while some kind of reception is always contained within cultural production, its potential spatial and temporal dimensions have changed over time with the availability of different cultural technologies. These changes will also be investigated as part of the shift from a mode of repetition to one of replication.

In his book *Culture*, Raymond Williams provides a useful

typology with which to distinguish between different kinds of technical reproducibility or types of copying (1981: 88). He distinguishes between 'that class of material means of cultural production which depends wholly or mainly on inherent, constituted physical resources', that is, the body, and 'that other class which depends wholly or mainly on the use or transformation of non-human material objects and forces'. In relation to the first class, the dependence upon 'inherent, constituted physical resources' means not only that the artist's physical presence in front of an audience is required for a cultural work to come into being, but that the work's 'material' existence is coterminous with its performance; spoken poetry, storytelling, dance and song are examples of cultural forms produced with the use of such means. Within this class of means of cultural production, then, copying takes the form of physical or bodily repetition; furthermore, the producer and audience share the same location, and the relation between them is immediate and direct. The organisation of the two facets of cultural reproduction in this way is described here as a mode of *repetition*.

The implications of this mode for the realisation of cultural value are described by Benjamin in his article on 'The art of storytelling' (1970) where he evokes the 'new beauty in what is vanishing' through an exploration of the practice of storytelling. To Benjamin, the aura of the storytelling form, which he sees as the basis of the epic, was embedded in a peasant and artisan culture in which tradition was deeply respected and in which the oral transmission of counsel and wisdom, 'the epic side of truth', was an important thread in the maintenance of the fabric of community. Furthermore, every 'real' story necessarily 'contains, openly or covertly, something useful' (1970: 86); in this sense, this mode of cultural reproduction is integrated with, or is symmetrical with, social reproduction.

Benjamin defines storytelling as 'the art of repeating stories' (1970: 91): 'The storyteller takes what he tells from experience – his own or that reported by others. And he in turn makes it the experience of those who are listening to the tale' (1970: 87). The storyteller draws on experience and in narrating turns that experience into the experience of the listeners. The listeners attend to the story in a mode of reception – what Benjamin terms relaxation – which allows them the possibility of retelling the story, and, in consequence, the narrative of the story is constituted through 'its layers of a variety of retellings' (1970: 93). In the most general sense, then, memory or a shared and usable past is the tradition of retellings within which stories acquire their aura as works of art. This is what lies behind Benjamin's comment that, 'The uniqueness of a work of art is inseparable from its being imbedded in the fabric of tradition' (1970: 225). Each individual story – each telling – is a unique event within a general mode of repetition.

The unique aura of a work of art thus derives from its repetition within a rooted, spatially and temporally particularised context, and is realised within a personal and particular mediating practice between producer and audience. In this way, the notion of aura is implicated in an understanding of history, not as a chain of cause and effect, but as a kind of tradition in which there is no radical separation between past and present. This is described by Benjamin as Messianic time, a simultaneity of past and present in an instantaneous but particular time and place. In this and other ways, then, repetition, as a cultural mode of reproduction, was both shaped by and helped to shape a particular mode of social reproduction.

This inter-relationship can be further explicated by looking at the social limits which helped to produce this process of repetition. It has been suggested that the existence of the art work was both spatially and temporally limited by the need for the physical presence of the performer, in this case the storyteller, but it was also constrained by the (social and cultural) conditions of the performance. These conditions can be understood in relation to the two dimensions of reproducibility identified earlier. On the one hand, while the 'same' poem, story, dance or song could in principle be repeated or copied by anyone, this means of cultural production was often combined with the differentiation and specialisation of creative labour through some kind of recognition of the functions of the artist. Thus, although, as Williams notes, it is important to remember that 'dancing and singing, in their most general forms, have been and have remained, in complex as in simple societies, the most widespread and popular cultural practices' (1981: 90) most societies have seen the emergence of an increasingly complex set of cultural divisions between artists and audiences, and the development of artistic techniques requiring a high degree of specialisation in relation to this class of material means.

16

On the other hand, other restrictions still have conventionally been placed on the audience for certain cultural works, often by means of some kind of association with particular rituals requiring limits in terms of time and place of performance, or constraints on the social composition of the audience, including, at the most general level, those necessary for the maintenance of the community. The audience for this mode of repetition was therefore limited in both size and composition. In general, then, these social limits to the organisation of cultural reproduction, given meaning in ritual and tradition, served to exclude certain groups from participation in the specialised forms of repetition associated with this means of cultural production. Nevertheless, because of the reliance upon physical resources, there was, and is still, a generality of access to at least some of the techniques involved in this means of cultural production, and a similarly wide, if not wider, degree of access in terms of reception.

Turning to techniques in the second class of means of cultural production, Williams makes the following distinctions of type:

i) combination of the use of external objects with the use of inherent physical resources . . .
ii) development of instruments of new kinds of performance . . .
iii) selection, transformation and production of separable objects, which then carry cultural significance . . .
iv) development of separable material systems of signification, devised for cultural significance . . .
v) development of complex amplificatory, extending and reproductive technical systems, which make possible not only new kinds of presentation of all the preceding types, but also new kinds of presentation of practices still otherwise based on the use of inherent and constituted resources.

(Williams, 1981: 91)

The first two types are relatively continuous with the first class in terms of the possibilities they offer for reproducibility in so far as they still contribute to a performance of sorts. However, the separability of the signs of creative labour from the performer and the fixing of those signs in either objects or material systems of signification mean that the third and fourth types offer new possibilities for reproducibility – including systematic, exact

17

copying or *replication*. That is, once the art work has a fixed material form in which the signs of creative labour are embedded, it can, subject to the reproducibility of the techniques employed in its construction, be copied by someone other than the originating artist. It is this possibility – what Benjamin refers to as mechanical reproduction, but will here be called replication – which has been extensively developed by commercial interests.

However, the actual effects of the development of this class of means of cultural production were initially limited. In the medieval period, for example, cultural production usually continued to assume the form of the manufacture of cultural artefacts that were singular and unique. Except for the multiple images produced by the use of woodcuts – a technique which produced considerable variation of texture and grain between different prints – and the limited number of manuscripts that were reproduced in multiple, but always variable, form by the clerical copyists of the Church, the courts and the universities, most cultural artefacts were singular and, usually, bound and limited to a specific context (a particular church, for example). Nevertheless, it is generally accepted that from the invention of movable type in the mid-fifteenth century onwards, a series of technical developments – first, metal engraving techniques and lithography, and then photography, film, sound recording techniques, offset litho and video recording – contributed towards a transformation in the organisation of cultural reproduction. As Benjamin observed (1970), this now typically took the form not of the production of a singular artefact as an end in itself; rather, the aim was the production of an original, of something that could be copied exactly – that is, replicated – for distribution.

It is as a consequence of these developments that, as Williams argues, reproductive technology informs 'a major cultural mode' (1981: 96) in modern societies. The characteristics of this cultural mode will be explored in this chapter by looking at the way in which, as Benjamin suggests, the commercial exploitation of this technology was organised around the production of originals that could be replicated, that is, as a mode of replication. This is not to suggest that the technologies mentioned above had inevitable cultural effects of standardisation or homogenisation; rather, their use was the site of struggle for innovation and diversity. On the one hand, these modern technologies presented a threat to the older social institutions of cultural and social reproduction, such as the Church and the state, and their introduction resulted in struggles over access to the means of cultural production, the organisation of licensing, censorship – particularly in relation to 'official information' and 'obscenity' – and other forms of control. Williams suggests that these struggles, while most evident in direct cultural production, were most complex in education, where the direct controls of established institutions were easier to maintain, and the influence of market forces was less.

On the other hand, the new forms of market culture deriving from the technologies of replication also presented a challenge to the already existing repetitive folk (largely oral) culture. This relationship is often seen in terms of an imposition of a standardised mass culture from above. Benjamin suggests, however, that there was a broad social basis to the decay of aura, which he relates to the decline of community and the increasing political and cultural significance of the masses and their desire: 'to bring things "closer" spatially and humanly, which is just as ardent as their bent toward overcoming the uniqueness of every reality by accepting its reproduction' (1970: 225). Both such tendencies were informed by and contributed to a ' "sense of the universal equality of things" which has increased to such a degree that it extracts it even from a unique object by means of reproduction' (1970: 225). This drive to equality is thus related by Benjamin to both the increasing penetration of commodity fetishism into the fabric of everyday life, and to the masses' desire for the removal of inequality, part of which consisted in their attempt to overcome spatial, temporal and social distances, such as those between high and low (economically and culturally), past and present, there and here (Simmel, 1990; Lunn, 1985).

As noted above, the new types of means of communication furthered this aim in so far as they made it technically possible for identical cultural works to exist across space and time, and, through their very form, contributed to the removal of conventions which had previously ordered the second dimension of reproduction, that is, the cultural reception and impact of cultural works. However, such conventions were to be replaced by others, including most importantly those relating to the notion of originality which, it will be argued, replaced the centrality of aura in the interpretation of cultural works; that is,

19

in locating their audiences in an increasingly wider and more diverse range of locations and contexts, modern means of cultural production contribute to and seek to legitimate their own spatial expansion. The social ordering of the uses of the technologies of replication in terms of originality will be investigated here in some detail by looking at the author-function (Foucault, 1979), the legal framework of copyright and the associated constitution of cultural goods as intellectual property. The use of publicity and promotion in mediating relations between the fields of cultural production and reception in relation to the notion of novelty will be considered in the next chapter.

However, it will also be argued that once the cultural work was separable, mobile, the social and cultural conditions of distribution and access – including the techniques of inter-pretation – became more difficult to limit; as Benjamin suggests, 'in permitting the reproduction to meet the beholder or the listener in his own particular situation, [the process of mechanical reproduction] *reactivates* the object reproduced' (1970: 223; my emphasis). In short, he suggests that the exploitation of the possibility of replication increases the possible diversity of reactivations at the point of reception in this general mode of reproduction. Certainly, the industrialisation of cultural pro-duction did make cultural goods available to an increasingly large number of people in an increasingly varied set of contexts: there was an expansion of the sphere of cultural consumption, which can be seen in terms of extended distribution, and an increased mobility of cultural objects as the ties of time and space have been loosened (Williams, 1981; Innis, 1950; Carey, 1989; Harvey, 1989; Berland, 1992).[2]

In particular, the development of the fifth type of material means of communication (that is, reproductive technical systems) radically increased the complexity and possible diversity of these processes of reactivation. It includes technologies not only for the production of cultural goods, but also for their distribution and reception, increasing still further the potential degrees of independence possible at the point of reception. Paradoxically, then, as they extended the possibilities for the commercial exploitation of cultural production, these examples of Williams' second class of means of production also meant that an increasingly independent and more diverse set of conditions came to be effective at another moment in the cycle of reproduction. However, before this destabilising situation can be considered, it is necessary to see how the technologies of replication were initially developed.

ORIGINALITY, COPYRIGHT AND INTELLECTUAL PROPERTY

Williams (1981) suggests that the emergence of the system of patronage was the first stage of the production of cultural works for conscious economic exchange. It saw a move in the position of the cultural producer from that of a specifically instituted practitioner who was an integral part of a social organisation such as the Church or court, to that of a mobile individual professional worker, who was for hire by a patron, either an individual or an organisation. Within this system, a patron provided the artist not only with finance but also with protection or social recognition, and thus helped to create a favourable context within which the artist's work could be received. In return, the patron's own esteem and reputation were enhanced to the extent that the cultural works produced by the sponsored artist were seen to be of a publicly recognised quality. During this period, the early modern, the cultural producer might alternatively have had the position of an artisan – an independent producer who offers his (for it usually was men who were able to take up these positions) own work for sale directly on to the market. However, in what Williams describes as the post-artisanal phase, the producer began to sell his work to either a distributive or a productive intermediary.

In their study of painting, White and White (1965) analyse the first stages of this phase in terms of a shift from systems of patronage to systems dominated by dealers, galleries and critics. They note how, in eighteenth- and nineteenth-century Italy and France, large numbers of wealthy merchants became interested in acquiring paintings as markers of prestige, cultivation and status, as well as for their own pleasure. Simultaneously, many people had become artists, hoping for the successful careers that patronage made possible. Under the patronage system public exhibitions had not been common but, when they were held, brought together enormous numbers of canvases for a relatively short time so that potential patrons could see who they wanted to take on as protégés. However, during this period, more painters wanted patrons than the system could accommodate, and more paintings were produced than could be adequately shown: the system never developed, within its own confines, the ability to place this hoard of unique objects for money. A much larger audience for paintings was needed and could be mobilised, and dealers began to recognise, encourage and cater to new *social markets* rather than to *individual patrons*; that is, dealers facilitated the rise of a relatively large, geographically dispersed, anonymised audience.

White and White note that one consequence of this was the elevation and privileging of the culural producer as an author, who was now freed from direct, personal dependence upon the wishes of an élite set of patrons. They thus imply that the creative autonomy ascribed to the modern notion of the author was one response to the requirement placed upon the cultural producer to meet the relatively impersonal and decontextualised demand which characterised the early stages of production for the market; that is, it was a consequence of the producer's relative freedom not only from the demands of employers *but also from the audience* (for a contrasting view, see Adorno, 1976). Others too have argued that it was precisely the internalisation of the abstractness of the audience as an unknown market and the incorporation of the unpredictability of the orientation of that audience that emancipated the cultural producer. As the function of the cultural work in everyday life became much more indeterminate, or else variously determinable, so the cultural producer's role became much more abstract (Radnoti, 1986).

However, all this is not to suggest that the emergence of market relations did in fact see the freeing of the cultural producer from relations of economic dependence, but rather that the terms of that dependence were altered in such a way as to allow the possibility of significant autonomy for the cultural producer (Williams, 1981). This autonomy was related to the radical division between producer and audience which this conception of the cultural producer confirmed. This dislocation within the mode of cultural reproduction provided, in turn, the conditions for a growing divergence or, in Williams' term, 'asymmetry' between social and cultural reproduction, an asymmetry which was institutionalised as the cultural work came to be defined in terms of purposelessness or lack of functional utility.

This definition was closely linked to the emergence of an understanding of the cultural producer as an author. The privileges accorded to the author have been examined by Foucault (1979) who notes how, in the secularised ritual of Romanticism, the uniqueness of the cultural work itself was more and more displaced by the empirical uniqueness of the creator or of his (and once again the use of a masculine pronoun is not accidental here, see Chapter 8) creative achievement. Foucault suggests that the emerging methods for defining an author – or rather for determining the configuration of the author from existing texts – derived in large part from those used in the Christian tradition to authenticate the texts in its possession; these included the definition of the author as: a standard of quality; a field of conceptual or theoretical coherence; a stylistic uniformity; and a definite historical figure in which a series of events converge. It was within these terms, closely bound in with the emerging Romanticist conceptions of the individual, biography and subjectivity, that authorship was accorded the cultural function of effecting aesthetic discrimination between works: that is, works came to be defined by the quality of the subjective imagination and vision displayed; more specifically, they were ascribed originality to the extent to which they were marked by a distinctive individual stamp.

The author-function thus acted as the locus of asymmetry between cultural and social reproduction, and, simultaneously, provided a means by which the creative labour process could – albeit in the hazy and indeterminate terms of individual originality and genius – be linked to the creative work. Further-more, this link was to be consolidated through the ways in which the author-function was used to help determine the constitution of cultural works as intellectual property through the use of copyright law. It was in terms derived from the functioning of the author in aesthetic discourse that individual works and movements entered the market as 'property'; in short, it was through the author-function that cultural value became a thing, a product and a possession caught in a circuit of property values. What was at stake in this circuit was the limitation of reproduction; it was through the constitution of cultural works as intellectual property, and the allocation of limited rights of reproduction, that the potential instability inherent in reproduction made possible by modern technologies of culture was contained.

The ways in which the author-function was put into law differed within different juridical systems. So, for example, what might be called an author's rights regime developed in France in which authors were accorded a special category of personal rights. This was done by explicitly linking the ownership of intellectual property rights, including the rights of reproduction or copying, with a particular conception of the author as creator. In *Ownership of the Image* (1979), Bernard Edelman examines the nature of this connection, and suggests that it was grounded in the French moral right tradition, that is, the principle of the rights of personality, including the rights of paternity (the 'right to be identified') and integrity (the 'right to object to derogatory treatment of work') (Clark, C. 1986: 203): within this tradition, the work of art could be legally defined as property because it was regarded as the creative expression of what the artist already owned: his self or personality. Thus, it was in relation to the rights of personality that the rights of reproduction were contained in France.

This regime stands in contrast to what might be called a copyers (or copyright) regime in England and in the USA (and in most common-law countries). In this regime, the rights of reproduction are vested in copyright owners rather than directly in cultural producers. Indeed, in England it was only in the eighteenth century that 'the author in his [*sic*] own right appears on the scene' at all (Birrell, quoted in Feltes, 1982: 54). Until then, authors' rights to their texts had only been recognised in common law, and 'copyright' had signified only a stationer's sole right to print and sell copies. 'Property was the right to make copies – not the right of authorship', and copyright was like 'a perpetual lease of personal property . . . for one specific purpose, that of publishing' (Birrell, quoted in Feltes, 1982: 54). It was only with the Statute of Anne (1709) and the series of legal decisions culminating in the judgment in the Donaldson case in 1774 that there came to exist an alienable property right in the text itself. However, while these legal struggles meant that copyright came to be defined as a monopoly of a work, rather than as previously the basis of the monopoly of the book trade, it was still defined as 'a concept to embrace all the rights to be had in connection with published works, *either by the author or the publisher* (Patterson, 1968: 151, quoted in Saunders, 1988: 140; my emphasis). The relationship between author and publisher was left to the terms of their contract for the transfer of economic rights of property, and support for the preservation of the author's moral rights of reputation was relegated to the field of tort – for example, of defamation, injurious falsehood or passing off.[3] Nevertheless, this did not mean that the notion of the author has been without support in the Anglo-American tradition, but that this support has been more indirect than in the French case.

A central distinction in the Anglo-American regime is that between the idea itself, which was not subject to copyright, and the material expression of an idea which was copyrightable.[4] The terms of this distinction between an idea and its expression (in a material substrate capable of reproduction) were initially defined in relation to originality, a quality which, as has been argued, was linked to the author-function. However, this link was necessarily somewhat indirect; for example, in the case of *University of London Press Ltd* v *Universal Tutorial Press Ltd* (1916) Mr Justice Peterson said,

> The word 'original' does not in this connection mean that the work must be the expression of original or inventive thought. Copyright Acts are not concerned with the originality of ideas, but with the expression of thought, and, in the case of 'literary work', with the expression of thought in print and writing. The originality which is required relates to the expression of the thought.
>
> (Quoted in Flint, 1985: 18)

Indeed, according to Frow, originality itself was defined in two linked, although slightly contradictory, ways. This is particularly clear in American law.[5] On the one hand, originality in expression has been distinguished in terms of the causal relationship between an author and the material form in which a work is embodied. Originality in this sense has been explicitly differentiated from novelty:

> Originality is not to be equated with the creation of something which had not hitherto existed; it is the word used to describe the causal relationship between an author and the material form in which a work is embodied.
>
> (Whale, quoted in Frow, 1988: 10)

The Borgian implications of this were summarised by Judge Learned Hands:

'Borrowed the work must indeed not be, for a plagiarist is not himself pro tanto an "author"; but if by some magic a man who had never known it were to compose anew Keats's *Ode on a Grecian Urn*, he would be an "author", and, if he copyrighted it, others may not copy that poem, though they might of course copy Keats's.'

(Quoted in Frow, 1988: 5)

From this point of view the legal criterion of originality demanded no more than that the work display 'something irreducible, something which is one man's alone'. This meant that what was protected was not distinctiveness of expression, not an inherent difference from other expressions, but only whatever distinctiveness derived from the originality of an act of authoring. On the other hand, the 'something irreducible' was also linked to a second definition of originality which was located in the work itself; the law is here interpreted as making a demand for some more than trivial variation to distinguish the work from other works. However, because this is a minimal requirement, 'copyrighted matter need not be strikingly unique or novel, and any distinguishable variation resulting from an author's independent creative activity will suffice' (quoted in Frow, 1988: 9). Significantly, though, it is the copyright category of the 'work of art' (as opposed to other works of the mind) which is seen to require originality in both senses, and thus requires both some indication of the producer's contribution – creativity – and some variation in the nature of the work itself – distinctiveness.

The general point here, however, is that both the French and the Anglo-American regimes of copyright, albeit in ways which are both informed by and help to constitute the broader ideological character of their national cultures, can be seen to have played a special part in the differentiation of creative labour by drawing on the Romantic myth of originality and creativity institutionalised in the author-function. In other words, in both the French and the Anglo-American copyright traditions the legal and the aesthetic were not opposed, but were reconciled in such a way as to secure special conditions, status and recognisability for the creative worker as author. Both regimes served to regulate the exploitation of the possibilities of replication which were offered by the new technologies of culture in a way which simultaneously strengthened the aesthetic functions of the author and protected commercial interests.[6]

The implementation and operation of the author as a legal, commercial and hermeneutic category were further supported by the institutionalisation of the roles of distributive and productive intermediaries. To return to the example of the fine art world, distributive intermediaries such as dealers can be seen to have gradually taken on an active role in the transformation of cultural value into exchange value. This role became increasingly complex as the market grew in size, since potential buyers of the work could no longer be assumed to share a common set of tastes and body of conventional knowledge with artists. In this context, intermediaries began, in the eighteenth century, to construct a shared aesthetic discourse in the sense that they collectively worked to define the standards by which cultural works were selected for distribution and promotion; this meant, in turn, that the exhibition system acquired a new significance for the organisation of artistic texts and their interpretation through the operation of the author-function.

The functioning of the exhibition system was supported by critics who helped, through public explanations and evaluations, to build up an interest in, and demand for, the work of a gallery's artists (Becker, 1982). The gradual institutionalisation of the role of critics, and the creation of distinctly high culture organis-ations, provided the social basis for the eventual emergence of what Rosalind Krauss has called a 'culture of originals' (1988). Such organisations were instrumental in grading the authenticity of cultural works in ways which not only recognised the specificity of the cultural work through the author-function, but also introduced a degree of routine or predictability to cultural production in so far as many authors came to internalise known market relationships in the form of an élite public and produce work which acknowledged the determinations of this public. This development might appear to undermine the argument put forward earlier that the notion of the author as a creative, autonomous individual was related to the emergence of an abstract, unknown audience, not a specific, élite group. It will be argued in Chapter 5, however, that this contradiction is apparent rather than real as a result of the ways in which this group's identity was, in part, defined precisely through its members' self-definition as individuals with a capacity to respond to the abstract, open, dissonant, non-everyday and non-this-worldly character of the works to which they attributed originality (Bourdieu, 1984).

This 'culture of originals' made use of a distribution system in which the people and organisations who distributed cultural works made editorial choices: they refused to distribute some works, required changes in others before distribution, or (most subtly) created a network of facilities and a body of practice which led artists in the world whose works they distributed to make works which fitted easily into that scheme. In general terms, the system came to be organised by reference to a received and traditional body of specialised knowledge to which the dealer and other intermediaries had exclusive access by virtue of education and experience. The circulation of this knowledge came, in turn, to help organise the public sphere in which it was created.

Becker suggests that critical discourse was especially influential in what he terms 'artistic revolutions' since it explained 'what the previous standard was, and how the new work now shows that the standard was too restricted and that there are in fact other things to enjoy' (1982: 112). White and White (1965) cite a representative example of the kind of criticism which explained Impressionist painting to the French art-buying public:

'In the field of color, they have made a genuine discovery whose origin cannot be found elsewhere. . . . The discovery properly consists in having recognized that full light decolorizes tones, that sunlight reflected by objects tends, by virtue of its clarity, to bring them back to the luminous unity which dissolves its seven spectral rays into a single colorless refulgence, which is light. From intuition to intuition, they have succeeded . . . in splitting the light into its beams, its elements, and in recomposing its unity by means of the general harmony of the colors of the spectrum which they have spread on their canvases.'

(Edmond Duranty, quoted in White and White, 1965: 120).

In this kind of way, criticism provided the parameters within which certain kinds of development were recognised as artistic innovation while other changes were passed over.[7] When critical interpretations of change as innovation were successful, the buyers, enjoying the works as they had learned to, communicated to others, both in their talk and by example of their own acquisitions, the possibilities of a new style or school, thus making the dealers' arguments more persuasive and securing the (financial and critical) legitimacy not only of a specific author's work but also of the aesthetic discourse itself.

In general terms, then, the distributive intermediaries began to develop processes of selection and promotion within the aesthetic discourse which had the effect of systematising the process by which cultural works realised exchange value through market distribution. However, conflicts arose during the course of the development of this discourse, some of which were concerned with the economic problems which the emergent market created itself. So, for example, the interests of the intermediaries who operated distribution systems frequently came to differ from those of the artists whose work they handled: a dealer might want to hold a work for years while its financial value grew, while the painter would prefer the work shown, purchased and placed where he could benefit from its being discussed by an audience which appreciated what he was doing and could contribute useful ideas and criticism. In addition, certain distributors began to act as moral and political gatekeepers for cultural goods, since this enabled them to build up their own reputation among the public in such a way as to give demand for the products they distributed some consistency. Nevertheless, despite possible conflict, since most artists wanted the advantages of distribution they tended to work with an eye to what the system characteristic of their world could handle (Becker, 1982). Timothy Clark's work on modernism, a movement which prided itself on the radical challenge it offered the traditional art world, provides confirmation of this:

> Market conditions encouraged the dealer to speculate in the long-term 'creativity' of those artists he favoured; and artists in turn learnt to market that particular commodity with some skill – nursing and refining it in a steady sequence of shows, interviews and promotional literature, trying to strike the right balance between innovation and product reliability, sniffing out the market's approximate wishes while maintaining (to the death) the protocols of individuality and artistic freedom.
>
> (Clark, 1985: 260)

On the whole, then, while there might have been some disagreement among the members of the artistic professions about the particular characteristics which merited attention at any particular time, the general standards of quality were collectively negotiated by a professional cultural élite, made up of producers, distributors and critics, members of the art form's market on the basis of notions of originality, creativity and authenticity which were routed through the application of the author-function.

What is being suggested here then is that the institutions and discourses that collectively functioned to construct the object 'art' were not distinct from but allied to the determinations of the marketplace which themselves established and confirmed the commodity status of the work of art. Notions of what constituted 'good art' in this system were not based on the consensus of a homogenous mass of art viewers but rather were formed within the calculated practices of reviewing, publishing and exhibiting art for a specific market. Moulin (1979, quoted in Miege, 1989) provides a suggestive analysis of the inter-relationship of such processes when he argues that in such systems – not only painting, but also sculpture, literature and music – marketing strategies 'combine the manipulation of signs of authentic rarity with manipulation of rarity'. The aim of such strategies is, 'on the one hand, to establish a certain type of rarity as artistic and, on the other, to create artificially the rarity of what has been established as artistic' (Moulin, 1979, quoted in Miege, 1989: 43). The first strategy is exemplified by the elaboration of restrictive notions of authenticity dependent upon authorial originality,[8] while the development and use of educational, cultural and linguistic barriers to act as a brake on the expansion of the market are representative of the second strategy.[9]

Rosalind Krauss (1988) provides a number of case studies of such strategies in relation to the critical discourse of modernism in her collection of essays, *The Originality of the Avant-Garde and Other Modernist Myths*, including, in her study of Rodin's work, an analysis of the state's collaboration with the market in the construction of the myths of originality. When Rodin died, he left his entire estate to the French nation, including not only all the work in his possession, but also all the rights of its reproduction. Thus, she suggests, '*The Gates of Hell*, cast in 1978 by perfect right of the State, is a legitimate work: a real original we might say' (1988: 151). However, according to Krauss, the Chambre des

Députés decided to limit the posthumous editions to twelve casts of any given plaster. She suggests that this explicitly artificial limitation indicates a (continuing) strategic manipulation of rarity in the aid of aesthetic authenticity, and asks,

> what are we to make of our squeamishness at the thought of the future of posthumous casting that awaits Rodin's work? Are we not involved here in clinging to a culture of originals which has no place among the reproductive mediums?
>
> (Krauss, 1988: 156)

Access to this culture of originals has been restricted as a consequence of the ways in which cultural works came to depend for their meaning on their relation to a complex configuration of other works; one result of this restriction was that the possession and display of such techniques of interpretation came to operate as a form of social closure (Abercrombie, 1991). More generally, the distinction between the audience for high culture – that is, 'onlookers', people outside those in a position either to appreciate or buy high cultural goods, who would know of high culture mostly through rumour and report – and the effective market, a smallish subset of that audience, was manufactured through the use of restrictive cultural barriers. Indeed, in many ways, the social and cultural value of high art, and its distinction from popular culture, relied upon the institutionalisation of this division between potential audience and actual market (see Chapter 8 for an analysis of the gendered dimension of this division).

Arguably, however, there were certain aspects of replication as a mode of cultural reproduction which cut across such divisions, notably its internalisation of an audience constituted through a common organisation of time and space (Giddens, 1990; Anderson, 1990; Anderson, 1991). So, for example, Benedict Anderson (1990) argues that these structurings of time and space within a cultural mode of replication associated with print technology underpinned the imagined community of the nation which was being formed during the eighteenth and nineteenth centuries. He suggests that the novel contributes to the emergence of a new conception of simultaneity. This understanding of time was distinguished by its portrayal of acts performed by actors who, though they are largely unaware of one

31

8406

another, are represented as part of the same imagined world by virtue of the fact that their activities are represented as taking place at the same time. In his terms, the novel is 'a complex gloss upon the world "meanwhile" ' (1990: 71), a simultaneity of here and elsewhere in consequential time. The resulting notion of a social organism bound together and moving through the same time, Anderson suggests, is a 'precise analogue of the idea of the nation, which is also conceived as a solid community moving steadily down (or up) history' (1990: 72).

However, this effect is not attributed to the novel alone, but also to the newspaper, which is seen by Anderson as a one-day bestseller exemplar of the novel format. As he notes, the effectivity of the newspaper as a medium of the imagined community of the nation is dependent upon the paradox of,

> an extraordinary mass ceremony: the almost precisely simultaneous consumption ('imagining') of the newspaper-as-fiction. . . . It is performed in silent privacy, in the lair of the skull. Yet each communicant is well aware that the ceremony he performs is being replicated simultaneously by thousands (or millions) of others of whose existence he is confident, yet of whose identity he has not the slightest notion. . . . What more vivid figure [than the newspaper reader] for the secular, historically clocked, imagined community can be envisioned?
>
> (Anderson, 1990: 79)

Through the manipulation of the mass simultaneity of reception made possible by technologies of replication, newspapers act as a technical means for 'creating that remarkable confidence of community in anonymity which is the hallmark of modern nations' (1990: 79).

Anderson thus points to a number of similarities between the fictional effectivities of the novel and the newspaper. To the extent that the readability of the (realist) novel and the newspaper both depend upon and inform what came to be widespread cultural principles, including those of shared simultaneity in space and time and temporal causality, it thus makes sense to talk of novelistic fictions or even a novelistic culture (Heath, 1982) associated with the technologies of replication cutting across the high culture/popular culture divide. However, there were differences of degree and divergences within this mode of cultural reproduction. As Anderson himself notes, the newspaper is a *one-day* bestseller: the intensive manipulation of the possibility of the simultaneity of reception in this case meant that time was increasingly understood in terms of succession rather than a series of inter-linked cause and effect trajectories. Through its construction of calendrical coincidence, the newspaper provided the legitimation of the random inclusion and juxtaposition of events. It thus displayed a tendency towards the presentation of simultaneity in homogenous or empty rather than consequential time. As such it was indicative of the ways in which the stabilisation of the possibilities of replication offered by the emergence of the third and fourth types of means of cultural production was always unstable; the meaningful organisation of artificial rarity upon which the notion of originality depended was always precarious.

More generally, in much, perhaps most, cultural production creative labour was not valorised in terms of originality, but functioned as merely one component in the recipe that dictated the essential requirements of production to be included in each version of a formula. Within such modes of cultural production, the cultural producer was required to produce plagiarisms of character and style as well as variations of routine plots and formulaic narratives, rather than so-called original work. As will be discussed in the next chapter, iteration, obedience to a pre-established schema, and the administration of innovation as novelty, were the principal mechanisms used to link the management of the labour process to predictable grades of quality.

Moreover, while this labourer too was protected by the legal regime of copyright, the terms of the reconciliation between the legal and the aesthetic were never secure. Indeed, they have required continual modification in the light of the changing possibilities of copying opened up by reproductive technologies. The French tradition, for example, presented particular difficulties for those seeking to secure a legal basis for the recognition of property rights in the developing industries of photography and the cinema.[10] At first, property rights in photographs were denied on the grounds that the camera did not involve any creative activity of the subject and was a mere mechanical reproduction of reality. However, this position was reversed under the economic pressure of the cinema industry: as photographic technique moved beyond its craft beginnings and became a significant sector of capitalist production, photography received legal protection on, 'condition of bearing the intellectual mark of its author, the imprint necessary to the work's having the characteristic of individuality necessary to its being a creation' (Cour de Cassation, Chambre Civile, quoted in Edelman, 1979: 14–15). Furthermore, the increasing capitalisation of cultural production and the growing complexity and socialisation of the labour process associated with the development of the new reproductive technologies contributed to a new significance for productive and distributive intermediaries, further complicating the terms on which authorship could be attributed. The role of such *brokers* or managers is described by Bernard Miege thus:

> The producer in fact is not only an intermediary between cultural labour (the singer, the writer, the engraver, the director, etc.) and the industrial capital ready to take on the role of technical reproduction of the unique work executed by the former (the record presser, the printer, etc.); and furthermore, as principal if not sole provider of capital, he is not content to transfer the products 'wholesale' to those with the job of distributing them. In fact, his intervention is decisive in that operation which consists in making out of unique and contingent (so far as their chance of success is concerned) cultural use value products which can be exchanged on a market. To do that he not only concerns himself with marketing problems, when he does not handle them directly, but he also intervenes in the conception of the product.
>
> (Miege, 1979: 304)

The increasing power of such intermediaries acting as representatives of capital was gained at the expense of the privileges of the cultural producer as author. Where necessary, this growing power was confirmed through changes in the copyright regime.

So, for example, film, as the product of a complex social and technical process with a marked division of labour between actors, scriptwriters, director, producer, etc. was resistant to the equation of legal personality with human personality that had initially provided the ideological basis for French property law. The response which this promoted, according to Edelman, was the 'socialisation of the subject-creator' through the vesting of legal rights of authorship in the collective subject constituted by the representatives of the capital used to produce the film. The result was what Edelman characterises as an 'extraordinary mutation' which 'turns an artist into a proletarian' at the same time as it vests in capital all the attributes of the creative author. He quotes a ruling from the Cours de Paris (1939):

'Considering that legal protection of artistic property can, in the quite special and still new category of cinema creation, be fully assured for the producers, since the work would not exist without its intellectual labour ..., considering that the *producer*, that is, the physical or moral person whose profession is the realization of cinema works, incontestably manifests himself through *creative activity* in the order of the intellect required of every author: considering that he imagines and expresses the ideas that will constitute the canvas, that he exercises a determinant influence over the entire direction and execution, and that it is under his *creative direction*, whether personal or delegated, that he exercises his influence over hundreds of specialist *assistants* who are duly remunerated at a fixed rate or according to contract, who are in any case interchangeable with other employees with the same specialist skills, and who will proceed to the *more or less intellectual or mechanical task*; ... could not have the consequence of all those who contribute to the sequence of the work's successive stages being given a personal right over the exploitation of the film.'

(Quoted in Edelman, 1979: 57–8; his emphasis)

Here, the organising function (that of the producer) exercised on behalf of capital is classified under the sign of 'art' (that is, it is aestheticised) in order to establish capital's right to ownership of the image; the 'original' moment here is thus that of investment. By contrast, the 'creative' labour of others involved in the process of film production is proletarianised (it is standardised to the point of interchangeability) in order to deprive them of such a right. This ruling thus represented a legal legitimation of the increasing significance of productive intermediaries in the organisation of cultural reproduction while still, just, preserving the founding terms of creativity and originality.

Moreover, it has been argued that, at the same time that the modern technologies of reproduction were emerging, the audience was perceived to have increasingly sophisticated responses to the forms of standardisation of cultural product they facilitated. These responses in turn contributed to the proliferation and transformation of the relative significance of standardisation, originality and novelty within cultural reproduction. For example, Eco has argued that

> the feuilleton, founded on the triumph of information, represented the preferred fare of a society that lived in the midst of messages loaded with redundancy. . . . In this sphere, the 'informative' shock of a short story by Poe . . . provided the enjoyment of the 'rupture'. In a contemporary industrial society, instead, the social change, the continuous rise of new behavioural standards, the dissolution of tradition, require a narrative based on redundancy. Redundant narrative structures would appear in this panorama as an indulgent invitation to repose, a chance of relaxing.
>
> (Eco 1985: 165)

One consequence of this broad change, he suggests, is that cultural producers came to build an awareness of their intended audiences' (socially and culturally determined) desire for standardisation into production. At this level, too, then, that of cultural form, the notion of originality was challenged. Indeed, at all three of the levels identified here – those of technical process, social specificity of creative labour and cultural form – the actual processes of cultural replication can be seen to have undermined the limits which had been imposed through the regime of rights associated with the author-function and the culture of originals. The commercial response to this challenge will be the focus of the next chapter.

NOTES

1 This criticism – that Benjamin's work sometimes displays aspects of a technological fetishism – is the basis of some of Adorno's criticisms.
2 So, for example, McQuail (1989) suggests that the development of

print tended to delocalise the audience, make it less time bound and diversify its basis.

3 The new Copyright, Designs and Patent legislation, constructed in part to bring British legislation in line with European law, extends certain aspects of the moral right tradition to the UK. However, even these are subject to consent and to waiver, whereas in French law the right is inalienable.

4 John Frow notes that the object that we would usually think of as the 'original' – the painting, the manuscript, the master tape –

> is [in legal terms] already a 'copy' of the (immaterial) 'work'. The 'work' that is copied thus has no separate material form, and no existence prior to the moment of its fixation in the copy; but as an elaborated expression it is also different in kind from the 'ideas' it expresses. It has a peculiar mode of existence which is neither concrete nor fully abstract.
>
> (Frow, 1988:5)

5 The account which follows draws heavily on Frow's (1988) and Nicholl's (1988) accounts of recent developments in American copyright law.

6 The distinction between an idea and its expression not only provided a basis for the commercial requirement for limited monopoly rights; it simultaneously defined the so-called public good character of cultural works by supporting the free circulation of ideas. As Vincent Porter (1979/80) notes, even within French law, once a work is published, the author enters into a contract with French society – as expressed in French copyright law – as well as with capital. In many cases the two interests are divergent. The author's right in a work has a limited time span, which varies according to the nature of the work, and certain acts, such as copying for the purpose of study, are legally permitted and these exceptions run against the commercial interests of the author.

7 Becker writes, 'The history of art deals with innovators and innovations that won organizational victories, succeeding in creating around themselves the apparatus of an art world, mobilizing enough people to cooperate in regular ways that sustained and furthered their ideas' (1982: 301). He also suggests that criticism was important in the emergence of photography as an art in the early twentieth century in terms of both the differentiation of particular practices from similar practices in non-artistic enterprises, and in the development of a subject matter and style departing definitively from imitations of painting (1982: 339).

8 A current example of this is to be found in the contemporary photography market, in which only those photographs which are defined by the critical discourse as 'close to the artistic moment' are ascribed the status of art (Krauss, 1988: 156).

9 See Chapter 8 for a more detailed discussion of the role of selective internalisation of the audience in the manipulation of rarity in the discourses of aesthetic modernism and the avant-garde.

10 Photography presented a particular problem for this tradition because it was one of the earliest examples of Williams' fifth type of cultural means of production – a reproductive technology which allowed 'new kinds of presentation of practices still otherwise based on the use of inherent and constituted resources' (1981: 91). Moreover, it made use of a relatively direct rather than notational mode of signification to do so.

3

REPLICATION, NOVELTY AND REACTIVATION

The last chapter explored the implications of the emergence of market-led production for the forms of reproducibility and thus criteria of aesthetic quality associated with the new technologies of cultural reproduction. This was broadly conceptualised as a shift from a mode of repetition to one of replication. It was further suggested that the legal framework of copyright, in which cultural goods were constituted as intellectual property, set the terms in and through which exclusive rights of copying were determined. This constitution was related to the emergence of the author-function, seen as a key mechanism through which the manipulation of artificial rarity was managed in the increasingly routinised organisation of cultural production for élite consumption. It was also noted, however, that the development of the later reproductive technologies, such as photography and cinema, posed a challenge to this regime of rights. It is the nature of this challenge which forms the subject of this chapter; in particular, the implications of this challenge will be explored by considering the ways in which the market distribution of cultural goods impacts upon their production in what has been termed the culture industry (Adorno and Horkheimer, 1982). The focus will be on the social organisation of the second dimension of reproduction, that is, the relations between producers and audiences within the mode of replication. More specifically, the focus will be on the role of distributive intermediaries, distribution relations for 'unknown' audiences, and with the influence that this complex distribution system has on the production of cultural goods and the terms of their constitution and exploitation as intellectual property.

NOVELTY AND PRODUCTION FOR THE MARKET

Becker notes that,

> When artists support themselves from non art sources, the distribution system has minimal influence; when they work directly for a patron, it is maximised; when they create works for unknown audiences, the influence comes through the constraints imposed by the intermediaries who operate the necessarily more complex and elaborate distribution system.
>
> (Becker 1982: 94)

It was argued in Chapter 1 that the development of modern cultural technologies profoundly destabilised relations between the moments of cultural production and reception; nevertheless, there have, historically, been a number of attempts to limit the indeterminacy of these relations (Thompson, 1990). The focus in this chapter will be on the ways in which attempts have been made to limit this indeterminacy through the internalisation of the audience as a market or, in other words, on attempts to mediate the relationship between supply and demand through the construction of the audience as a potential market.

In this respect, it is important to recognise that while the market at its simplest refers to an arena of exchange in which individuals attempt to maximise their own advantages, in so far as it becomes institutionalised, it also serves to co-ordinate and even transform the activities it appears merely to bring together:

> The cultural industry is not in the end a response to a pre-existing demand. Rather, basing itself on the dominant conceptions of culture, it must as a first stage, at the same time as it puts new products onto the market (or rather a whole interlocking package of new products) create a social demand, give it a consistency, in other words, lead certain social groups selected as commercial targets to prepare themselves to respond to the producers' offer.
>
> (Miege, 1979: 300)

As production for the audience-as-market market takes priority over any other, the seeming rationale of the market – the buyer's choice – comes to operate within an always already selected range.

However, the process of internalising the audience as a market is not static, but is, rather, dynamic. General movements of social and cultural relations can effect the entry of new audiences into the cultural market. Williams (1981) identifies three principal sources of such innovation. The first of these is the rise of new social groups,[1] which bring in new kinds of both producers and consumers, and support new kinds of work. For example, the growth in the service classes, and their emergence as a significant target market, have been seen as particularly significant in determining recent changes in contemporary culture (Lash and Urry, 1987; Featherstone, 1991; Urry, 1990; but see Chapter 9). The second source identified by Williams is the redefinition of an existing group or fraction of its conditions of existence: the emergence of youth as a social and cultural group in the post-war period and the development of youth cultures and a more widespread pop culture is the obvious example here (Martin, 1981; Hall and Jefferson, 1976). Transformations in the means of cultural production, which provide new formal possibilities, and new conditions of consumption, provide Williams' third source of innovation. So, for example, the development of video for home use helped to constitute children as a market for commercial cultural production.

This suggests that it is important to recognise that the relation between the culture industry and the audience is neither fixed nor simply one-way, and that the market as a system of exchange is always and necessarily receptive to innovations. However, the internalisation of groups as appropriate targets by the culture industry is always a mediated response to, and not a direct outcome of, these factors. This mediation is shaped by a number of factors, including compatibility of work with the technical, economic and social means and determinants of its types of production, including 'known demand', which tends to be defined within market planning as demand as it has already been crystallised. The response of creative labour to this mediation then further structures the relations between producers and audience. One facet of this mediation was explored in the last chapter, by looking at the ways in which the notion of originality structured the manipulation of artificial rarity in relation to a notion of the audience-as-public in the institutions of high culture.

However, such strategies are not employed in relation to what is often called mass cultural production. This is, in part, because a central mechanism in the organisation of the audience-as-market within mass cultural reproduction is the commercially motivated tendency to increase the size of the total audience reached, either on a one-off basis or by increasing the frequency of consumption of a range of known products by a relatively fixed audience. An obvious example of the first strategy is the blockbuster: by carefully planning all aspects of a bestseller or blockbuster, including large-scale promotion and control over distribution, the culture industry aims to control the risk of failure while maximising the potential for profit. Such blockbusters are characterised by heavy advertising and promotion before the product itself is released, tie-ins between different media, and the use of stars, all of which stress the unique characteristics of the cultural product. In contrast, the most common example of the second strategy is the standardised production of serial cultural goods, such as detective or romantic fiction, in which creative labour is required to produce variations of standard formulae: so, for example, 'Publishing thirteen new titles each month, the company strives to have happy endings, exotic settings, but no premarital sex' (Coser *et al.*, 1982: 201–2).

Indeed, so central is this type of standardisation that Eco (1985) has argued that seriality or iteration is typical of production for the mass market in general. He discusses the example of detective fiction in some detail, reinforcing the point made earlier about the importance of redundancy in modern cultural works:

> the reading of a traditional detective story presumes the enjoyment of a scheme. The scheme is so important that the most famous authors have founded their fortune on its very immutability.
>
> Furthermore, the writer plays upon a continuous series of connotations (for example, the characteristics of the detective and of his immediate 'entourage') to such an extent that their reappearance in each story is an essential condition of its reading pleasure. And so we have the by now famous historical 'tics' of Sherlock Holmes, the punctilious vanity of Hercule Poirot and the familiar fixes of Maigret, on up to the famous idiosyncrasies of the most unabashed heroes of the hard-boiled novel.
>
> (Eco, 1985: 162–3)

He distinguishes between different strategies of seriality; these include: the retake, sequel or prequel, in which characters from a previous story are recycled; the remake which is a telling again of a previous story (or, in popular music terms, a cover version); and the series itself, which, he suggests, works upon a given situation and a restricted number of fixed pivotal characters, around whom the secondary and changing ones turn.

This type of standardisation, which attempts to achieve a dialectic between predictability and novelty, is exemplified by the series format in broadcast television. Such a series typically involves repetition across episodes combined with an element of novelty in the way in which the problematic is played through. It is precisely in the foreseen and awaited predictability that the audience's pleasure is believed to be based. The moment of predictability provides a distraction which consists in the refutation of a development of events, in a withdrawal from the tension of past-present-future to the focus on an instant. This moment is desired precisely because it is repeated. The pleasure such repetition evokes is a response to both the return of the same which such predictability offers and the subtlety of the strategy of variation which presents the same as different.

Each new episode or story is a 'virtual new beginning': the character exhausts the narrative material that he or she is given and requires more parcelled out week after week, year after year. Such characters learn nothing – think of *I Love Lucy*, for example; they neither grow nor change significantly: the narrative returns them to the same situation and frame of mind in which they began the previous week. In topological terms, the character moves round a loop; for example, as, Patricia Mellencamp writes, the series premiss of the *I Love Lucy* show, which was portrayed in brilliant performances then denied weekly, was that Lucy was (not) star material:

> Every week for seven years, in reality, Lucy, the chorus girl/clown, complained that Ricky was preventing her from becoming a star. For twenty-four minutes, she valiantly tried to escape domesticity by getting a job in show-business; after a tour-de-force performance of physical comedy, in the inevitable reversal and failure of the end, she resigned to stay happily at home serving big and little Ricky.
>
> (Mellencamp, 1990b: 261)

As Eco also notes, the flash-back is a sub-type of this serial loop, in that through its use, characters are made to relive their pasts continually; a film such as *Back to the Future* offers a feature length pastiche of this strategy.

In this and other ways, the proliferation of forms of seriality or iteration challenges the presentation of simultaneity of here and elsewhere in consequential time associated with originality and the author-function discussed in the last chapter; temporal distinctions themselves, while still integral to the serial, are obscured within the very form of the series. Indeed, it has been suggested that it is the blurring of the differences between temporal modes which characterises television as a cultural apparatus; all modes are subsumed within a 'disciplinary time-machine' (Mellencamp, 1990b: 241). In this context, it is not narrative, but catastrophe, the ultimate drama of the instantaneous, which constitutes the absolute limit to the temporal dimension of the internalisation of the audience (Doane, 1990a).

More generally, it can be suggested that the manipulation of innovation as novelty, not originality, is present not only in the very structure of series, but also in other forms of standardisation which characterise cultural production for the mass market. It can be seen, for example, not only in different strategies of seriality but also in the planned organisation of renewal and obsolescence in cultural tastes associated with fashion. This is achieved through the definition of certain changes (and not others) in cultural goods as significant development by means of selective, but intensive, publicity and limited distribution. The construction of fashion in taste in this way allows a maximisation of audience by creating a particular form of scarcity through the manipulation of availability and the construction of a need for constant renewal as novelty.

However, all these examples of the ways in which the implementation of the technologies of replication have been contained by the manipulation of novelty are marked by contradictions. Given that a key function of cultural goods is to act as positional goods (Veblen, 1925; Bourdieu, 1984, although see Campbell, 1989), that is, to act as markers of relative status, there is an inherent instability in this process of expanding the audience-as-market.[2] As noted above, in some kinds of commercial production, this process was stabilised by the restriction of access to the codes and conventions required to 'appreciate' art. But such a possibility was not readily available to the producers of mass-produced cultural goods, who were and are, in general, much less closely aligned with the institutions of aesthetic authority and education than producers of 'unique' or semi-reproducible cultural goods. The only sector of the culture industry which is able to sell its products to a 'mini-mass' public is publishing, owing to the enormous expansion of literary studies in educational institutions which occurred early this century. As Terry Lovell writes,

> the institutionalisation of English studies generated an essential component of the literary market, a pool of competent readers. Producers of the literary novel are participants in one of Becker's 'art worlds' which contain among their members not only their producers but also the suitably trained recipients. The competent readership for the contemporary novel as literature is supplied above all by students who have specialised in the study of English in schools and colleges.
>
> (Lovell, 1987: 137)

For most other sectors in the culture industry, the links between cultural and social reproduction are much less direct (see Chapters 5, 6, 7 and 8 for a fuller discussion of this). Nevertheless, they attempt to manage the instability inherent in the process of maximising the audience for cultural goods through the differentiation of target markets within the total available audience, that is, through market segmentation. The logic here is to seek to maximise audiences while at the same time manipulating access to cultural commodities in order to create scarcity in ways which facilitate positional differentiation. While this process has occurred gradually, almost as a matter of course during the expansion of the audience-as-market, this process of market segmentation has often been triggered by competition between as well as within media.

The audience characteristics traditionally perceived as the most suitable criteria for use in targeting as market segments are socio-economic. However, existing patterns of cultural tastes and preferences are increasingly believed to have a role. One conceptual development which is related to the construction of target markets is the notion of a 'taste culture', which has been defined as an aggregate of similar content chosen by the same people (McQuail, 1987). The term was introduced in market planning as a way of exploring the role of non-demographic factors in the organisation of the audience-as-market, and as part of the recognition of the often fleeting and overlapping nature of audiences within a market. It is used to group individuals according to acts of media choice seen to display similarity of content or style – in short, according to market notions of taste – rather than to demographic variations, and has begun to be used as a basis on which to plan new products. It provides one indication, albeit as yet not fully developed, of the ways in which the construction of the audience-as-market is beginning to be organised in terms of the specificities of audience responses to cultural goods themselves.

Underlying all these examples of the construction of the audience-as-market lie the techniques of promotion, publicity and marketing. Nicholas Garnham (1979) suggests that these techniques, specifically developed in order to increase the chances of commercial success for the whole range of goods or services, take on a particular significance in the culture industry. This is because the costs of copying in relation to the costs of conception and prototype production are relatively low for cultural (as opposed to other kinds of) goods; that is, the commercial rewards to be derived from a successful cultural commodity are especially high because the marginal returns from each extra sale will tend to grow. In general, the application of techniques of promotion can be seen as one of the first stages in creating a 'second skin' to the cultural commodity, culminating in the creation of brands (Lash *et al.*, 1990; see next chapter).

However, there are particular problems associated with promoting what are, more or less, one-off goods, as Coser *et al.* note in their study of American publishing:

> The goal in distributing books is to get the message to the right people. Until a book is opened, however, no one can tell what its message is: thus, the main problem in promoting books is to get people to want the message they have not yet received – no small task.
>
> (Coser *et al.*, 1982: 200–1)

To compound the problem of getting people to want a message they have not yet received, what the culture industry's audiences think, what really moves them in what ways, is something, which, as Becker suggests, 'no one knows in . . . a quick and direct way; in fact, for all the devices of audience research, it is something no one at all knows for sure' (1982: 123, 125). This radical indeterminacy can be explained in terms of the plurality and instability of cultural processes as value-creating activities, and the difficulty encountered by producers in controlling valorisation, a problem exacerbated by the possibilities of reactivation opened up by the new technologies of replication. At the most basic level, audience membership itself is not a matter of compulsion or necessity, but is principally voluntary and optional. In addition, the problems raised by this indeterminacy are further extended as the traditional concept of the audience as a group or set of people receiving the same content at the same time and place is called into doubt by current developments in technologies of culture, including the multiplication of media channels and the transnational flow of content, the detachment of cultural works from fixed and accountable systems of distribution, and the development of interactive media based on computer technology.

Hirsch (1972) has argued that, in the face of these problems, different means of reducing uncertainty through promotion are adopted by different sectors of the culture industry according to the relative unit cost of the output. He argues that in sectors where unit costs are high, such as film, attention is paid to techniques which will not only reduce the uncertainty surrounding the production and distribution of each item but also promote the distribution of the whole service. He sees the star system in classic film production as a means of achieving both objectives. In contrast, in sectors, such as popular music or book publishing, in which the unit cost of each item of output is relatively low, a technique of systematic 'over'-production is adopted, with the aim of deliberately writing off failures against successes. For 'over'-production to be successful, potential buyers must be made aware of what is being offered, but it does not make commercial sense for this to be done through the individual promotion of each item; so, a number of more complex promotional strategies are adopted instead, including the use of differential publicity. Thus, for example, a selection of individual items will be put forward for promotion in the mass media, particularly television and radio, but also magazines and newspapers. They are promoted either directly, as in the case of record plays or by serialising, adapting or excerpting from books, or indirectly, through criticism, interviews and news items about the authors or artists involved.

One problematic effect of this from the point of view of entrepreneurs is that these sectors of the culture industry are situated in a position of dependence on an outside organisation. Simon Frith, for example, argues that a fundamental problem for the record industry is that 'the sales needed depend on competitive marketing mechanisms that the record makers don't, themselves, completely control' (Frith, 1983: 102). Thus, for example, 'To sell a record, companies must, in the end, get a sound to the public and to do this they have to go through a disc jockey, the most significant rock "gatekeeper" ' (Frith, 1983: 117). In Hirsch's terms, then, the media become 'gatekeepers' or 'strategic checkpoints' for other sectors of the culture industry, regulating innovation and channelling demand through their own priorities. However, as Frith suggests, the relationship between gatekeepers and their audience is itself a dialectical one; for example, 'The most important disco gatekeeper, the disc jockey, is employed to mediate the disco public's tastes back to the record companies as well as to select (and sell) the resulting records to the disco public' (Frith, 1983: 129).

However, there is widespread variability in the criteria employed by mass-media gatekeepers in selecting cultural items to be awarded coverage. Hirsch writes,

> While the total number of products to be awarded media coverage may be predicted in the aggregate, the estimation of which ones will be selected from the potential universe is problematic.
>
> The organizational segregation of the producers of cultural items from their disseminators places definite restrictions on the forms of power which cultural organisations may exercise over mass-media gatekeepers to effect the selection of particular items for coverage.
>
> (Hirsch, 1972: 648)

For example, radio DJs are independent of the record company, not just legally, but because they have to please their audience, and the two goals – attracting and keeping listeners, and selling records – are not necessarily compatible. Indeed, there may be a conflict between the two, not least because the pleasures of listening to the radio and those of listening to records at home can have very different cultural significances for the audience.

In an attempt to rationalise this process, cultural commodities may, rather than being promoted as individual items, be put forward by producers as part of a list or catalogue, the units of which are marketed as a package, thus spreading the risks associated with the uncertainty of success associated with cultural production (Miege, 1979). One example of this is the marketing of books, which by the twentieth century had come to be seen in terms of their singularity, by book clubs. Radway's study of the Book-of-the-Month Club (1992) documents the realisation by Harry Scherman, one of its founding partners, that if books were to be sold by mail, not only would advertising and solicitation have to be spread across a number of volumes, the idea of a series of books would have to be sold by giving the series a comprehensive use and application for the potential customer:

> 'You had to set up some kind of authority so that the sub-scriber would feel there was some reason for buying a group of books, so that he'd know he wasn't buying a pig in a poke, and also that he wasn't buying books which were suspect.'
>
> (Quoted in Radway, 1992: 519)

Radway suggests that he succeeded in this aim by establishing a selection committee of 'eminent experts' who were deputised to pick 'the best book published each month'; that is, he offered the audience the promise that these new books, because they were part of this series, were assured of becoming classics.

One further strategy in the constitution of the audience-as-market must also be noted here; this is the use of advertising as sponsorship for some forms of cultural production. According to John Sinclair,

> Advertisers have increasingly come to seek markets appropriate to their particular products and have so chosen their advertising media according to whether they can give access to the desired target audiences. This has had profound effects upon patterns of media development in this century, and the rise and fall of different communication media has been determined less and less by

technological innovation itself than by the capacity of new technologies to be adapted to the changing state of play in who wants to advertise to whom.

(Sinclair, 1987: 72)

According to this argument, advertising has effects for cultural production from the moment at which the balance shifts from advertising acting as a support system to a primary communicative function to a situation in which the communicative function's value is estimated in terms of its benefits to advertisers (Williams, 1981). It is at this point that the role of marketing and advertising as an element of reproduction in general becomes significant for specialised forms of cultural production.

Perhaps the most forceful analyst of this process is Dallas Smythe (1981) who argues that the economic function served by the media is to 'produce' the audience which can then be sold as a commodity to the advertisers. His basic insight is thus that one of the significant factors structuring the commercial development and organisation of the major media is the assembling of audiences for sale to advertisers. This suggests, in turn, that the use of advertising to finance cultural production has meant that the principles of the organisation of the audience-as-market described above have been modified by the interests of advertisers in reaching audiences who are target consumers – what can be seen as the organisation of the audience-as-consumer.

This modification occurs because advertisers are not neutral in their desire to reach all members of the potential audience and do not allocate their media budgets straightforwardly according to the likes and dislikes of media audiences. So, for example, there is no direct correspondence between the size of the audience for, and the amount of expenditure on, different titles in the press (Curran, 1986). Instead, advertisers have their own criteria for judging the worth of the media's output; they usually wish to reach, and will pay more to reach, particular segments of the market. Their judgements are based, not on qualitative indices of audience appreciation of cultural goods, but, rather, on a range of marketing measuring standards, including the advertisers' opinion about the effectiveness of different media as agents of persuasion. Obviously, such standards are not unchanging; on the contrary, changes in marketing perspectives, research procedures and data inputs have produced changes in how advertisers have spent this money. In general, though, advertising provides a competing set of commercial criteria for the selection and promotion of cultural goods; or, to put this another way, competition for advertising has transformed the notion of the audience which is internalised in some forms of cultural reproduction and has led to the constitution of the audience-as-consumer in competition with the constitution of the audience-as-market (see Chapter 6 on broadcasting for a further discussion of this).

CREATIVITY, COPYRIGHT AND BRANDING

In general terms, then, it has been suggested that there has been an increasingly pervasive use of the strategies of seriality, iteration and standardisation; this has been associated with an intensification of the transformative role of productive and distributive intermediaries. One consequence of this is that, as a result of market planning, work may be selected at so early a stage, on the basis of a few examples or of some projected demand, that production no longer originates with, but is commissioned from, the primary producer. This suggests that the cultural producer's protected position as originator has been undermined by the commercial exploitation of the possibilities of replication offered by the technologies of culture in so far as they employ strategies of regulating innovation as novelty. The development of market relations can thus be seen to have been a factor in both the emergence and the decline of the author-function as a form of asymmetry in cultural reproduction.

It has, for example, been suggested that the character produced for the series has brought about the death of the author; Edelman writes that

> the character represents the culmination of a certain type of writing. With the character, the writing circle closes – one could even claim that the author disappears. The author alienates himself [*sic*] within an infernal machine of his own making. The writing takes on a form beyond that of its own origin, a product that moves about freely on a stage, playing out its non-human role. The transgressive gesture of writing disappears.
>
> (Edelman, 1987: 36)

51

Furthermore, recent changes in copyright law suggest that the legal protection afforded the cultural producer as author is under threat. For example, the recent French software legislation of 1985 has modified the moral rights regime which had initially accorded the author absolute rights of alteration or withdrawal in relation to his or her work. Authors of software are presumed to have assigned their work to their employers together with all the other rights afforded to authors when the work has been created in the exercise of contracted functions. The author also cannot 'oppose adaptation of the software within the limits of the rights he has assigned nor exercise his right to correct or retract' unless there is a specific contractual agreement allowing him to do so (quoted in Saunders, 1988: 133). Moreover, and perhaps more significantly, a shift in the criteria – from creative will to intellectual effort (and this is defined, rather minimally, as the making of a choice) – for deciding upon the originality of a work means that the aesthetic distinction between an original and an unoriginal work of the mind has become almost impossible to sustain legally (Edelman, 1979).

Frow (1988) suggests that the notion of originality has recently been similarly redefined in American law in the context of recent technological developments; he notes that in the case of cartography, for example, the possibility of protection of virtually identical maps is seen to reside in the labour of production which has gone into them.

'When the creative process is re-examined by the wisdom of judicial hindsight, it is, like a conjuror's trick that has been explained to children, almost always a disappointment. There is, we discover, no magic to it after all. It's only work.'
(Whicher (1963), quoted in Frow, 1988: 11)

This 'discovery' has mixed implications. On the one hand, it suggests that the concept of originality is no longer legally sustainable, and this can be seen as an indication of the collapse of legal support for the distinction between the labour of an author (as originator) and other forms of labour. On the other hand, as Frow notes, what this might mean is that originality can be rethought in materialist terms: the 'causal relationship between an author and the material form in which a work is embodied' would be an investment of labour power. In this sense, it allows a recognition of the ordinariness of creative labour and demystifies the myths and metaphors of artistic expression.

However, while the concept of author-as-originator as developed in the critical–aesthetic discourse of authorship may no longer be internally linked to copyright, this is not to say that the status and conditions of creative labour are necessarily the same as those for other kinds of labour, merely that these differences are maintained by other, perhaps more indirect, means. Clayton and Curling (1979) make an interesting argument in this respect. They suggest that it is possible to explain the fact that some labour within television is remunerated on a wage basis and other labour on a rights basis in terms of the special claims which can be made for that labour which is seen to provide the basis for discrimination between television programmes *as commodities*. They write,

> That labour which is thought to produce significant difference between television commodities (ie that which significantly influences audience ratings) will *tend* to be remunerated (in addition to a basic fee) on a rights basis; while that which is thought to produce little difference, but which is repetitive, is paid solely on a wage basis. . . . We use the word *tend* for two reasons; first, because rights only accrue when a programme is reused; second, because of the operation of the credits system which names many of the workers to whom rights will not accrue under the present system.
>
> (Clayton and Curling, 1979: 48; their emphasis)

They note that the operation of the credit system is interesting because while the attribution of authorship is necessary for critical and financial reasons, the further differentiation of products by the assembled names of the credit list does not have the same function. It is, though, necessary for the circulation of labour within the institutions enabling the assembly of 'named' workers into programme-making groups. This naming of labour can, however, be exploited by creative workers as the basis from which their contributions to projects can be assessed; the significance of this for the organisation of the creative labour market will be touched upon in the next chapter.

In what follows, however, this argument will be used to explain shifts in copyrighting, and thus rights of use in intellectual property, in terms of the growing significance of certain kinds of representations or signs of creative labour to the circulation of many kinds of cultural works as commodities. In general terms, it is suggested that creative labour is able to retain privileged conditions in so far as it is able to lay effective claim to having made a contribution to the commercial 'effects' of a cultural good, including, most notably, that of producing audience ratings. The importance of audience ratings is linked to the increasing importance of the internalisation of the audience-as-market and as-consumer.

Such an argument requires the identification of the mechanisms by which creative labour can win credit for having contributed to such effects. A preliminary investigation suggests that the factors which go towards the making visible of different forms of creative labour in this way are various, but include the strength of labour organisations, and the critical practices of naming and evaluation, but, perhaps most importantly, the inter-relationship of that discourse with the audience's ability to decipher the signs of creative labour in the completed cultural work. Historical changes in the conditions for such recognition will be explored here by looking at Benjamin's comparison of cult and exhibition value (1970).

Benjamin has argued that the experience of aura can be seen in terms of

> the transposition of a response common in human relationships to the relationship between the inanimate or natural object and man. The person we look at, or who feels he is being looked at, looks at us in return. To perceive the aura of an object we look at means to invest it with the ability to look at us in turn.
>
> (Quoted in Lunn, 1985: 170)

In some ways, this can be seen as a crucial aspect of the early stages of the process of internalisation in modern cultural technologies: as one means by which the indeterminacy created by the radical split between producers and audience opened up by the technologies of replication was limited. In contrast, however, works which are designed to display exhibition value do not return the audience's look; instead, the experience of their quality is derived from the ways in which works explicitly function as objects of a look which cannot be returned. They are judged in terms of their style, image or capacity to give off effects, which, in turn, is related to the surface or 'flat' features of cultural works, that is, their transferability or dislocation from the contextuality of narrative and shared space and time.

Within modes of cultural reproduction organised for the creation of exhibition value, creative labour is able to gain recognition only to the extent to which it is able to lay claim to the production of such effects. These effects are related to the capacities of the audience, including the skills of apperception, in which the audience is able to see characteristics of the object not previously visible. For example,

> in photography, process reproduction can bring out those aspects of the original that are unattainable to the naked eye yet accessible to the lens, which is adjustable and chooses its angle at will. And photographic reproduction, with the aid of certain processes, such as enlargement or slow motion, can capture images which escape natural vision.
>
> (Benjamin, 1970: 222)

This technical intensification of sight is seen by Benjamin to be a consequence of the more general process discussed in the last chapter by which 'reality is adjusted to the masses'.

More generally, Benjamin has argued that, with the growing independence of the conditions for reactivation associated with the technologies of replication, a less concentrated and more distracted state of mind characterises the reception of cultural goods. The mastery of skills and the tactile appropriation of the world can no longer be accomplished through contemplation, he argues; instead, noticing the object in an incidental fashion, in an almost absent-minded state of distraction, the audience can tacitly appropriate the material as a matter of habit. Moreover, with the possibility of receiving cultural works outside the confines of ritual and tradition, the audience gains confidence in its own expertise: 'The greater the decrease in the social significance of an art form, the sharper the distinction between criticism and enjoyment by the public' (Benjamin, 1970: 236).

It appears that recent copyright rulings are beginning to take recognisance of these changes in the reception of cultural works made available through the new technologies of replication. Earlier copyright practice had proposed a particular model of communication from the sender, whose work was considered fully embodied in the completed work, to be understood when 'consumed' by the reader. In this way, it was informed by and supported an aesthetic discourse which privileged the moment of authorship as determinant of value in the circulation of the cultural work within a cycle of cultural reproduction. However, the commercial exploitation of the new technologies of replication has required a new emphasis on the processes of reception rather than the authorial moment as the basis for defining the terms of intellectual property. For example, Nicholls (1988) argues that the ruling in the case of *Atari* (the owners of the *Pacman* video game) v *North American Phillips Consumer Electronics Corp.* (the owners of the video game featuring *K. C. Munchkin*), 1982, in which the originality of the Munchkin character was disputed, reveals a new awareness of the importance of the state of the receiver to decisions about the criteria for the allocation of exclusive rights of copying. It seems that the criteria used to allocate exclusive rights of copying are increasingly understood in relation to a notion of novelty, which is defined in terms of distinctiveness as experienced by the intended audience, rather than the creative will or expression of the cultural producer. In the case described above, the Circuit Court ruled that

> 'Video-games, unlike an artist's painting or even other audio-visual works, appeal to an audience that is fairly undiscriminating in so far as their concern about more subtle differences in artistic expression. The main attraction of a game such as *Pac-Man* lies in the stimulation provided by the intensity of the competition. A person who is entranced by the play of the game, "would be disposed to overlook" many of the minor differences in detail and "regard their aesthetic appeal as the same".'
>
> (Quoted in Nicholls, 1988: 42)

The use of criteria which refer to the receiver's participation ('appeal', 'attraction', 'stimulation', 'intensity of competition', 'entranced'), at the expense of the producer's expressivity (signs of which become 'minor differences of detail'), suggests that the capacities of reactivation facilitated by the new technologies of replication at the moment of reception may be coming to be legally recognised to have a new commercial significance in the constitution and exploitation of intellectual property.

More generally, other rulings have begun to undermine the previously existing legal distinction between cultural and other material goods. For example, the American Software Act (1980) began the erosion of a basic distinction between copyright and patent by suggesting that useful objects were eligible for copyright. In judicial cases such as *Diamond* v *Diehr* (1981), the court held that

> 'when a claim containing a mathematical formula implements or applies that formula in a structure or a process which, when considered as a whole, is performing a function which the patent laws were designed to protect (for example, transforming or reducing an article to a different state of things), then the claim satisfies the requirements of [the copyright law]'.
>
> (Quoted in Nicholls, 1988: 40)

This finding goes against a long-standing tradition which had meant that copyright could not protect useful objects or inventions. Within this tradition, it had been accepted that if an object had an intrinsically utilitarian function, it could not receive copyright. (Useful objects can be *patented* if they are original enough, or protected by trade secret Acts.) In the USA, this stemmed back to 1908, when the Supreme Court ruled that a player piano roll was ineligible for the copyright protection accorded to the sheet music it duplicated. The roll was considered part of a machine rather than the expression of an idea. However, this recent ruling, together with the growing importance attached to reception more generally, suggests that the criterion of purposelessness which was traditionally a distinguishing characteristic of the cultural work is no longer as important in setting the terms of legal regulation of rights of use of intellectual property, and may indicate that the very general differentiation between the cultural and the social is itself being eroded (Baudrillard, 1988, 1990; Lash, 1990).

It is in this changed context – the increasing significance of exhibition value, and greater legal attention to the actual activities of the audience – that certain representations of creative labour still appear to be able to win recognition of their contribution to the market success of cultural goods, and thus are able to secure special working conditions, including a degree of working autonomy. In general terms, as Becker notes,

> The reputation of the artist and the work reinforce one another: we value more a work done by an artist we respect,

just as we respect more an artist whose work we have admired. When the distribution of art involves the exchange of money, reputational value can be translated into financial value.

(Becker, 1982: 23)

This exchange has been strategically developed by stars or personalities, who provide many sectors of the culture industry with one of the surest guarantees of success through the self-conscious management of appearances, publicity and promotion. Indeed, in many ways, the star-function can be seen as a transformation of the author-function in the later stages of corporate production for a market in that the imprint of the star acts as a means of linking the signs of creative labour with the exhibition value of the work produced.

Miege is cautious, however, about the benefits of this system and the Matthew effect which it promotes, for cultural producers in general;[3] he writes,

This situation only really profits the small group of artists who dominate and direct the societies of authors and who, thanks to the stardom they enjoy, are in a position to reclaim a part of the surplus value produced. For the majority of artists this autonomy is a pure facade; it allows them to be paid at a rate markedly lower than the value of the labour process which underpins most cultural production.

(Miege, 1979: 304)

Nevertheless, in certain periods the dynamics of certain culture industries have precipitated an intensification in the importance attached to stars: for example, Frith writes that,

In the 1970s ... [the record companies'] intensive competition for the services of rock superstars (the apparently guaranteed bestsellers) gave these stars unprecedented power to write their own contracts – power that reflected both the ideology of rock (the demand for artistic control) and its mass sales.

(Frith, 1983: 110)

And the rise of rock stars in the 1970s had a parallel development in book publishing during the 1980s, where the promotion of potential bestsellers on television – as in the case of Jacqueline

Susann – intensified the competition for authors (see the next chapter for a more detailed discussion of this). In addition, the tendency to promote goods as part of a catalogue across (rather than simply within as discussed above) media, that is, in the form of a group of multi-media products (film, book, record, cassette, compact disc, videotape as well as merchandising products), gave the star an increasing importance which has been reflected in the growing significance attached to the sale of subsidiary rights across the culture industry (Miege, 1989), and is, as will be discussed in the next chapter, marked by a shift in power.

It is often argued that the emergence of exhibition value is entirely the result of marketing, and the fact that there is no attempt to ensure that cultural goods produced within such systems of evaluation are attributed with the ability to return the look is seen to invest commercial interests with a new kind of power. This is sometimes understood to be a consequence of the ways in which the construction of the audience-as-market and as-consumer has meant that the relationship between producers and their audiences is increasingly commercially calculative, rather than premised on disinterestedness. Moreover, it is argued that the significance of the already existing relationships between the members of the audience is seen to have diminished; that is, they are designated as a set of individual and equal consumers, who are organised as a serial rather than associative community. From a commercial perspective, it is argued, the primary significance of audiences is their attention-giving behaviour, expressed in acts of purchase or viewing, listening and reading choices. Such data come to provide the criteria for the success or failure of cultural goods, rather than internally generated standards of aesthetic quality. Other writers have emphasised the audience-as-market's dependence on what is made available to it or have conceived it as a body of non-participant spectators largely manipulated by media producers.

However, it is important not to overstate the significance of the construction of the audience-as-market and as-consumer by ignoring the continuing importance of the audience-as-public in some forms of contemporary cultural reproduction. For example, the audience for broadcasting is still partially constituted as a public through the deliberate profiling of audiences for public service channels. Rather than talking about the disappearance of the audience-as-public, it may be more appropriate to consider its (gradual) decline within a more general consideration of changes within the public sphere. In this respect it is important to bear in mind the tendency for 'the public' to become more localised, issue-and interest-specific, and less identified with a single informed public élite. So, for example, social and political movements have contributed towards the development of a number of counter public spheres linked to diverse forms of cultural production (Felski, 1989; see Chapters 8 and 9 for further discussion of this).

Moreover, Ien Ang (1991) argues that such pessimistic arguments are heavily dependent on institutional knowledges of audiences; that is, they draw on, and take at face value, knowledges which construct the audience as an objectified category of others to be controlled. Their conclusions are therefore limited; they assume what they purport to establish. She argues, in contrast, that institutional knowledge does not, and indeed cannot, understand the concrete practices and experiences of audiencehood; it is ultimately unable to supply the institutions of cultural production with the definitive guarantee of control that they so eagerly seek. She suggests that in the case of television, for example, the audience is 'an invisible and mysterious interlocutor' and, as such, is necessarily unstable. Indeeed, it has been suggested, more generally, that aggregates are less open than organised publics to planning and prediction by producers, since individuated reception does not necessarily involve participation in any organised collectivity, and both direct control by authority and the degree of institutionalisation of response are much lower. Indeed, Ang suggests that the social world of actual audiences consists of 'an infinite and ever expanding myriad of dispersed practices and experiences that can never be, and should not be, contained in any one total system of knowledge' (1991: 155).

Thus, while exhibition value is clearly the subject of commercial manipulation, it is by no means clear that this value is actually realised at the moment of its reception in these terms. That is, while the object is no longer attributed the ability to return the look, the object can still be reactivated in the process of reception, and as a consequence the mode of reproduction associated with the market implementation of technologies of replication is unstable. This is evident in the cases discussed above which suggest that it is struggles over the use or reactivation of cultural goods which are at the heart of attempts to redefine the terms on which rights in intellectual property are allocated, including the attempted substitution of novelty for that of originality as the basis for allocation. In conclusion, then, this chapter has suggested that, while the systematic character of the asymmetry of cultural production made possible by the author-function has been undermined, both the ability of creative labour to make itself visible in exhibition value, and the independence of the determinants of reception for the realisation of cultural value, mean that the commercial exploitation of the new technologies of replication is still necessarily limited by the internal instability of cultural reproduction.

NOTES

1 Although Williams uses social class, the term 'social group' has been used on the grounds that Williams' emphasis on class is unduly restrictive.
2 As Urry (1990) has noted there is a countervailing tendency in that some forms of cultural consumption are enhanced by collective reception; nevertheless, who makes up that collectivity is still an issue.
3 Miege (1979) cites a report prepared for the Council of Europe to back up the claim that the growing importance of stars has seen a growing gap between cultural producers as regards remuneration.

4

BRANDING, TRADEMARK AND THE VIRTUAL AUDIENCE

(with Nicholas Abercrombie, Scott Lash and Dan Shapiro)[1]

This chapter will provide an account of recent changes in the organisation of the culture industry. The framework it adopts draws on both the analysis of changes in the popular music sector developed by Richard Peterson and David Berger (1975) and the elaboration of this framework proposed by Paul DiMaggio (1977). It will be argued that while both accounts are important for the ways in which they make links between the social relations of cultural production for the market and the characteristics of cultural works, neither takes sufficient account of long-term transformations in the characteristics of the cultural work itself – notably, those associated with the increasing importance to its circulation of exhibition value – in their analyses of changes in the organisation of the culture industry. It will further be argued that the culture industry is increasingly organised in terms of a regime of rights characterised by branding, in which the manipulation of innovation as novelty is subsumed within the more general phenomenon of the simulation of innovation. This regime is associated with the development of the right of publicity and the constitution of cultural goods as intellectual property through trademark rather than through copyright law, and is an adaptation to the increasing importance of exhibition value in cycles of cultural reproduction.

In their influential article published in 1975, Peterson and Berger put forward the view that there is a relation between homogeneity or innovation in production and market structure. More specifically, they show that from 1948 to 1973 popular music production was characterised by stagnation and product homogeneity during periods in which there were high degrees of seller concentration. By contrast, periods of creative ferment and product innovation followed increased competition in the marketplace. In an attempt to explain this, they suggest that the degree of competition among firms affected the roles that producers and artists played in the creative process, and imply that it is the relationship between competition and creative autonomy which determines the degree of innovation in production in any particular period. During periods of oligopolistic control, creative decision-making is relatively centralised and artists and producers have minimal autonomy; during periods of competition, artists play a more important role in the recording process and producers themselves demonstrate increased independence from management.

As part of this argument, Peterson and Berger assume that managers of culture firms place a high value on predictability. As noted in the last chapter, this is particularly difficult to achieve in cultural production because of the insistent need to generate 'a constant stream of unique (if often similar) products with a severely limited life span' (DiMaggio, 1977: 441), what DiMaggio calls routine product generation. This represents an inherent source of instability in the culture industries. Nevertheless, Peterson and Berger argue that managers in the culture industry seek to maintain commercial success by adopting strategies which both inhibit competition by controlling their markets (in particular, as discussed in the last chapter, by managing promotion and distribution) and controlling and co-ordinating creative workers. Their aim is to ensure that innovation remains routine, predictable and guaranteed to produce material acceptable to the widest possible range of individuals in the controlled market. That is, they actively refrain from 'unnecessary' product competition through significant innovation and associated deroutinisation of creative work. This management strategy was discussed in the last chapter in terms of the creation and manipulation of novelty in cultural production.

DiMaggio seeks to assess the validity of this argument for the culture industry as a whole, and, in this way, aims to assess whether or not mass culture, that is, standardised production of homogenous cultural products, is likely to become increasingly widespread. He argues that because of the inevitable instability associated with the need for product generation in all sectors of the culture industry, they necessarily involve what he calls brokerage administration. Brokers – the productive and distributive intermediaries of the last two chapters – mediate the aspirations of artists for creative expression and the desire of management to be able to predict and control. However, creative workers, and their products, can only be accurately evaluated *post hoc*, on the basis of their success. During the process of production itself, the broker's criteria of evaluation are ill-defined:

> The pure broker is subject to regular communication with management and must observe a set of norms and traditions prescribing loosely the attributes of a marketable product; at the same time, the pure broker has considerable discretion in contracting and dealing with creative personnel.
>
> (DiMaggio, 1977: 443)

Unlike bureaucratic and craft forms of administration (Stinchcombe, 1959), brokerage administration is not defined by a legal relationship and lacks standards for evaluating both professional competence and the acceptability of the final product; instead, it is characterised by 'ambiguity, informality and negotiation' (DiMaggio, 1977: 442).

DiMaggio further distinguishes three types of brokerage. The first, mentioned above, a pure brokerage system, is one in which the broker serves 'both management and creator, acting as mediator, double-agent, and advocate for both, with ultimate loyalty to the former' (1977: 443). The second type, centralised brokerage systems, are, DiMaggio suggests, to be found in sectors dominated by a few firms; in these systems, brokers and artists are subordinated to management, and management personnel are involved in the creative process itself. In contrast, managers abdicate control over acquisitions and production to the broker in the third type, entrepreneurial brokerage systems; further-more, brokers may, in turn, abdicate production decisions to creative workers themselves. This third type of brokerage system is said by DiMaggio to be characteristic of highly competitive sectors of cultural production.

DiMaggio thus extends Peterson and Berger's argument by suggesting that brokerage systems are key mediating elements in the relationship between economic concentration and degrees of innovation in cultural production. In addition, he points out that, while his own typology makes use of Peterson and Berger's assumption that horizontal concentration is the principal determinant of industrial structure, it is in fact only one of a number of possible determinants including state-imposed forms of regulation, monopsony (control of the market by a few buyers), vertical integration, conglomerate concentration and inter-nationalisation. This is an important qualification to the argument proposed by Peterson and Berger, and the significance of some of these other factors will be discussed later in more detailed accounts of changes in cinema, publishing and television in the UK.

DiMaggio also recognises that market segmentation may have an impact on the diversity of products that an industry produces. Indeed, he introduces an admittedly schematic understanding of different strengths of market segmentation – minimal, strong and loose – into his analysis in order to distinguish three ideal types of cultural production systems – mass, class and pluralistic. He concludes by suggesting that contemporary American culture represents a mix of these three types, and will continue to be so constituted in the foreseeable future as a consequence of continuing competition within the culture industry. This factor – market segmentation – has been considered in the analysis put forward in the last two chapters through a discussion of the dynamic character of the process of internalising the audience. This chapter will suggest that, in addition, yet another factor needs to be taken into account in any consideration of change within the organisation of the culture industry, namely, the (changing) characteristics of the products – that is, cultural works – themselves. In other words, it is suggested that issues of cultural value have to enter into the analysis of culture industries, not only in the qualitative assessment of performance, but also as factors in institutional arrangements and changes, and thus in economic success (Shapiro et al., 1992).

It was suggested in the last chapter that the institutionalisation of certain kinds of market practices has led to the routinised implementation of forms of commercial selection. It was further suggested that the internal calculations of the market have formed the basis for a shift in the criteria of aesthetic quality as production for the audience-as-market has taken priority over any other; in other words, the set of 'norms and traditions' which prescribe the attributes of a marketable product has been undergoing qualitative change. This shift was discussed in terms of the increasing importance of exhibition value, which in turn was related to the growing importance of promotion and the increasing significance of the media as the primary institutional regulator of innovation (Hirsch, 1972). It will be argued here that the dominance of exhibition value is in itself one factor which has come to shape the systems of brokerage adopted within the culture industry, and that this long-term, secular change cuts across, and shapes, the cyclical pattern of concentration followed by competition which Peterson and Berger identify. More specifically, it will be suggested that the rise of exhibition value has contributed to a shift from what might loosely be called fordist to neo-and post-fordist forms of cultural reproduction. This argument will be developed by drawing on secondary sources and through the use of data collected from a collective research project into five sectors in the British culture industry (Abercrombie, 1990; Lash *et al.*, 1990; Lury, 1990; Shapiro, 1990; Shapiro *et al.*, 1992), including cinema, publishing, television and advertising.

This research drew extensively on debates about flexible specialisation and post-fordism (Aglietta, 1979; Piore and Sabel, 1984). However, it is clear that the applicability of the notion of mass production associated with discussions of fordism to the culture industry is limited, since, as discussed above, it is characterised by relatively innovation-intensive systems of production and makes use of a brokerage system of administration in which many aspects of the work process are governed by professionalised workers in accordance with empirical lore (Stinchcombe, 1959). Nevertheless, given this qualification, it will be suggested here that the distinction between fordism, neo-and post-fordism is useful in that it allows a consideration of the particular institutional arrangements that obtain in different economic sectors, and thus provides a framework within which to consider DiMaggio's other factors affecting industrial structure; furthermore, it highlights the role and causal significance of processes of market segmentation.

CINEMA

The film industry provides perhaps the clearest affirmative case of a shift towards post-fordism and the development of flexible specialisation (Christopherson and Storper, 1986). Most sectors of the culture industry came late to fordism, but in cinema it emerged early, from the 1920s in the USA (with the vertically integrated combines of Hollywood during 1920–1948) and, briefly, immediately after the Second World War in Britain (with Rank, 1942–1949). Production and exhibition were integrated in organisations that were able to use exhibition profits to undertake a planned programme of production in which functions as diverse as scriptwriting and costume design were centralised, and a large proportion of the staff worked in full-time waged or salaried posts.

However, this relatively stable system of production was threatened by the decline in mass consumption of cinema in the 1950s (in part associated with the emergence of television as a domestic medium).[2] According to Christopherson and Storper (1986), this created a situation in which vertical disintegration of production was adopted to minimise transaction costs. This produced flexibility in three ways. First, there has been 'upstream' disintegration of creative or 'above the line' costs: actors, directors, writers, producers, etc. Long-term arrangements, in which once-and-for-all contracts were coupled to sustained role commitments, were largely replaced by hiring on a per-project basis (Faulkner and Anderson, 1987). One consequence of this for creative workers has been that a career now has to be built from a succession of temporary projects and a performance history or profile has to be created from an identifiable line of credits. Second, there has been downstream disintegration of 'below the line' technical costs; once again, a freelancer is forced to enter into a series of contracts to acquire a cumulative line of credits and build a record of accomplishment. Third, there has been disintegration of facilities – movie theatres, studios, film libraries, camera, sound and lighting, and so on – in an attempt to minimise fixed overheads.

The result of this process of disintegration has been a transaction-rich nexus of markets and small firms, with high rates of reconstruction, although, as is often noted, multinational conglomerates still dominate the industry (Amin and Robins,

1990). Faulkner and Anderson's research (1987) provides some indication of how reputation is built within these markets. They suggest that transactions within such markets are organised through networks in which collective attributions of an individual's contribution to performances are used as a basis for decision-making:

> As a result of being observed exercising these talents when given assignments, an artist or technician accumulates a history of performance results. The results are part economic, part artistic, and part collegial industry-relevant outcomes imputed or attributed to the contributions of an individual in the community, within which the work of ambitious people is likely to be assessed by many other qualified and ambitious people. Attributes translate into professional reputation and into a distinct industry identity: the person slowly becomes a *personage*, a valuable commodity to buyers.
>
> (Faulkner and Anderson, 1987: 889)

What is significant for the argument put forward here is that the basis on which transactions are made includes imputed contributions to performance results; the terms of the visibility of this contribution clearly must thus change with changing notions of artistic quality. If this is so, it is imputed contributions to a project's *exhibition value* which now contribute to the industry identity of creative workers.

Faulkner and Anderson further argue that one cause and consequence of the significance of networks is that the distinctive identities and past successes of personnel are increasingly important to decision-making practices in the film industry. They point out that a career is a two-sided affair: buyers and sellers continuously monitor, audit and certify the performance capacities of one another in the market. On the one hand, buyers match the performance profiles of creative and technical workers to individual projects. On the other hand, projects are assessed for the possibilities they offer for satisfying the artistic and career objectives of professional creative workers including directors, cinematographers, screenwriters and composers as well as actors. Careers are thus the product of multiple relationships among combinations of buyers and sellers joined to multiple productions. The disintegration of both above- and below-the-line creative workers has directly facilitated the flexibility of such relationships; moreover, the discretionary power accorded to successful creative workers to pick and choose between projects, or even, in certain exceptional cases, bring projects into existence, has been heightened by their ability to create distinct identities through the manipulation of the effects associated with exhibition value.

This is most clear in the case of stars, whose very mode of existence has been transformed in relation to the manipulation of such effects.[3] It is commonly argued that stars produce an 'invitation' to cinema. This invitation is seen to be produced by the creation of a star phenomenon in subsidiary forms of circulation which is incomplete (only the voice, only the still photo, only the face) and paradoxical (showing the star as both ordinary and extraordinary). This phenomenon thus proposes cinema as the completion of its lacks, the synthesis of its separate and scattered fragments. Moreover, this process is seen by Ellis (1982), among others, as repeating a fundamental aspect of the cinematic apparatus itself: its representation of an absence that is present:

> In this sense, the star image is not completed by the film performance, because they both rest on the same paradox. Instead, the star image promises cinema. It restates the terms of the photo effect, renews the desire to experience this very particular sense of present-absence.
>
> (Ellis, 1982: 93)

Ellis further argues that it is the fictionality of the star's cinematic performance, together with its comparative rarity, which not only animates the desire that plays around the star's image but also holds it in place. Other moments in the circuit of circulation, Ellis suggests, are deliberately proffered as intended truths about the performer:

> The star's performance in a film reveals to the viewer all those small gestures, particular aspects of movement and expression, unexpected similarities to acquaintances or even to self.... The journalistic apotheosis of these moments witnesses the feeling that the star is caught unawares in them.... They mark the absorption of the star into the fictional character.... This is different from the

69

star's image in other forms of circulation where the elements of intentionality are very marked. The fanzine photo is obviously constructed for the look; the magazine interview or the radio broadcast participate in forms of direct address where the star is present as an intentional 'I'.

(Ellis, 1982: 99)

Ellis does not indicate how this economy of desire might have changed since the days of the Hollywood studios. However, while the comparative rarity of the cinematic image remains (despite the availability of video), the truth status of other moments in the circulation of the star image has been destabilised as a consequence of the increasing pervasiveness and self-consciousness of forms of promotion and the expansion of the performative principle in contemporary consumer culture. Each moment in the (what was once the subsidiary) circulation of the star image has been increasingly and self-consciously fictionalised. In a further twist, the fiction of film itself is increasingly understood as a form of promotion: this process is taken to its limit in Madonna's feature-promotion film, *In Bed With Madonna*.

The consequences of this for the star are mixed. In some ways, it has contributed to the lessening of the significance of the photo effect to stars and thus, indirectly, to cinema; the special significance of the cinematic performance begins to pale as it fails to synthesise the newly independent fragments of the star image. Its impact is necessarily weakened once a belief in the reality of the absent 'ordinary' person is abandoned. The desire that was offered access to its object only on condition that it was presented as absent was fuelled by the claims to truth offered in the subsidiary circulation of the star image; these claims are no longer either so intended or received. Similarly, the fetishistic moments described by Ellis in which the performer was seen to be absorbed into the fictional performance have lost their significance; they are no longer credible once acting is seen to operate as a (specialised) form of fictionalised self-creation and promotion. The decline of this mode of stardom is indicated by the claim that Elizabeth Taylor was the last 'real' star (although see below); but it has not disappeared – Meryl Streep, Warren Beatty, Robert de Niro and a few others still shine in the firmament.

At the same time a new kind of star is emerging; these stars are sustained through the strategic and self-conscious manipulation of performative intentionality across media; their appeal derives from their capacity to make the actual virtual and the virtual actual, and their radiance flickers with an oscillation between two and three dimensions. Jack Nicholson, Madonna and Arnold Schwarzenegger are the most obvious current examples of this phenomenon. Within this mode of stardom, the 'value-added' from an artist comes not from the management of the distance between their image and their creative abilities, but from its collapse. The previous distinction between acting and image, between creative achievement and ascriptive condition, is effaced – for Madonna, her image is precisely her achievement (and, as will be discussed later, her property). A review of *In Bed With Madonna* notes that, 'with its self-consciously grainy 16mm black-and-white backstage footage, we see La Ciconne argue, scream, undress, shout, pray, laugh, suck and scowl in a manner sold as natural'. But this is not intended to fool:

> despite the chronology of her career, Madonna is a film star first and a pop star second. It matters not whether she is on or off stage – what is significant is that she is in front of a camera, and thus in full performance mode throughout. 'Why would she want to say anything off camera? She doesn't want to live off camera', mumbles Warren Beatty, hitting the nail on the head. Neither you nor I will ever see Madonna in her private moments, and why would we want to? From the vocal acrobatics to the jaw-dropping deep-throat performed on a passing [*sic*] bottle, it's all an elaborate pantomime. *In Bed With Madonna* is proof positive that Madonna can act.
>
> (Kermode, 1991: 102)

What this comment suggests is that Madonna's star appeal is better revealed in her acting of the promo-fictional character Madonna than in that of a character part in any feature film – she revels in her own intentionally fictive acts; the moments of revelation occur when the actuality of Madonna the star is subsumed by the virtuosity/virtuality of Madonna the promotion.

As Barry King (1985) argues, the emergence of this new kind of star is related to a series of more general changes in the criteria by which acting is evaluated. He suggests that contemporary stardom is 'a strategy of performance that is an adaptive response to the limits and pressures exerted upon acting as a discursive practice in the mainstream cinema' (King, 1985: 27). More particularly, he suggests that there has been a shift from the evaluation of acting in terms of impersonation, in which the persona of the actor should disappear into the part, to evaluation in terms of personification, in which the performance of a part is subsumed by the actor's persona. While King recognises that the persona of the actor as star has always entered into the construction of a character, he suggests that it has now become the baseline for the evaluation of a performance:

> The moment of the star image is, in fact, the moment of a proprietorial claim to such effects as though they were a property of the star as a person, a claim which subsists not primarily in what is represented on the screen, but in the subsidiary literature where the image is rendered as a 'real life' property of its bearer, the actor as star.
>
> (King, 1985: 40)

King suggests that the privileging of impersonation was related to an organisation of film production in which control was exercised by the director. This control has, however, been challenged by changes which are related by King to what he calls hypersemiotisation, but which was discussed in the last chapter in terms of Benjamin's notion of apperception. As part of these changes, close shooting invests greater meaning in the star as a signifying entity, involving in the process of signification a detailed focus on parts of the actor's body, such as the eyes, mouth and hair, and habitual expressions. King suggests that, as the scale of observation is increased, the range of behaviours approaches the uncontrollable in directorial terms. As a consequence of this, King suggests, there is an increasing emphasis on what is unique to the actor, displacing emphasis from what an actor *can do qua* actor on to what the actor *qua* person or biographical entity *is*. Actors thus become increasingly committed in their on- and off-screen life to personification in the hope that, by stabilising the relationship between person and image on screen, they may seem to be the 'natural' proprietors of a marketable persona. Arnold Schwarzenegger's body-building and Michael Jackson's use of cosmetic surgery as part of a bigger project of literal self-creation can be seen as examples of the bodily attempt to manage this process; more generally, an attempt is made to create a personal monopoly of a particular personality. In this process, the previously existing terms of the constitution of cultural works as intellectual property are challenged.

The shift in modes of evaluating acting is seen by King to have been exacerbated by the trend towards short-term contractual employment for actors. He suggests that personification provides a mechanism through which the star's contribution can be represented as resting on his or her private properties as a person, thus reducing the possibilities of being replaced. However, legal support for a monopoly in the exploitation of such personal attributes has not always been forthcoming. In the USA, for example, the right of privacy, recognised as an individual personal right, provides the private person with rights of property to his name and likeness. However, until recently, famous persons were seen, legally, to have waived their rights to privacy and thus could not claim such rights in their person.

In the 1942 Texas case, *O'Brien* v *Pabst Sales Co.* documented by John Viera (1988), plaintiff David O'Brien, a famous football player of the time, sued the Pabst Blue Ribbon Beer Company. This company had been distributing yearly football calendars with photographs of football players, including O'Brien, amidst advertisements for Pabst beer without securing the players' permission. However, the Court found that even if

> the mere use of one's picture in truthful, respectful advertising, would be an actionable invasion of privacy in the case of a private person, the use here was not, as to plaintiff, such an invasion, for as a result of his activities and prowess in football, his chosen field, and their nationwide and deliberate publicizing with his consent and in his interest, he was no longer, as to them, a private but a public person, and as to their additional publication he had no right of privacy.
>
> (Quoted in Viera, 1988: 141)

Such rulings indicate a legal awareness that media images or personalities exist in the minds of the public, and their value, as intangible intellectual property, derives from the public's willingness to buy copies of this image; as Viera writes, 'Media images exist society-wide in a shared cultural plane' (1988: 145).

However, such views have been modified as a result of rulings in support of claims made by 'public persons', notably stars, to ownership of their image, and are beginning to coalesce in a so-called right of publicity. Yet even here, although there is great variation and even flat contradiction between states, the question of the role of the public in the creation of the value of an image has re-emerged. So while the right of publicity, if it is converted from a personal to a property right through the individual's exploitation of his or her image via merchandising when alive, can be inherited, the question of ownership surfaces in relation to issues of descent and transferability. As a court ruling in a dispute relating to the use of Elvis imagery asked, the key question here is 'Who is the heir of fame?'. In this case, the court held that 'fame often is fortuitous and fleeting. It always depends on the participation of the public in the creation of an image', and stated that 'the memory, name and pictures of famous individuals should be regarded as a common asset to be shared, an economic opportunity to be available in the free market' (*Memphis Development Foundation* v *Factors Etc. Inc.*, 616 F.2d 956, 957, 960, quoted in Viera, 1988: 151). In contrast, the Personal Rights Protection Act in Tennessee explicitly provides that an individual has a property right in name, photograph, personality and likeness that survives death; similarly, the Celebrities Rights Act in California applies such rights to deceased 'personalities', defined as 'any natural person whose name, voice, signature, photograph or likeness has commercial value at the time of his or her death' (quoted in Viera, 1988: 153).

A further issue relating to the possibility of a star's ownership of his or her image derives from the fact that the emphasis on personification means that while a star's persona is itself a character, it is one that transcends placement or containment in a particular narrative and exists in cinematic rather than filmic time and space. This might be thought to strengthen the claims of stars to rights in their own image, at least in relation to other creative workers such as directors. However, King suggests that the use of the strategy of personification by stars in an attempt to control their effects is undercut by the extent to which the formative capacity of the cinematic apparatus continues to confine them to being a bearer of effects that they do not or cannot originate. However, as the examples of Michael Jackson and Madonna indicate, even the effects of this capacity are diminished with the rise in importance of other media as sites for the circulation of the star's persona.

The increase in the importance of other sites raises yet other problems, however, including those associated with attempts by stars to restrict the exploitation of this decontextualised or transferable image. Elizabeth Taylor, for example, brought a suit against ABC on the grounds that a fictional made-for-television film would cause irreparable damage to her by exploiting her name, likeness, and public and professional reputation and image. She claimed that 'I am my own commodity and industry. ... This is my industry and if someone else portrays me and fictionalizes my life, it is taking away from my industry' (*The Hollywood Reporter*, quoted in Viera, 1988: 157). Taylor's central claim was that docudramas about her life compete against the films she chooses to appear in for an audience's attention, that is, that she is, in effect, forced to compete against herself. In this case, however, the court held that Taylor's right of publicity should not outweigh the rights of others to free expression.

At a less than celestial level creative workers have limited ability even to make claims to such rights. Indeed, Faulkner and Anderson argue that another consequence of the emergence of webs of recurrent transactions among such experience-rated personnel is that transaction-specific segments begin to emerge. Such segments are characterised by restricted access and high densities of market transactions among participants with similar career profiles. Their development thus contributes to the disparity between 'winners' and 'non-winners', as the successes make use of (accumulating) resources to achieve recurrent contracting in the market. Faulkner and Anderson conclude that there is marked inequality in such contracting systems; as one of their informants noted, ' "This industry operates with a very short list" ' (1987: 905).

The characteristic mode of film production in such disintegrated systems, then, has a small group of entrepreneurs, sometimes a director alone or a director with a producer, aiming to assemble a 'package'. This package consists of an idea worked into a script, together with commitments from key personnel such as stars, camerapersons, editors and composers. This package is then touted round to various possible sources of production funding, including distributors. If a distribution guarantee and enough money are raised, the production goes ahead. Increasingly, it is an agent or an agency which will put together such packages, sometimes to further the career of one

client or because of a fortuitous combination of clients represented by one agency. Indeed, the increasing power of the agent
contributes here, as in some other sectors of the culture industry,
to an unusual feature: a complex management structure, existing
separately from any corporation, whose principal value-adding
function is to manage the reputation of its clients. It can be
argued that the rise of such agencies is one indication of a
convergence between advertising and certain sectors in the
culture industry, in that, in both cases, such agencies create
packages or brands which enhance a product through their
presentation of effects which are intended to 'produce' audiences
either for that product itself or others (Smythe, 1982). In this
sense, the advertising industry provides a model for cinema and
other sectors in the culture industry.

However, there are also tensions between different parties
within and across the industry sectors about how this model is to
be emulated. Ties between agents (in conjunction with actors,
directors and producers) and distributors (commonly the major
studios, banks, inside 'professional' investors and outside
partners) are now commonly formed on a per-picture basis, and
the fact that studios sponsor many more projects than are
completely funded gives them leeway and discretion. Some
projects die in story conferences, others fall apart as outlines or
scripts or fail to attract the attention and commitment of other
investors, while others still are made but fail to secure adequate
promotion and distribution. The common basis on which such
decisions are made is that of their assumed probability of success
in the market, but agents, producers and distributors may have
conflicting interests in the constitution and control of this
market: David Puttnam's short term of office as studio head of
Columbia Pictures has, for example, been put down, in part, to
his conflict over the financial terms of contracts between the
studio and stars and their agents.

Ellis (1982) argues that some films, blockbusters in particular,
have increasingly come to be judged in terms of their capacity to
act as a logo, trademark or have a distinct product image. In
these cases, the particular film-product is not the only product
that can be sold through the creation and circulation of this
image: it is also used to sell a series of other products – records,
clothes, toys, books, magazines, confectionery, among others.
However, while, for example, stars commonly feature as part of

this product image, there are cases in which the furthering of a star's persona may not be served by the product image developed around a film; this is an extension of the conflict identified in the last chapter between the constitution of the audience-as-market (for cultural products) or as-consumer (for cultural and other products). The use of animated characters or special effects animals/machines can be seen as a response to this potential conflict between product image and persona: Mickey Mouse is the shining example of the well-behaved performer here. When real-life performers are involved, the best contracts tend to be reserved for those who can be relied upon to produce products that fit the preferred product image.

In general terms, then, the diseconomies of scale in the previously hierarchical form of organisation have been displaced by economies of agglomeration (Scott, 1988) which are knit together through systems of brokerage in which agents have an increasingly powerful role. These changes in the sector structure have been accompanied by changes in the product along the lines noted in the last chapter. On the one hand, there has indeed been an emphasis on the blockbuster: a successful blockbuster such as *Star Wars* or *Alien* can offset the losses from less popular films, revitalise the fortunes of studios and establish the distinct identities of industry personnel. While such a strategy might be seen as no more than a return to the routine product generation which characterised classic studio production, such projects require distinctive, often spectacular, characteristics or characters; that is, they must have a high degree of product differentiation from the others that surround them to be successful. They become general cultural events through their massive but skilful use of publicity, expenditure on which often exceeds that on the film's production and is intended to create the conditions for the successful exploitation of a product image. On the other hand, there has also been increasing specialisation: many films are now produced for smaller market segments, including, for example, young people. Such films offer competitive rates of return owing to relatively low breakeven points. The groups targeted for specialised production tend to be those that have a relatively large amount of disposable income, so there is a certain circularity in the process: cinema now tends to address its films towards those fractions of the market that recognise themselves in various forms of leisure activity, one of which is cinema attendance. This encourages the use of certain forms of intertextuality such as pastiche, and contributes to the increasingly rapid turnover in fashion in ways which, in turn, add to the effectivity of exhibition value in contemporary cultural reproduction, and thus intensify the processes described here.

PUBLISHING

In publishing, by contrast to cinema, even the transition to fordism was quite recent for many firms, and did not happen until the integration of hardback and paperback publishing in the 1970s. However, many firms currently display a form of neo-fordism; specifically, there is a high concentration of multi-divisional firms, in which divisions of the same firm compete against one another, but ownership and some functions remain integrated. So publishers now often consist of multiple imprints, often making use of the name of firms which have been taken over; these may be run as separate profit centres in a decentralised fashion. In this kind of set-up, editorial meetings routinely include other departmental representatives, including those from marketing, sales, production and rights. Decisions to publish are now thus typically the complex result of a collective process rather than the experienced whim of an individual as had been the case in the classical, or heroic, days of publishing.

However, in publishing too, some degree of disintegration has occurred. Warehousing, invoicing, distribution, design and copy-editing as well as printing and binding are now sometimes externalised, and increasingly organised in terms of just-in-time production. In addition, some of the functions of commissioning editors and rights and contract departments are now being sub-contracted out, often to newly empowered agents. Moreover, while there has been remarkably little change in the five-firm concentration ratio since the early 1960s, there has been a disproportionate increase in the number and output of smaller publishers – Headline and Bloomsbury are two examples of the most recent wave: the 50 largest groups accounted for about 80 per cent of book sales in 1979 and for less than 70 per cent in 1988. Furthermore, there is some evidence to support the claim that at least some of these new firms display some aspects of flexible specialisation in that they are both more likely to make use of outsourcing and direct their products at small, specialised markets.

In general, however, despite or perhaps because of disintegration, many of the large firms appear to be characterised by centralised forms of brokerage: indeed, meetings were a theme of our publishing interviews:

> Editors have to be under an editorial director and spend their time in meetings. Editorial directors, of course, are far too busy organising the meetings actually to get any books themselves, except they might dash out to see an important editor or something.
>
> (Senior managing editor)

Similarly, one editorial director described the changes in his work when his rather traditional firm was merged with a more dynamic, profit-oriented concern in the following way: 'When I started out . . . when I took a book on . . . it didn't have to go through a meeting at all. I just filled in the forms and proposed numbers.' In the new regime, however,

> we started the system which we now have that the editor who wants to put up a proposal has actually not only got to ask marketing colleagues about it, but has to get them to put down numbers and sign to those numbers.

However, the ultimate controls appear to be financial. Moreover, the source of this capital is changing as increasing numbers of companies are actively involved with what many respondents called 'City money', leading to greater pressure for both higher and, significantly, more rapid rates of return.

While publishing firms have for a long time had working capital provided by the banks, they were also well practised at internal financing through retention of profits. This was related to their ownership as family firms: profit rates were not expected to be high and returns on investment in an author were typically long term rather than immediate. In general terms, there was a tendency to accept high risks and lower immediate profitability and turnover in hopes that once a book was part of the backlist, it would continue to find new buyers (Bourdieu, 1977, quoted in Coser *et al.*, 1982). Moreover, the family sometimes also provided continuing finance. Such practices were dependent upon the effective operation of the author-function and the stability in audience taste ensured by the maintenance of links between education and cultural élites in the public sphere, including the development of the academic subject English literature and secure funding to a public library system. However, more recently, as the public sphere has fragmented as a result of both internal and external pressures, families have been selling their stakes in publishing companies: a number of companies are now publicly quoted and more have had shareholdings bought by outside interests (other than publishers). Furthermore, several of the fairly large recent start-ups have merchant bank finance as equity participation.

This change in ownership patterns has coincided with the introduction of more rigorous internal financial regimes and practices which require rapid returns on investment; this, in turn, has prompted a higher rate of product turnover and the minimisation of long-term risk-taking practices. It is also associated with the tendency selectively to raid backlists for works whose potential sales have been under-exploited, and, in conjunction with internationalisation, has contributed to the intensive promotion of literary properties across a wider range of territories. There has, furthermore, been increasing interest in the exploitation of rights in literary products across other media, and, as a consequence, the importance of subsidiary rights in film, magazine serialisation and television has grown enormously. In these ways, then, the spatio-temporal parameters of the reproduction of publishing as an industry have been transformed.

One particularly noteworthy aspect of these general changes is the 'squeeze' of power from distributors to production firms at one end, and from authors to production firms at the other. With booksellers, it is a case of the concentration of distribution giving commercial capital considerable leverage over production capital: as one informant noted, 'the temperature has gone up considerably'. This is reflected both in discounting arrangements – stretched from 30 per cent to as much as 50 per cent – and in the growing influence of booksellers, with sophisticated point-of-sale information systems, over what is published and how it is promoted:

> for the first time ever booksellers know more about the sales of their books than the publishers do. Publishers used to tell booksellers things. Now booksellers, through electronic point of sale, say that our fiction is going up, and our health and diets going down, and business books aren't doing well.
>
> (Marketing director)

Traditionally, publishers were interested in talking to booksellers about the titles they were about to publish: for example, quarterly sales conferences brought publishers and large booksellers together and the latter were consulted about such questions as cover design, but their view was not decisive. However, booksellers are now becoming involved higher and higher up the publishing chain; occasionally, this is to the extent that they will have influence on publishing policy – what kinds of book to publish and even whether or not to publish a particular title. While some publishers are unhappy with this, others see the closer relationship with the bookseller in more positive terms: the bookseller is believed to provide the customers' view and this is increasingly seen as essential knowledge for the publisher. In this way, interpretations of the audience-as-market (rather than as audience-as-public) are coming to have an increasingly important role in commissioning decisions.

At the other end of the squeeze by distributors, there has been the increasing power of successful authors to command huge advances. This is in part associated with the integration between hardback and paperback firms, but it is also tied to the disintegration of editorial functions on to agents. The result has been a diminution of the in-house editorial role:

> There was a time when editors were the top of the heap; they are not the top of the heap now actually. Editors have gone down, I believe, within the publishing house in status very considerably. . . . It has happened very gradually, because all sorts of people have intruded themselves over the top, the accountants, the market forces, and one thing and another.
>
> (Senior managing editor)

Agents have always represented authors, finding a suitable publisher, intervening between author and publisher, and negotiating the best terms for the author. The modern agent, however, goes much further than this. She (for it is very commonly) will not only work to get the best financial deal for authors: negotiating advances, royalty terms, and the maximum of finance for as many rights – paperback, serialisation, film, foreign publication, and so on – as possible; but she will also attempt to influence production decisions, particularly the physical appearance of the book, and try to secure a good promotions budget for the author. In addition, the agent will also take on the primary nurturing role, giving encouragement and advice to the author and suggesting rewrites.

Once again then, as in cinema, a creative management system has developed independently of specific firms, providing an organisational basis for entrepreneurial forms of brokerage; and once again, this development is, at least in part, both a cause and consequence of the increasing importance attached to notions of exhibition value. This management system has provided a context in which the successful author can acquire the status of a star as in cinema. Such author-stars are often no longer recognised through their creative achievement, that is, their appeal does not primarily derive from the ways in which their books (or related products) are read as expressions of their self, but, rather, as in the case of cinema, by means of their ability to act as the focus of an image property: Catherine Cookson, Barbara Cartland and Jackie Collins are prime examples here.

TELEVISION

Television in the UK was born fordist, partly because of the capital costs and the scale of organisation involved, but more importantly because of the structure imposed on it by the state and inherited from radio. The BBC was a classic Chandlerian hierarchy, although, since its inception, it has been continually modified to try to cope with the special problems of the management of creative labour (Burns, 1979). This form was (and is) further overlain by the state with mechanisms of external control such as the BBC Board of Governors and its legally defined constitution. Independent television, established in 1955, took another state-invented form: a state-sponsored and (through the ITA/IBA) state-supervised commercial network of regional monopolies.

Taken together, the systems were a curious mixture of duopoly and dual monopoly: the BBC with a monopoly of licence revenue and ITV with a monopoly of advertising finance, but with the competition between them for audience share affecting – in different ways – their actual income (see Chapter 6). So, for example, the rapid popularity of ITV in the late 1950s shook the BBC's security, and led to a questioning of some aspects of its hierarchy of control; in this case, centralised brokerage gave way to more entrepreneurial techniques. New creative talent was hired, and there followed a burst of acclaimed innovative programming; however, the late 1960s saw the imposition of a new corporate strategy in which, as in the case of publishing, financial accountability was foregrounded (Burns, 1979). Later, there were more state-imposed changes: when the BBC gained a second channel in 1964, oriented to an élite high culture market segment and other complementary audience segments; and with the establishment of Channel 4 in 1982.

The most recent changes in regulatory arrangements required by the Broadcasting Act (1990) contribute to the already visible move in the direction of flexible specialisation, though this is still more evident in some parts of the sector than in others. There has, for example, been externalisation of employment through increased use of freelance staff and of agencies, and with this has gone a decline in job security, and in union membership and influence. For example, most ITV companies have forced flexible deals on their own workforces, and the BBC has embarked on succeeding rounds of both labour and cost cutting, and of restructuring intended to focus resources more directly on programme-making; standard contract lengths have also been reduced. Teams are increasingly gathered together for a particular production only, and specialise in a particular type of production. The use of contract services and facilities houses has greatly expanded, even in the BBC and the large ITV companies.

Furthermore, the publishing model – adopted for Channel 4, and an increasingly important aspect of the other channels because of the imposition of the independent production quota – has institutionalised a distinction between production functions on the one hand and 'common carrier' distribution and editorial functions on the other. This has led to a growth in small production companies, some specialised, some general-purpose opportunist, and some *ad hoc*, although there are signs that the near monopsony purchaser relation of Channel 4 to independent production has had the effect of making the lives of many such companies harsh and short (Amin and Robins, 1990). To some extent, then, there has been a move towards production in small 'disintegrated' outfits in which commercial and creative functions are united, or where, at the least, creative staff are required to have financial and marketing considerations in mind as an integral part of the job.

Nevertheless, in many ways television can be seen as a case of arrested development (Shapiro *et al.*, 1992) in that state regulation has effectively constrained the effectivity of market relations, and moderated the tendency towards vertical disintegration identified in cinema and publishing. Furthermore, the continuing dominance of a public service ethic has limited the role and significance of exhibition value in broadcasting in that it preserves the authority of the producer at the cost of reducing the importance attached to the production of audiences. In addition, it has been suggested that certain characteristics of the medium necessarily restrict such developments: so, for example, it has been argued that performers on television are less likely to be able to become stars (Ellis, 1982); indeed, a distinction has been made between the stars of cinema (Dyer, 1979) and the personalities of television (Lusted, 1991). Both draw upon the myth of the individual, but while, as noted above, the cinema foregrounds notions of difference and distance, television affects connections of intimacy with its audience through forms of direct address; the performer thus lacks the necessary mystique required for (the traditional mode of) stardom. However, if, as suggested above, such mystique is less and less necessary for the operation of the star-function, the luminosity of the celebrity-personality is likely to wax brighter.

The difficulty of achieving stardom on television has also been attributed to the relatively standardised nature of programming in broadcasting – discussed in the last chapter in terms of seriality – as opposed to the emphasis on the single or unique text in the cinema. However, it will be argued here that it is precisely this feature, that is, the use of iterative or redundant narratives, which provides the basis for the increasing use of a related valorisation technique, namely the character as an image property. The use of characters in this way has been aided by the emergence of trademark law as the governing principle of character protection in popular formats, at least in the USA;[4] indeed, it has been suggested that the trademark has begun to replace copyright in certain areas of cultural reproduction as the preferred means of legal protection for intellectual property (Gaines, 1990a).

In her article 'Superman and the protective strength of the trademark', Jane Gaines (1990a) suggests that copyright began to fall out of fashion as early as the 1954 Sam Spade case. The case focused on whether Warner Brothers' motion picture rights to the novel *The Maltese Falcon* should include the right to enjoin author Dashiell Hammett from using the character in sequels. The courts demurred and gave Spade back to Hammett. However, in the process they defined characters as *potentially* mobile pieces in relation to the work: the character had to constitute the work as a whole in order for it to be protected by copyright. Characters which did not meet this requirement, that is, those seen as potentially transferable across works, were thus potentially unprotectable by copyright, and the exclusive rights of the property owner were consequently called into doubt. In contrast to copyright, trademark law allows for the protection of the character independently of any relation to the work of which it is a part. Furthermore, and again in contrast to copyright, with its emphasis on originality and authorship, trademark law protects both title and character simply *if they emanate from the same source*. In short, the name of a character can, through the use of trademark, become independent of its context of origin and name any other product; these products can, in turn, become an element of the identity of the character.

As a consequence, there has, since the Sam Spade case, been a tendency, at least in the US, to use trademark law in preference to copyright as the preferred means of securing the profitability of popular titles and characters. A trademark provides a legal shield around the name, logo, slogan, shape, or character image and, in conjunction with product licensing,[5] makes it possible for the original proprietor to transfer this sign to second and third parties for a limited period of time in exchange for royalties. It has increasingly thus come to set the terms for the constitution and exploitation of intellectual property both within and, crucially, *outside* the culture industry; that is, it supports the exploitation of the image property across all forms of production. To this extent, copyright has been replaced by trademark as the preferred legal remedy to the crisis of replication posed by the new technologies of culture.

As Gaines suggests, the displacement of copyright by trademark is indicative of a conflict over cultural values: most generally, between authorship and sponsorship as the principle of protection, but also between rounded and flat characters. As outlined above, copyright law can only be used to protect effectively the rounded as opposed to the flat character; this might be thought to help secure the rounded character's prospects of survival in contemporary culture. However, rounded characters have other limitations from the point of view of the intellectual property owner: as noted in Chapter 2, they have to develop and change along the chronology of classical narrative time; that is, they are defined in and through life choices which only bring them closer to their own death. In contrast, flat characters are not constrained by any such inevitability. Indeed, as Eco (1979) remarks, the flat character of Superman is defined precisely by his abstention from experiences which might produce change or personal growth; significantly, for example, sexual encounters are presented as explicitly threatening to his very being.[6] With every human-like act Superman would approach death and so consume himself as intellectual property. As Gaines wryly notes, 'the profitability of the literary property requires this impossibility: a semihuman character who is immortal and a story which never really ends' (Gaines, 1990a: 181). Flat characters come closest to meeting these impossible demands; they are 'inconsumable' in Eco's terms. Superman's actions will never extinguish him; rather, he is intended to repeat them endlessly. As such, they provide a sound investment for the intellectual proprietor. Moreover, as was noted in the last chapter, it is with the repetitive flow of the series – and especially the television series – that the flat character has found the ideal form for ensuring his or her immortality.

Flat characters can either be animations or played by actors. If they are embodied, there is potential for conflict between the interests of the performer-as-star and the owners of the trademark; the very human form which the character assumes in live-action manifestations is a potential danger to profit. Gaines notes that while legal commentators have generally concurred that cartoon characters cannot lose their identities to actors, the Lone Ranger and Bela Lugosi (Dracula) cases (in which the actors' rights to the roles they had played were asserted) provide cautionary warnings. In the latter case, Bela Lugosi's contract with Universal Pictures gave the latter the right to reproduce and exploit any and all the actor's 'acts, poses, plays and appearances of any and all kinds' and to use the actor's 'name and likeness, photographic or otherwise' (quoted in Viera, 1988: 147) in connection with the advertising and exploitation of the photoplay *Dracula*. The court deemed that Lugosi himself had owned the rights to other uses of his particular character expression (as opposed to uses of the character type), including merchandising rights for the name, likeness and appearance as Count Dracula. However, the Court also found that Lugosi had failed to convert his image-value into a property right, and his personal rights expired with him in 1956 and could not pass to his heirs. Nevertheless, this ruling suggests that the actor playing the part of a character can challenge the monopoly that the trademark owners have on their image properties since the actor could conceivably argue that he or she had an ownership in the role with which he or she had become synonymous through the application of the right of publicity. More generally, though, what Gaines' analysis suggests is that the flat character of the iterated or series narrative has as much potential to provide the basis for an image property as the cinematic star, and that television provides an ideal medium for such characters' lives.

In general terms, then, these accounts of changes in the cinema, publishing and television sectors of the culture industry suggest that there has been a move towards neo-and post-fordist forms of reproduction, with varying degrees of vertical disintegration. However, at the same time as vertically disintegrating, many of the key culture industry players are horizontally integrating (Amin and Robins, 1990). Moreover, conglomerisation is intimately bound up with internationalisation – of ownership, sales and co-production deals; national cultural boundaries are increasingly permeable. Moreover, it was further suggested that degrees of owner concentration are overlain by diverse forms of brokerage and state regulation. This seems to imply that it is not possible to assume the direct relationship between degrees of concentration and the extent of innovation proposed by Peterson and Berger (1975).

Furthermore, it has been suggested that changing constructions of cultural value make it inappropriate to employ static notions of innovation. Instead, it has been argued that what might be called *branding*, the forging of links of image and perception between a range of products, has become an increasingly significant production strategy within and across the culture industry: the aim being to achieve repeated exchange in a predictable manner (Lash *et al.*, 1990). Branding can be realised in a number of different ways: across a series of products within a sector, across a range of products within the culture industry as a whole, and also, crucially, outside the culture industry itself. As outlined above, branding operates through the strategic creation of the effects associated with exhibition value, and can be recognised in the star, the character as an image property, and associated forms of promotion and packaging, all of which contribute to what can be described as the simulation of innovation (Lash *et al.*, 1990) in contrast to previous regimes for the manipulation of innovation as either originality or novelty.

In so far as the achievement of branding is coming to define the culture industry, it can further be suggested that its various sectors are operating, not as businesses *per se*, but as business services, 'adding' value through their organisation of the effects through which audiences are produced for other products. In this sense, advertising provides a model for the culture industry. At the same time, advertising, classified as a business service, is coming to see itself more in terms of 'commercial communication' (Saatchi and Saatchi's description of its own activity). It has come to see the production of advertisements not only as a means of selling commodities, but as the creation of artefacts.

This recognition was institutionalised in the UK with the introduction of account planning, in which an advertisement is planned for an account by testing it out on small groups of consumers. These small groups of consumers view the advertisement collectively while it is in a design stage and, by way of group discussions, play a crucial role in determining the final form of the advertising campaign. One of our interviewees noted that the consumers who participate in account planning act in effect as 'creative judges'; they look at advertisements not in terms of consumption so much as in terms of entertainment: advertisements are judged as 'artefacts', 'abstract things' (agency director). This tendency is given public legitimacy in the media's treatment of advertising: advertisements are evaluated as art in *The Late Show*, and the annual advertising industry prize-giving has taken its place on television alongside the BAFTA film and television awards and the publishing industry's Booker prize. Moreover, the evaluation of advertisements in these terms is exploited by corporations through the licensing of product logos or trademarks; for example, R.J. Reynolds and Philip Morris can license their *Camel* and *Marlboro* trademarks for leisure wear

(Gaines, 1990a). Account planning is thus emblematic of the implosion of the economic – advertising as a business service – into the cultural – advertising as a sector of the communications or culture industry (Lash, 1990).

In the most general terms, branding can be seen as the locus of an attenuated fiction effect, what Margaret Morse (1990), in a discussion of television and its analogues, the freeway and the mall, terms distraction (a term presumably deriving from Benjamin, 1970). She identifies the general preconditions of distraction in the phenomenon of mobile privatisation (Williams, 1981); as part of this tendency, the culture industry is characterised, as noted earlier, by a deep, and multiply determined, contradiction between centralised production and privatised reception. As a consequence of this contradiction, contemporary cultural production is both 'adamantly intentional and resolutely non-interactive' (Ang, 1991). When this dynamic is combined with the internalisation of a notion of an increasingly self-reflexive audience-as-market or audience-as-consumer, it results in the *virtual inclusion* of the audience.

The virtuality of this inclusion is evident in a number of processes. Sometimes, it is invisible, as in the testing of cultural works before their distribution:

> The major networks test new products *before* they are aired, hoping to 'take the guesswork out of TV production' (J. Nelson, 1987: 88). Test audiences push buttons or switch dials so that technicians can trace overall audience response to each moment of a previewed program. . . . Programs are then refined in response to these encounters.
>
> (Berland, 1992: 40)

The application of this technique means that cultural works come to provide a vehicle for the audience's unwitting self-consumption (Berland, 1992). In other cases, this self-consumption is more conscious; as when, for example, the audience's participation is artificially added in to the broadcast transmission, as in the case of the use of 'canned' laughter in sit-coms, and when *actual* members of the audiences themselves appear in the cultural product, as participants in quiz shows such as *Blind Date* for instance. In such shows, participants show a clear awareness of their role, and indeed can be seen to be playing up to the part expected of them. The Radio 1 show *Steve Wright in the Afternoon* provides one of the most concentrated displays of such techniques, including the repetitive use of simulated phone calls from imaginary characters, such as Mr Angry, based on stereotypical representations of phone-in individuals.

Margaret Morse (1990) suggests that what has been called here virtual inclusion is a defining characteristic of television itself, not simply individual programmes. She sees television as a cyborgian 'machine subject' which is part partner and part spectacle in the process of communication, situated both outside and inside the home. Television is seen to be characterised by a fiction of discourse in that the television transmission offers itself to the audience as a quasi-subject, addressing its audience members personally and directly as a 'you'. Morse also contrasts the conventional story space of cinema with the discourse space of television in which a virtual form of direct address is played out across a variety of genres, including news, sports and chat shows. In this discourse space, narrators as hosts, presenters, news and sports-casters either look directly out of the screen at the viewer position, or, alternatively, an economy of looks between the host, interviewees and representatives of the audience creates phantom crowd and phantom audience effects. Morse notes that this representation of discourse as sociality offers the viewer, 'a fictive sociality, a poor simulacrum of human exchange, but without its pitfalls or obligations' (1990: 13). She thus concludes that television, a medium structured to prevent dialogue, has developed a fictional form of dialogue which displaces the desire for subjectivity itself.

Virtual inclusion can also be seen to structure the constitution and exploitation of intellectual property. It underpins, for example, the increasing importance of secondary rights (which amounts to the selling *of* audiences within and outside the culture industry) rather than primary rights (which are rights linked to sales *to* audiences);[7] the cases of the use of music in advertising (think of Coca-Cola, Pepsi Cola, Lévi Strauss) and in television and film provide the most obvious examples here. The importance of virtual inclusion is also evident in the operation of trademark in the US which requires the proprietor to establish the widespread use of an image property *in order to establish a claim*; the consequence of this is that, as Jane Gaines notes,

Unwittingly, the consumer then participates in a kind of

90

marking off of the territory of culture, which designates particular sign areas as out of bounds for users, some of whom are the very consumers whose use-practices have helped establish the claim.

(Gaines, 1990a: 185)

Yet, as a result of the diversity of types of reception possible in the context of reactivation, virtual inclusion is not actual incorporation. On the one hand, as noted in the last chapter, what audiences actually do with cultural products is not predetermined by producers; the processes of reactivation are not contained by this process of inclusion. So, for example, Janice Radway's research into the practices of the readers of popular romance fiction stories suggests that consumers of branded products have well-developed (if not high-brow) aesthetic criteria and differentiate among products on the basis of (their view of) product quality (Radway, 1987). On the other hand, the very success of branding, as the regime of rights associated with virtual inclusion, brings about its own demise; as Jane Gaines points out, the threat that faces Superman is not of non-use or abandonment, but of emasculation brought on by popularity itself as a direct result of fifty years of product merchandising and licensing:

> Built into the Lanham Act of 1946 [the US Trademark Act of 1946] is a seldom-invoked provision which gives the US Federal Trade Commission the power to cancel a trademark in the name of competition if, through the success of its proprietors, it really does become the household term they set out to make it. Thus it was that Abercrombie and Fitch lost 'safari' and Bayer lost its monopoly on 'aspirin', which went the way of thermos, zipper, escalator, cellophane, ping-pong, yo-yo, brasserie, and shredded wheat: all from protected trademark to generic *descriptive* term available to competitors. The specter of a final peril for the protectors of SUPERMAN is raised by the concern in the plastic laminate business; because the trademark may become generic through universal recognition, SUPERMAN might face the fate of 'formica'.

(Gaines, 1990a: 188)

91

In conclusion, then, it has been suggested that the culture industry has always been concerned with the creation and exploitation of intellectual property; and that the emergence and development of the new reproductive technologies have provided a focus for struggles over the exploitation of the rights of reproduction in such property. It was further suggested that attribution of authorship has historically provided a basis for both the adjudication of such rights through copyright and the management of innovation through the identification of originality, but that, in the most recent stages of production for the market, its commercial, legal and cultural authority have been undermined. The creation of brands in the advanced stages of production for the market has been seen here to have replaced the operation of the author-function; that is, it has been suggested that branding is intended to operate as a new regime of rights within which a particular kind of innovation is managed. More particularly, it is suggested that branding is a form of flexible specialisation which is specific to the culture industry in which the simulation of innovation through the manipulation of the effects of exhibition value is increasingly important; as a consequence, simulation is becoming increasingly innovative.

NOTES

1 The co-authors of this chapter are all colleagues in the Sociology Department at Lancaster

2 This is thus an example of the instance noted by Williams (1981) in which transformations in the means of cultural production provide the conditions for new formal possibilities in production for the market.

3 The twin strategies of stars and genres have long provided the basic mechanisms for categorising films and were adopted from as early as the 1920s. So, for example, generic information was signalled to the audience through the titles of films, their slogans and review synopses, and their images on posters and in papers and magazines, and the process of circulating a star image was initiated by the centralised studio agency of the 1930s and 1940s: stars would 'feature' in newspapers and magazines; they would appear in advertisements endorsing products; and they would be heard on radio, in news, chat shows and fiction programmes.

4 British trademark law is much less helpful to intellectual property owners in this respect; there is, for example, a provision in British law against 'trafficking in trademark'.

5 Gaines notes that Weston Anson cites Theodore Roosevelt's 1913

royalties earned from the sale of 'teddy' bears (which supported the National Parks system) as the earliest American use of licensing, followed by the radio, television and film licensing campaigns for Buck Rogers (1929), the Walt Disney character licensing programme, the Lone Ranger and Shirley Temple (1930s), Hopalong Cassidy and Tom Mix (1940s), and Zorro and Davy Crockett (1950s).

6 Michael Jackson's project of self-creation can be seen as an indication of what is required if a live person aspires to the immortal status of a flat character.

7 This point is taken from an unpublished paper, 'Youth/Music/Television' by Simon Frith (1991).

Part II

TECHNOLOGIES OF REPRODUCTION

5

MECHANICAL REPRODUCTION: PRINT, LITERACY AND THE PUBLIC SPHERE

The following three chapters will focus on the historical emergence and development of three major technologies of culture, defined by the processes of mechanical, electronic and micro-electronic reproduction. Together, these technologies comprise the principal institutions and techniques by which specialised groups disseminate symbolic content to large, heterogeneous and geographically dispersed audiences in contemporary societies. The three chapters are ordered chronologically in terms of the moment of appearance of the technology upon which they focus in order to chart the productive history of the means of cultural production.

In general, this history will be presented in terms of the development of the organisation of the means of communication and the social relations of their cycles of production, distribution and reception, that is, their modes of reproduction. More particularly, each means of production will be investigated in terms of the *relationship* between the two more specific meanings of reproduction identified earlier, that is, between the technical potential of copying that they employ, and the relations between producers and audiences that they make possible.

This task is initially approached through a discussion of the impact of technologies of culture on reproducibility in the first sense, that is, ease of technical copying, but cannot be reduced to this level: technical invention does not itself lead to new cultural and social institutions and practices. Indeed, a technical invention as such has comparatively little social significance; it is only when it is selected for investment towards production, and when it is consciously developed for particular uses that it moves from being a technical invention to an available technology and

97

its significance begins (Williams, 1981). In each case, the focus of analysis will be on the strategies through which reproductive relations in the second sense – that is, relations between producers and audiences – provide a particular set of conditions for the implementation of techniques of copying. These relations provide a means of analysing the implementation of technologies of culture, and in particular their social accessibility. It will be argued that this implementation has not been uniformly expansive, but rather has been uneven and contradictory in its effects.

It will be suggested that the central mechanism through which the potential of these technologies has been limited is the internalisation of specific concepts of an audience, including, for example, the audience-as-public or audience-as-market. This mechanism, it was argued in Chapter 1, was adopted as a means of reducing the indeterminacy introduced in modes of cultural reproduction by the development of technologies of culture making possible the separability and mobility of cultural works. The central tension that will be focused on in this and the next two chapters is that between the technological capacity for copying of cultural works and the economic, social and cultural limits placed on such reproducibility through the internalisation of specific concepts of the audience.

There is some debate about the date of the first emergence of the mass media. Some have argued that the communication system of the Catholic Church in early medieval Europe should be seen as the earliest extensive form of mass communication and persuasion. However, the introduction of printing in the late medieval period represents a more significant moment in that it facilitated the development of a form of media which operated as an autonomous institutional apparatus; this marks a key stage in what has been described by Williams (1981) in terms of the emergence of a significant asymmetry between cultural and social reproduction.

It is clear, however, that the rise of the Papacy as the most powerful feudal court in Europe was not based on military strength, but on the power of the Papacy to persuade people to consent to its authority, and to induce monarchs, feudatories and senior churchmen to submit to and uphold its authority. Medieval media – the emergent educational system, literate culture reproduced through manuscripts, the developing bureaucracies of medieval monarchies, and art, architecture, liturgy, ritual and religious teaching – played a critical role in this building of consent. As a consequence of this ecclesiastical dominance over book production, the content of literate culture was largely religious and orthodox, and was structured in a way that legitimated and maintained Papal authority; indeed, at this time 'culture' itself carried the sense of 'worship'. This situation can thus be characterised in terms of what Williams (1981) has called cultural integration in the sense that, while there was some kind of differentiation between cultural and social reproduction, the two fields were largely congruent or symmetrical.[1]

Important changes occurred in the production and distribution of élite, literate-based culture during the late Middle Ages which threatened this symmetry. These included: new techniques for the manufacture of paper (which made possible a substantial increase in the output of manuscripts since it entailed the replacement of laborious processes for the preparation of parchment with the simpler, quicker and cheaper techniques of paper production); the employment of far greater numbers in the production of manuscripts; and a revolution in the organisation of medieval publishing. These changes occurred largely in response to the emergence of an urban bourgeoisie created by broader developments in late medieval Europe, that is, in response to changes in audience organisation. As a result, the copying of manuscripts became a developed industry dominated by university and commercial scriptoria, with its own industrial organisations. These initially took the form of guilds and an international network of retail outlets serving the European book market.

These changes meant that, while the ecclesiastical hierarchy still sought to regulate book production by exerting influence within universities and by direct proscription of 'undesirable' books and pamphlets, it was no longer able to exercise direct censorship through control of the means of production as it had when monasteries dominated book production. The consequent growth in manuscript culture threatened the unity of the late medieval Church, since it facilitated the dissemination of an alternative, secular interpretation of the world that challenged the moral authority of Papal rule. This development, in turn, contributed to the beginnings of distinct national cultures which subverted the universalism of Papal hegemony.

In some ways, then, it is tempting to regard the development of the printing press in the mid-fifteenth century as nothing more than an extension of previous innovations; a technical improvement which merely assisted an already developing asymmetry betwen the Church and an emerging political élite. However, this obscures the significance of the invention and implementation of metal type. This significance derives from the radical extension of the dissemination of symbolic content that it made possible as a consequence of the capabilities it offered as a technology for the rapid development of writing as a *separable* material system of signification (Williams, 1981). While the development of print should be seen as a response to the growing demand for books and the market opportunities this created for a more efficient mode of production, its effects were themselves *productive* of the particular form which the growing asymmetry or divergence between cultural and social reproduction took, and thus of the character of the emerging challenge to the existing dominant social order. In particular, the rise of print, and the inability of the authorities to impose effective censorship, contributed to the growing confrontation between word-based and image-based forms of worship and religious involvement.

The separability of cultural goods, that is, printed material, from its context of production made possible by print technology is seen by Thompson (1990) among others to be central to what are seen as the defining features of this and other systems of mass communication: the institutionalised production and diffusion of cultural works; the institution of a break between production and reception; the extension of availability of cultural works in time and space; and their public circulation. As Thompson notes, cultural works, 'are literally *mediated* by the technical media in which they are fixed and transmitted' (1990: 220; my emphasis). Most obviously, the direct effects of print were both to increase enormously the output of book production (it is estimated that the adoption of the new technology resulted in a productivity increase of well over 100 times per capita engaged in book production), and to reduce book prices drastically, thereby extending access to a book culture.

The impact of the shift from script to print in effecting the transition from orality to literacy was fundamental. Williams (1981) has isolated four stages in this process, as writing moved from: first, a supporting and recording function in societies in which oral composition and tradition were still predominant; through second, a stage in which this function was joined by written composition for oral performance; and third, a further stage in which composition was additionally written only to be read. Increasingly, also, the oral 'literature' of pre-literate or marginally literate societies was gradually transferred to this new material technique, and transformed through it. In the fourth and familiar stage, most or virtually all composition was written to be silently read, and was, for this reason, generalised as literature.

Elizabeth Eisenstein too (1979) argues that the introduction of print was an epoch-making event, for it provided a new technological means of retrieving, recording, codifying and transmitting information to an enlarged audience. Its impact, she contends, helps to account for the scale and permanence of the revival of learning that got under way in this period and it had a number of important consequences for the production and dissemination of knowledge. It aided the preservation of the classical past and contemporary intellectual advances through what Eisenstein calls typographical fixity; and extended access to more cultural artefacts to more people. It also increased scholars' reach through time and space, and helped to break down barriers between work done in different fields, other disciplines and other traditions of knowledge. In these ways, it made possible an educational revolution in Protestant countries in early modern Europe, which in turn radically assisted economic development.

It is obvious then that the fixity and reproductive scale of printing made possible new kinds of continuity within, and access to, writing; that is, the technical reproducibility of cultural works offered by print, in the sense that multiple exact copies could be made, did contribute to a new kind of reproducibility in the sense of newly diverse relations between producers and the audience. However, this advantage has been counterpointed throughout the history of print by the radical disadvantages of the need for specific training to make use of its potential. Rather than being a development of an inherent or generally available human faculty, writing is a specialised technique wholly dependent on specific training, not only as became common in other techniques for producers, but also, and crucially, for receivers (Williams, 1981).[2] It is only in the last 150 years or so that a majority of people have, in any society, had access to this technique which carries a major part of formal learning. Much of the subsequent development of literacy can then only in one sense be treated as an 'expansion'. In numerical terms it was so, but the cultural specialisation of literacy led to significant internal hierarchies in access and interpretation. Moreover, literacy cannot be understood simply as the ability to read, since what this means is not as obvious as it might seem, as the dual meanings of the word 'literate' – descriptively, an ability to read and, categorically, the condition of being well read – indicate.

As has often been noted, the mode of distribution of any means of communication is thus not only technical – in this case, manuscript copying and then printing – but depends on a set of relations, in which the ability to receive, which is the true substance of distribution, is itself socially and culturally produced. Initially, while the invention of printing made technical distribution much easier, it did so in relations of relatively unaltered cultural distribution, that is, these relations were largely, although not completely, those which already existed, deriving from other forms of hierarchy. Later, however, they came to be structured in relatively independent ways and provided a particular set of determinations in themselves. An analysis of print technology as an example of mechanical reproduction therefore requires a review of the institutions and agencies of training and specialisation which sought to regulate access – or act as brokers – to the specialised and internally hierarchical skills of reception.

While the earliest forms of training were developed by and confined to very limited specialist (usually official) groups they were later somewhat extended in the continuing process of urbanisation and in merchant trade. As writing came to carry an increasing proportion of law, learning, religion and history, marked divisions, relating to, but not directly derived from, those already present in pre-literate societies, became, as it were, culturally stabilised. This form of stratification of access to cultural reproduction became more and more important. Indeed, it might be argued that in decisively increasing the importance of literate culture, the technical innovation of printing had the effect of contributing to a new kind of stratification, in which not only the cultural but also the social importance of the still oral majority culture declined.

However, the terms of this stratification were themselves the site of struggle. On the one hand, in some respects the new technology of print made certain forms of cultural (and social) reproduction very much more effective, over a wider territory, through the extension of a set of cultural techniques of interpretation, learning and self-development mediated by training, status and knowledge. On the other hand, it is also clear that the cycles of cultural reproduction associated with print technology were significantly more diverse than in the preceding period, since the possible uses of the new means of cultural production were never wholly controllable. The consequences of this 'deep contradiction' (Williams, 1981) between centralised production and dispersed reception have helped to define the specificity of modern cultural reproduction (Thompson, 1990). In the particular case of literate culture, there was soon conflict between the received and relatively rigid forms of literature and learning and a print industry which made possible a newly diverse and mobile production of printed material.

This view is supported by work on the growth of literacy, which suggests that there were contradictory forces at play in the distribution and reception of writing from very early in the development of print. So, for example, the popularity of the chapbook, the jestbook, the ballad and the broadsheet dates at least from the sixteenth century and this presupposes a reading audience, however small and irregular, of a general rather than élite kind. In his study (1976) on 'The cultural origins of popular literacy in England 1500–1850', Thomas Laqueur argues that the strikingly large number of people who could write in seventeenth- and eighteenth-century England cannot be adequately understood in terms of a response to the economic need for an educated workforce or even some wider conception of social reproduction: 'Neither economic necessity imposed by commercial or industrial developments nor schools founded by the higher orders to convert, control, or in some way mould the working classes can explain how literacy became so widespread' (Laqueur, 1976: 255). He prefers to explain the growth of literacy and the spread of literate forms of culture into all aspects of people's lives in terms of a desire to read which was prompted by increasingly diversified needs and opportunities. These included the wish not only to participate in the formalised relations of élite economic and political activity, but also to join in radical political protest, popular forms of Protestant religion, and to enjoy recreational forms of literature.

This struggle over the extension and uses of literacy had, of course, been evident before, as is clear from the history of condemnation and prohibition of books by the medieval Church, but changes in the means of production, and the developing asymmetry between social and cultural reproduction that it produced, led to new forms of attempted control. There was, for example, a new emphasis on prevention rather than retribution: in 1487 a Papal Bull prescribed a pre-censorship licensing system, and in 1559 the Index, the proscription by law of vernacular Bibles and a number of popular religious bestsellers, was introduced. Both measures were a direct reflection of the anxieties experienced by élite groups in the face of the new conditions of rapid and extensive reproducibility afforded by print technology.

In England, from 1531, a pre-censorship licensing system was established under secular authority; forms of this system lasted until 1695. This meant that publishers, printers, booksellers and authors could be prosecuted for evading licensing regulations (as well as for the capital offence of heresy). The Tudor monarchs issued patents of monopoly and privileges to selected printers, publishers and booksellers. By doing this they exercised indirect control over the ownership of print production and distribution, since the threat of the withdrawal of these valuable patents and franchises forced publishers to submit manuscripts for examination before publication, and to boycott undesirable material themselves. In order to protect these privileges further the recipients had a vested interest in reporting unlicensed printers, publishers and booksellers and putting them out of business. This approach was institutionalised with the establishment of the Stationers' Company by royal charter under Queen Mary. This Company, a corporate organisation of printers, publishers and booksellers, was given search, seizure and limited judicial powers of its own. Control was also exercised through the law of criminal libel which was modified under the Stuarts so that the printing and publishing of a 'libel' were judged to be as heinous an offence as writing it.

However, normative controls, which had been more important than law enforcement in this regulative system, gradually began to break down, and with the English Revolution came to a virtual, albeit temporary, collapse. This breakdown helped to give rise to the modern English newspaper press and an enormous output of print of all sorts. Despite attempts to reassert the traditional system of censorship following the Restoration, state licensing was finally abandoned by the authorities who were failing to cope with the growing increase in print output. The Stationers' Company had in any case ceased to be co-operative in the enforcement of regulations following a court case in 1677 which protected existing patents and monopoly rights from arbitrary withdrawal by the Crown. Armed with the protection of this decision, the majority in the Stationers' Company were more anxious to satisfy market demand than to maintain state censorship.

This point thus marks the initial moment of perhaps one of the most significant forms of internal division in the history of cultural reproduction, that is, the division between the interests of the state and the market in the regulation of the production of cultural goods (Williams, 1981). An important aspect of this division is the internalisation of opposing conceptions of the audience: in general terms, between the audience-as-public and the audience-as-market respectively. Significantly, however, in this case market demand was still often mediated through quasi-state or professional organisations of cultural producers and distributors, and it was their practices that came to define and constitute the cultural markets of industrial capitalism. Moreover, this commercial victory, important though it was, did not mean the end of direct attempts by the state to restrict the circulation of cultural goods.

New methods were introduced to contain the disruptive potential of print, and in particular the press which had grown in circulation since the English Revolution. Thus press taxation – taxes on newspapers, pamphlets, press advertisements and paper, introduced in 1712 – was designed to restrict both ownership and readership of the press to the 'respectable' sections of society. In addition, many of the traditional legal sanctions – the laws of treason and seditious libel, general warrants (only finally declared illegal in 1765) and parliamentary privilege – were retained, and financial subsidies, bribes and the management of news were further developed as means of controlling the press. However, although press taxation undoubtedly decelerated the growth of the commercial press it did not halt its expansion altogether. The rise of the regional weekly press was accompanied by a growth in the metropolitan press, and by a significant increase in total newspaper consumption. As part of this expansion, the period saw the emergence of a radical press under working-class control. This represented an important institutional channel through which a popular critique of society was developed and mediated in relation to a mass audience.

The commercial press became progressively more independent of the landed political élite in the late eighteenth and early nineteenth centuries as divisions between different groups within the ruling class became more marked. This process was furthered by two particular Acts of Parliament. In 1792, Fox's Libel Act blunted the ability of governments to harass the commercial press with seditious libel suits by making juries the judges of guilt in seditious libel prosecutions, while in 1843, Lord Campbell's Libel Act made the statement of truth in the public interest a legitimate defence against the charge of criminal libel. Both these Acts and, importantly, the piecemeal abolition of the press taxes in the period 1853–61 can, in part, be credited to a compromise between the interests of liberal bourgeois evangelicists and those of the commercial sector of the middle classes.

The effect of these measures, particularly the abolition of press taxes, was to transform the character of newspapers, through the displacement of political with commercial mechanisms for regulating the circulation of cultural goods. The consequent growth of advertising patronage and sales revenue allowed the commercial press to become yet more independent of the political élite, thus furthering the growing asymmetry between forms of social and cultural reproduction. This should not be understood simply as the lifting of constraints, however, but rather as the establishment of new forms of variable, but still effective, regulation. Thus, for example, the advertising dependence of all competitively priced newspapers in the mass market meant that the radical press was forced to move up market in order to attract the audiences which advertisers wanted to reach (Curran, 1986; Hall, 1986). It also meant that a whole new generation of newspapers came into being: regional daily newspapers, a popular national daily press which emerged at the end of the nineteenth century, and new national Sunday newspapers.

In general terms, the development of the internal division between market and state, marked by a resistance to forms of direct control and censorship by the state, was initially framed in terms of either bourgeois individualism or a radical populism, both of which made use of some notion of a public right of access to print technology. To some extent, then, it is possible to identify the emergence of an acceptance of a notion of the public good in relation to cultural works with the intensification of cultural commodification. This understanding of the moral and political rights of the public to access to ideas and information, and thus to unconstrained reactivation, has been highlighted in discussions of the special character of cultural works. Indeed, it is sometimes suggested that they have an intrinsically public status and, while this is true in one sense, at least of media goods, in that such goods are necessarily produced for a diffused large-scale audience, it is important to recognise that this public character is itself socially circumscribed by, for example, forms of regulation and control, including the internalisation of specific conceptions of the audience through commodification.

So, for example, while the acceptance of this right of access was clearly integral to the emergence of the ideal of the public sphere as the site of communication, reflection and decision-making, in actuality this right was defined restrictively in relation to the rights of the individual as either citizen of the bourgeois *polis* or consumer in a cultural market. So, for example, Hall (1986) argues that the increasingly commercial organisation of the press constituted the reading audience not as a public but as a cultural market; the consequence of this was that while the commercial press did increasingly depend on the popular classes, this was as a reading and buying market for its goods, not as a popular cause to be championed. At the same time, anxieties were expressed by political and cultural élites about the perceived vulnerability and lack of discrimination of the mass audience; this contributed to attempts to restrict the circulation of various types of writing on the grounds that the mass audience-as-public required protection from the commercial exploitation of its own demands and desires. This period thus saw a shift from statutory control of the circulation of texts – by a body appointed by and responsible to the Crown – to a regulative system based on individual rights, itself fractured by the competing discourses of citizenship and consumption.

This shift was evident not only in the press, but also in the reproduction of fictional writing within the development of a novelistic culture during the eighteenth and nineteenth centuries (Heath, 1982). The emergence of this culture can be traced back to the modern notions of authorship and creativity which began to be developed in the second half of the sixteenth century in contradistinction to the notion of craftsmanship (Murdock, 1980). At that time craft work was characterised by two essential features: a command over technical knowledge and skills which were acquired through a process of training and apprenticeship; and, crucially, the deployment of these skills to make products demanded by somebody else, either client, customer or employer. The stages of overlap and eventual transition between the status and conditions of the craftsman to the author thus coincided with the release from direct dependence on a patron, and shifted the social relations of cultural reproduction significantly into a post-artisanal or market phase. In this way, creative activity came to be defined precisely by its relative freedom from the demands of employers and audiences or rather employers-as-audiences; more positively than the lifting of constraints, even, it came to be organised in terms of production for not just an anonymous or unknown, but an *unknowable or indeterminate* audience, one that could not be fixed.

Yet how did this come about? While the emergence of market relations meant that writers no longer needed to be directly dependent on any of the various forms of patronage, the logic of the market should surely have meant that writers would ultimately have become 'literary proletarians', producing whatever would sell. Indeed, in many ways, 'independence' resulted, in actuality, in new, although more variable, commercial forms of dependence, with the role of the publisher assuming a new significance as the mediating link between writers and the market, buying or commissioning works and selling them to the public. Moreover, while initially the publishers primarily acted as distributive intermediaries (Williams, 1981), their role became increasingly productive, with the extension and consolidation of market relations. In practice, then, the role of the upper class patron of the arts was gradually superseded by a range of capitalist producers and intermediaries, including not only publishers, but also printers, booksellers, critics and reviewers, who, through a number of institutional and aesthetic means, mediated the novel's reproduction.

In these ways then, commodity production was not, as it was for artistic forms already in existence prior to this development, something alien to which the novel had to adapt, but a condition of its existence. However, there were a number of other factors shaping the relations between producers and audiences. For example, it is clear that the potential audience was small;[3] not only was there the restriction imposed by cost, there were also the barriers of low levels of literacy, lack of leisure time and of adequate lighting in the home. Moreover, the middle class itself initially supplied novel *readers* rather than novel *purchasers*. This was not merely because of the high price at which novels were sold, but because they were goods which were not seen as fit for possession but only for somewhat shamefaced consumption (Lovell, 1987). Indeed, it was partly for this reason that the early rapid expansion of novel production and consumption was tied in with the growth of the commercial circulating library.[4] It was the libraries rather than individuals who actually purchased the three-decker novels; in this way, they played an important part in securing the financial viability of what was an under-capitalised industry, facilitating its expansion to meet the demand for new fiction among a small but growing clientele.

Paradoxically, however, as the novel's audience grew with the rapid spread of novel-reading in the last quarter of the eighteenth century the literary credentials of the novel reached their lowest point. The widespread reproduction of the novel made possible by print was seen as a threat to literature and learning, and the novel was attacked on the grounds of its commercialism in literary journals and in a wide range of writing of all kinds. The criticisms voiced indicate that it was the very success of the novel in the market which undermined its literary status. Defoe, for example, derided the success of novelistic forms by comparing it with other forms of production:

> Writing ... is become a very considerable Branch of the English Commerce. The Booksellers are the Master Manu-facturers or Employers. The several Writers, Authors, Copyers, Sub-Writers and all other operators with Pen and Ink are the workmen employed by the said Master-Manufacturers.
>
> (Quoted in Williams, 1984: 183)

while Goldsmith warned of, 'that fatal revolution whereby writing is converted to a mechanic trade' (quoted in Williams, 1984: 183). John Wilson Ross proclaimed:

> Upon the narrow isthmus on which we stand, on one hand rolls the literature of the past, and on the other, the ocean of literature of the future. [We] hail . . . a new coming epoch in the world of letters – ECONOMIC LITERATURE.
>
> (Quoted in James, 1973: 33)

As these comments indicate, the doubts commonly expressed about the novel centred around its commercialism (although see Chapter 8); its commodity status and the attendant need for popular appeal were used against the novel by its detractors, who held that there was an inherent contradiction between literature and commerce, and between literary quality and popular appeal.

This contradiction presented a dilemma for the novel's publishers: on the one hand, in order to win a place on the terrain marked out for literature, the novel had to show that it could rise above its origins in the market, while on the other, commercial exposure and market popularity were clearly necessary for profit maximisation. Thus, in so far as it was specifically literature which was being offered for sale, there was a tension between commercial success and literary standing. More generally, since the cultural field was coming to be defined in terms of its autonomisation from the social, its integration with any form of socially reproductive demand was perceived as compromising within élite or high culture circles. The various strategies adopted by publishers of the novel can be seen as attempted resolutions of this dilemma. These strategies fall into two main groupings; these two groupings define the terms of the deepening segregation between the literary novel and other kinds of more popular fiction which were taking shape in relation to the emergence of a substantial working class readership.

The first strategy, which resulted in the consolidation of the high culture status of the novel in the nineteenth century, was the product of a number of institutional and aesthetic means which obscured the form's commercial origins. As Lovell (1987) has shown, while the novel remained a commodity, the manner of its production and distribution came to foreground its literary claims and mask its relationship to the market. As the potential audience expanded, production might have been reorganised along the lines on which it developed in the USA, with long print runs at low unit cost to encourage the buying habit. Instead the three-decker library system continued to dominate the production and distribution of much of the literary fiction throughout the nineteenth century in Britain and provided the institutional base for the development of a literary respectability for the novel.

While ostensibly cutting loose the novel from commercial demands, this was in actuality a system which was peculiarly amenable to a high degree of commercial and critical control and allowed the author and publisher to negotiate the potentially conflicting requirements of the novel as commodity and as literature. A high cover price increased the size of the author's income from royalty payments, while for the small number of quality publishers who monopolised the publication of the literary novel, the more or less predictable sale of a novel to the library at a high price permitted a modestly profitable venture on small print runs. (The library edition would usually be followed by a cheap reprint once library demand had been satisfied. The price of these reprints and cheap railway editions gradually fell over the century as publishing and printing costs fell and demand rose.) On the other hand, certain key gate-keeper roles in the system, including the readers for the literary publishers and, most importantly, librarians, were able to impose a prescriptive mix of moral, critical and commercial standards in the cause of literary credibility. So, for example, as has been well documented (Lovell, 1987; Tuchman, 1989), the buying power which Mudie's Select Library commanded gave its proprieter, Charles Mudie, almost dictatorial powers over the quality literary fiction industry.

At the same time as production for this kind of pre-defined market, as a purpose taking priority over any other, was increasingly widespread in literary culture, there were many examples of writers explicitly struggling against or effectively ignoring market trends. In many cases the writer was able to maintain an unusually privileged relation (for labour) to that form of demand or projected demand which was mediated by the market. Certainly, it is clear that the notion of the cultural producer as an autonomous individual, which has been derived from this period of a privileged élite literate culture, has been the focus of actual and attempted resistance to the social relations of the more general productive mode. As Radnoti writes,

The most widespread image of modern art is the artist standing at the crossroads of market temptations and his [*sic*] own inspirations. An artist is one who says 'no' to the world for he does not recognise his home in it.

(Radnoti, 1986: 80)

Terry Lovell (1987) argues along similar lines that the individuation of the cultural producer, together with the concept of creative genius, provided the soil for the Romanticism which came increasingly to define artistic production in the era of industrial capitalism. It implied a certain distance between producers and their social class, and emphatically denied any service role towards the capitalist state and its ruling class. (Lovell points here to the often noted tendency in the literary novel towards the expression of anti-capitalist sentiments.) The general outcome was the stabilisation of a form of professional independence within what were increasingly integrated and dominant market relations. As discussed in Chapter 2, this was related to the emergence of the author-function, and its definition in relation to notions of originality and creativity, supported institutionally through the implementation of copyright law.

Moreover, although the concept of authorship operated as an ideological category in the sense that it promoted a systematic misrecognition of the actual processes of production, the institutionalised existence of a licensed 'authorial' space had real and important consequences for the range and forms of cultural production. Even in contemporary society, where most relations of cultural production have been assimilated to the terms of the developed market, some have not, and it is significant that these are defended in terms of types of production which are important 'in and for themselves' and are still distinguished from production in more general terms.

At a deeper level, however, the denial of a service role was itself related to the particular type of commodification that developed within élite literary production. This can be seen in the way in which the status of the author as an autonomous agent actually provided an institutional locus for the cultural reproduction of a literary formation within which the aesthetic value of cultural goods related to their 'practically useless, imaginative element'. This status was dependent upon the maintenance of particular social and cultural conditions, including a dual constitution of the audience: in terms of anonymity through its constitution as a market and, simultaneously, through its definition in terms of a particular kind of reception, namely the adoption of critical distance. This second aspect is related to the historically specific formation of the audience as a self-reflexive public associated with the rise of the bourgeoisie.

On the one hand, the functioning of the author-function was integrally tied to the anonymity of the audience provided by cultural production for the market. It was in relation to an author producing for an unknown audience that goods could come to be defined in relation to 'aesthetic' purpose, as an, in effect, autonomous intention. On the other hand, the unknowability of this audience could not be secured by the market alone, but also required internal changes in the self-understanding of the bourgeois reading audience. Campbell (1989) has argued that this self-understanding can be seen in terms of the emergence of an aestheticism which can itself be traced back to a form of self-illusory hedonism in which the skilful use of imagination was developed and deployed in the calculating practice of 'willing suspension of disbelief'. Such a practice requires high levels of individual emotional self-determination and can be seen to be part of the more general creation of an aesthetic personality. These broad cultural changes contributed to the prevalence of the belief that an individual should have the sensory capacity to respond in a detached manner and the use of the work of art as a device in the practice of self-problematisation; its instituted incomprehensibility provided, 'a powerful technology for *withdrawing* from the world as a sphere of mundane knowledge and action' (Hunter, 1992: 354). Within this élite culture, then, the art work was understood as precisely that which is not useful or that which is distanced, or set apart from, everyday life. The operation of the author-function can thus be seen to be tied to a specific type of commodification in which an indeterminate or unknown audience was internalised simultaneously as market and as a disinterested public, with the latter masking the significance of the former.

One consequence of the adoption of this dual understanding of the audience was the restriction of access to the newly autonomised sphere of aesthetic valorisation. As a means for some individuals to distinguish themselves from others by problematising 'ordinary' experiences and conducting themselves as a superior mode of being, the ethic of aesthetics provided a basis for the symbolic distinctions through which the cultured middle classs identified themselves in opposition to other groups (Bourdieu, 1984). At the same time, as Terry Eagleton ironically notes, art could stand in the same relation to politics that it occupied in relation to commerce; that is, it could,

> cease to be a mere lackey . . . swearing fidelity to its own law; but this [was] not greatly disturbing, since the very social conditions which allow[ed] this to happen – the autonomisation of culture – also prevent[ed] art's potenti- ally subversive freedom from having much of an effect on other areas of social life.

> (Eagleton, 1990: 367)

However, while, as Lovell (1987) notes, the major symbolic institutions of capitalist society, those of the family, Church and school, are supported by sanctions which guarantee the exposure of individuals to their socialising process, cultural production intended for the market, even one which is simultaneously defined as a public, has few such sanctions:

> While the wants which 'commodities of the fancy' stimulate and address are developed in the course of the emergence of the socialised human being, and are therefore not independent of the society and culture within which that socialisation occurs, it does not follow that they can be addressed with impunity nor that individual and collective attempts to satisfy them are necessarily '. . . conducive to good order'.

> (Lovell, 1987: 153)

Furthermore, the mobility and diversity of cultural goods made possible by the new technology of print further intensified both the extent and the degree of indeterminacy at the point of the reactivation of the printed text. Despite these qualifications, however, it is generally recognised that the normalisation of particular forms of writing as high culture was, on the whole, successfully achieved through the developments in the discourse of aesthetic autonomy described above in terms of institutional, critical and textual strategies. These, however, were not the only strategies adopted within the publishing industry.

Despite the fact that many of the literary and sociological accounts of literary culture (Watt, 1957; Lovell, 1987) focus on the literary novel, the significance which it has been accorded is far in excess of its numerical and commercial importance. Sutherland (1978), for example, estimates that for each quality publisher publishing above the literary threshold, there were ten beneath at this time. These publishers had adopted another solution to the dilemma facing the novel: most of them had required the dropping of any claim to literary repute and the tapping of the recently emerged urban working class audience for literate culture. This occurred not through the manipulation of originality in conjunction with the author-function, but through the manipulation of various kinds of copying strategies, including serial publication (Bennett, 1982), plagiarism and generative retellings (see Chapter 3), and the internalisation of the audience-as-market.

During the nineteenth century, this sector of the audience was also, as were the middle classes, serviced, at least in part, by libraries: many working-class educational organisations threw open their book collections to the public for a small charge, and some commercial libraries, sometimes initially attached to tobacco and stationery shops, were explicitly targeted at the working and lower middle classes.

Albert Smith amusingly describes Smedlar's Library, found by Christopher Tadpole in a dingy London square. The dusty interior of the shop had piles of novels alongside the items of a tobacconist's trade, and against the window, 'Well-thumbed novels were opened enticingly at exciting pages, and displayed flat up against the panes, with the intelligence that they were "Lent to read" on top of them'.

(James, 1973: 7)

From about 1840, penny-issue fiction was published, and this was offered for loan, bound into as many volumes as possible in order to extract the maximum from the borrower. Up to 1850 newspapers, periodicals and even books could often be borrowed from the public house, although from about 1800 their place as suppliers of literature was gradually taken over by coffee houses (although in the north coffee houses were not so popular, and popular literary tastes were met by penny reading rooms). In addition, fiction and other literature was also increasingly available for sale at cheap prices. There was therefore a considerable range of sources for those who wished to read.

In its early stages of development, the backbone of the cheap literature industry was serial publication. These 'number books' ranged from immense Biblical commentaries to criminal biographies and standard novels. As a form it had opened up a range of new possibilities for the small printer. The eight pages could be printed as one sheet on a hand press, and lengthy volumes could be printed with almost no capital, since the income from one issue paid for the printing of the next. Unsold weekly parts could be stitched together to be offered as monthly parts, then bound and sold as a normal volume. In the early years of the nineteenth century the number trade prospered from the sale of serious works such as *Fox's Book of Martyrs* and *The History of England*, and while the publishers of serial fiction were smaller, the circulation of number novels was still considerable. A survey of the popular literature available in London in 1840 estimated that there were approximately 80 cheap periodicals circulating; out of these nine were scientific, four were political, five were considered licentious, four were devoted to drama and sixteen to biographies and memoirs. Twenty-two contained romances or stories (James, 1973: 30–1). The proportion of fiction was to increase gradually in the coming decades. Much of this increase can be explained by the expansion of the book-buying audience brought about by the reprint houses and undercutters who virtually flooded the market with regular cheap reprints and pirate copies.

Initially, popular publishers turned to the eighteenth century for historical series, criminal biographies, romances and 'erotica': by printing works on which the copyright had lapsed writers' fees were evaded. Plagiarism of works whose popularity had already been established by the middle-class audience was another common strategy for the cheap or popular publishers. Plagiarisms were first made in order to avoid prosecution under copyright law; while it was acceptable to carry long quotations (this was even encouraged by publishers as a means of advertisement), some form of adaptation was necessary after a certain length. Dickens' *The Pickwick Papers* (1836–7) was one of the most plagiarised novels of this period: it created a set of characters which, partly because of their links with the tradition of portraying comic types, became common property through a multiplication of adaptations, interpretations and dramatic versions: 'One met "Pickwick" everywhere – one rode in 'Boz' cabs, wore Pickwick coats and hats and smoked Pickwick cigars' (James, 1973: 52). Indeed, Louis James (1973) claims that, although comparatively few working-class readers read Dickens direct, he had a central place in the development of cheap popular fiction in that it was 'apprenticed to Dickens' plots and characters' (1973: 82).[5] Similarly, he argues that romantic poetry was one of the most consistently profitable lines of publication for publishers of cheap fiction at this time, partly because of its political overtones, and cites twenty-five cheap editions of Byron's various works as an example of this tendency, and this is excluding reprints!

Following this experimentation in popular taste through plagiarism of already successful quality fiction, popular publishers gradually began to put out fiction written specifically for the new working-class audience, notably serial novels and cheap magazines. In the development of this new mass market fiction the genres of the domestic romance, the fashion novel, stories of criminal life, and the historical and gothic novels were popular. Of these, the domestic novel became the dominant form after the decline of the gothic, representing the move towards realism, or 'life as it is', to use the tag which was frequently attached to the titles of these stories, as it developed in popular fiction in the mid-nineteenth century. This, however, was rarely enough to earn the title of literature for the works it described since this was reserved for literature consumed within the previously outlined relations between producers and audience.

In contrast, in this, the primary sector for the developing publishing industry, it is possible to see the emergence of a number of strategies specifically adopted for the mass circulation of cultural goods targeted at an audience explicitly constituted as a market rather than a public. Clearly evident is the importance of forms of copying, standardisation or seriality, which reduce commercial risk, while the relative insignificance of, and even disregard for, the author is also noticeable in the widespread use of plagiarism. As noted above, copying was sometimes direct, as in rebinding, multiple editions and remaindering, or through the reprinting of American and French novels, but was also transformative, through plagiarisms of character and style to generations of plot and story.

In general terms, the consequence of the commercial exploitation of these forms of copying was an emerging solidification of categories of different types or genres of popular literature, each defined in relationship to emerging patterns of market taste. In addition, there was a fertile intermingling between fiction and other cultural forms with transposable stories, characters, songs and dialogue across popular fiction, drama, ballads and news. All these strategies can be seen as examples of a relatively direct type of commodification, although even here it is important to recognise the complexity of this process as it operates at the various levels of edition, form, genre and style, making use of different proportions of standardisation and differentiation.

This brief overview of developments in the press, the emergence of the novel and its differentiation from popular fiction has looked at different strategies for the management of the cultural commodity at a time when the new forms of mechanical reproduction associated with print technology vastly extended the distribution and mobility of cultural goods. It suggests that there were limits placed on the reproduction of printed texts as a consequence of the contradictory implications of the conditions of the historical emergence of the cultural sphere. On the one hand, it was potentially a new sphere for exchange relations in that the new means of communication made possible the reproduction of cultural goods as objects to be sold. Yet, on the other hand, the terms of its differentiation simultaneously made it open to multiple forms of appropriation, not simply commodification, in ways which were potentially disruptive for the existing social and economic order.

It has been suggested that the emergent aesthetic discourse developed in such a way as to manage this process within novelistic culture; its terms and boundaries provide the limits for cultural reproduction. The principal focus within this discourse was the author-function, which acted as the generative function around which a culture of originals developed. However, this culture was dependent upon not only the privileging of particular textual forms, but also required specific institutional relations of production, distribution and reception. These relations were not external to the process of commodification, but instead provided the basis for a particular type of commercial production. The segregation internal to literary reproduction, between the novel and popular fiction, was grounded in the privileging of authorial originality defined in relation to an indeterminate public over and above generative copying or standardisation for a targeted market.

However, while the author-function has remained significant in the discourse of aesthetic autonomy, the development of more integrated market relations in literary production has meant that the productive role has been increasingly claimed by intermediaries in the relation between originator and audience. By the mid-nineteenth century the circulating libraries had outlived their usefulness and came to be perceived as restrictive; they were seen to be the key factor in keeping prices high and thus limiting commercial expansion. Several factors combined to break through this situation, and to revolutionise the distribution not only of magazines and newspapers, but of books. Important among these was the development of the railway system, for the bookstalls at the new stations, notably those of W.H. Smith, meant that the audience could be reached in a new way.[6] The cheap Parlour Library, and then the Railway Library, were distributed through this new outlet. The high-price circulating libraries slowly declined, and by the end of the century, cheaper libraries – such as Boots' from 1900 – were taking their place, with a larger constituency. The public libraries, growing slowly from mid-century, added an increasingly important sector to the reading audience.

However, as English literature began to find a place within the curriculum, especially at higher levels of the education system, a further new dimension was added to the institutional structure within which literary reproduction was organised. Educational institutions, unlike publishing and commercial libraries, are not directly subject to market forces, and thus modified to some extent the effects of commodity exchange on the development of literary reproduction. Although the proportion of living authors studied in universities and schools is small, the educational institutionalisation of English has meant that an essential component of the literary audience, a pool of competent, critical readers, was secured (Lovell, 1987; and see Chapter 3).

Generally, however, as the publishing industry has become more highly organised and more fully capitalised, the direct commissioning of planned saleable products has become much more of a normal mode. As outlined in Chapter 4, for many writers the most available social relations are those of casualised, fixed contract, employment, with the ideas for books coming from professional intermediaries such as publishers' editors. In this sense, publishing is coming to resemble the institutions of the electronic media, cinema, radio and television. However, in the case of the electronic media, the scale of capital involved, and the dependence on more complex specialised means of production and distribution, have to a significant extent blocked access to these media in older terms and made possible the imposition of the predominant means of corporate employment. As a result of this, the effective, if never absolute, origin of cultural production is now centrally sited within the corporate market. It is with the institutions of these new media and the relocation of authorship that the following chapters are concerned.

NOTES

1 This integration, however, was never complete: so, for example, medieval media helped the rise of a new power group in societies who used their control over communications to annex some of the power and influence exercised by the traditional leaders of feudal societies.

2 This is not to imply that speech, for example, is 'natural' or without specialisations, since there are hierarchies of speech which, for example, trivialise certain kinds of talk as gossip.

3 In the 1750s around 100 titles were published annually; by the 1790s the annual average had risen sharply to over 500, and to more than 2,600 by the 1850s and over 6,000 by 1900 (Williams, 1985a: 42–3).

4 Commercial circulating libraries began to appear in the 1720s in London and the fashionable resorts, and by about 1770 had assumed a key position in the economy of the novel.

5 See Norman Feltes, 'The moment of *Pickwick*, or the production of a commodity text' for a discussion of *Pickwick Papers* as the 'first commodity text' (1982: 58) in the transition to a specifically capitalist literary mode of production.

6 See Jody Berland, 'Angels dancing: cultural technologies and the production of space' (1992) for a general discussion of the importance of spaces of consumption in the organisation of cultural technologies.

6

ELECTRONIC REPRODUCTION: BROADCASTING, WATCHING AND PUBLIC SERVICE

Once again this chapter will chart the history of a technology of culture – in this case, that of broadcasting – to see how a means of cultural production was developed and exploited as an intervention in the sphere of the social. The primary focus will be an exploration of the social, political and cultural implications of the realisation of broadcasting in terms of its internalisation of a 'mass' audience. On the one hand, it will put forward the argument that the regulation of this internalisation was fundamental to the development of the forms of asymmetry between cultural and social reproduction which came to characterise broadcasting. On the other hand, it will also suggest that the forms of autonomy which characterise broadcasting derive, in part at least, from the cultural realisation of the technical possibility of universality of reception. A second, related, focus will be the extent and nature of access to communication actually made possible by broadcasting as the primary means of cultural reproduction in the mid-twentieth century.

The last decades of the nineteenth century and the first two of the twentieth century saw the emergence of a series of related technologies of communication. The principal incentives to their development came from problems of information exchange and control in expanding commercial and military operations. So, for example, telegraphy and telephony and, in its early stages, radio, were developed within a communications network which was serving the needs of the established and growing military and commercial complex. These technologies were thus initially developed for, and organised around, the communication uses of specific person to specific person within established structures.

This development was only somewhat later supplemented by support for a technology for the transmission of varied messages to a general audience: what is now known as broadcasting.[1]

These technological developments occurred during a period of rapid historical transformation. Hall (1986) describes this period as one in which a number of different levels of social and economic crisis were condensed into an issue of political and cultural authority by what came to be defined as 'the problem of democracy'. The 'problem' was how to contain democracy following the extension of the franchise, while at the same time maintaining popular consent in circumstances of economic upheaval and intensified international rivalry. More generally, the developments in communications technology were one response to an increasing awareness not only among ruling and commercial groups, but also among the general public, of new social and political conditions requiring new kinds of knowledge and communication. As Williams writes, 'In a number of ways, and drawing on a range of impulses from curiosity to anxiety, new information and new kinds of orientation were deeply required' (1974: 22).

The emergence and development of broadcasting meant that the general public was exposed to a mass means of communication in new ways, and there were certain opportunities – of access to public forms of communication, for example, – associated with this exposure. However, this access was largely restricted to the moment of reception, since the scale of capital investment involved,[2] and the development of complex and specialised means of production and distribution, blocked access to broadcasting production for most of those outside the dominant groups. As a result, the participation of subordinate groups in public communication was limited to the moments of exchange and consumption in relation to this means of cultural production.

Nevertheless, there was a much more even social distribution of the ability to receive the new means of communication than had been the case with the technology of printing. This is a consequence of broadcasting being a form of communication which can technically provide the means for 'direct' (rather than notational) transmission of meaning. It is thus potentially directly accessible in the sense that the skills involved in its reception are not restricted to those who have acquired specialised training, since the necessary skills are already developed in primary communication. Thus although the opportunity for mass extension to social communication that this technical possibility offered was, in actuality, limited in a variety of ways, broadcasting was still the first mass means of cultural production to contain the technical possibility of universal reception.

Since there were, in the abstract, several different ways in which broadcasting as a technical means might have been developed,[3] its actual development in terms of centralised transmission to individual homes must be understood in relation to more general processes of social change. Williams (1974) locates the particular form of broadcasting which eventually emerged as part of a new set of consumer technologies and sees its development as, in general terms, largely congruent with the wider social complex of the period which he describes in terms of 'mobile privatisation'. This, he argued, can be 'characterised by the two apparently paradoxical yet deeply connected tendencies of modern urban industrial living: on the one hand mobility, on the other hand, the more apparently self-sufficient family home' (1974: 26). In this context, broadcasting technology can be seen as one of the set of new consumer technologies, organised through the rapid commercial development of products for private purchase, that led to an increase in practices that were familial or individual rather than communal or public. The abstract possibility of broadcasting – varied messages to a general public – was technically stabilised as centralised transmission for privatised reception.

Scannell (1986) further argues that the primary work of national broadcasting systems was the mediation of modernity, an important aspect of which was the normalisation of the public sphere and the socialisation of the private sphere; he sees broadcasting's development as 'a mediating response to . . . large scale displacements and readjustments in modern industrial societies where custom, tradition and all the givenness of social life has been eroded' (1986: 29). This, he suggests, was accomplished through the continuous presentation and representation of public life and mundane life, not as separate spheres but as routinely implicated in each other, and as recognisable, knowable and familiar.

The mediation of modernity required a specific organisation of universal or mass distribution to be internalised, as a key social

condition, in the development of broadcasting, and the problems
of regulating the terms of this internalisation can be seen to have
shaped the history of broadcasting (Smith, 1976; Ang, 1991). As
a central aspect of this process of mediation, broadcasting has
continually had to face, 'the problems of . . . what image it should
contain within itself of the single and simultaneous manifestation
of the mass audience' (Smith, 1976: 46). This image has taken
different forms, but it has shaped the character and limits of the
emergent asymmetries of both commercial and state institutions
of broadcasting.

A significant factor in shaping the image which was adopted,
and thus a key determinant of the particular realisation of
broadcasting which developed, was the fact that, both in radio
and later in television, major capital investment was initially in
the means of distribution, and was at first only devoted to
production to make distribution possible, rather than being seen
as something desirable in its own right.[4] This investment had two
sets of motives, both of which were commercial in origin: first,
manufacturers saw a market in the sale of receiving equipment
for the family home; second, following on from this, the owners
of the means of transmission saw the sale of broadcasting entry to
the family at home as itself a potential commodity. Broadcasting
was thus realised as a channel of transmission for communicative
entry to the family at home; more particularly, it was funded and
organised precisely as a means of gaining and regulating mass
distribution in and of itself, or, to put this another way, its
product was not programmes as such, but rather centralised
distribution to privatised homes: 'the public was considered first
only as consumers of equipment and later as a saleable audience'
(Schiller, quoted in Smith, 1976: 57). In many ways, this
underlying imperative remains the same even today.

More generally, the early twentieth century saw a widespread
reconstruction of public understanding of the notion of 'the
masses', as this term was taken up and refigured in terms of
families, through, among other social mechanisms, the consumer
market. It was as both a consequence and a cause of this that a
particular conception of the family as the appropriate focus for
mass distribution entered into the development of broadcasting.
Ellis writes,

'The home' and 'the family' are terms which have become

tangled together in the commercial culture of the twentieth century. They both point to a powerful cultural construct, a set of deeply held assumptions about the nature of 'normal' human existence. The family is held to consist of a particular unit of parents and children: broadcast television assumes that this is the basis and heart of its audience.[5]

(Ellis, 1982: 113)

For Ellis, the internalisation of the mass audience in terms of the family has important implications for the characteristic forms of broadcasting production, some of which will be explored later in this chapter. However, the important point here is the way in which the establishment of the family as the unit of the mass audience inscribed a key social limit for the reproducibility of broadcasting and restricted the technical possibility of universal reception.

As a consequence of the development of broadcasting in terms of centralised production for privatised reception, an initial problem was that, technically, it had no direct point of sale (unlike most previous cultural commodity production, such as books, newspapers, paintings, concerts and films). Radio and television sets, the receiving apparatus, could be directly sold, but from the nature of the technology of broadcasting adopted there was no easy point of sale for actual programmes, and thus there was no direct exchange relationship between viewers and broadcasters. Funding for programme making has therefore been arranged in other ways: by direct state subsidy; by licence fees or subscription; or through advertising revenue, either directly for specific programmes through sponsorship or in systematically constructed breaks.

All these models of financing broadcasting production have certain features in common: first, they present broadcasting institutions with a relatively predictable income for up to a year in advance; second, this income is global, and not tied to a particular programme or programmes (Ellis, 1982). These features have contributed to certain characteristic ways of organising broadcasting production, including a relatively high degree of industrialisation and the use of financial subsidy across an institution according to a framework of mixed economic, political and cultural criteria – what Murdock (1980) calls 'the calculus of legitimation'. These two processes – of industrial-isation and institutionalisation – shaped the development of broadcasting as a form of integrated production within which the cultural producer was displaced from the privileged position outlined in the previous chapter.

The choice between funding options was fixed in general terms by the bargain struck between state and commercial interests within the nation state.[6] The option chosen clearly further determined the specific kind of mass distribution internalised in particular national broadcasting institutions, and the resulting distinction in modes of broadcasting reproduction is usually presented in terms of a contrast between 'public service' and 'commercial' production. The specific terms of the bargain are set by the form of mediated exchange relations agreed upon to finance production. In general, however, the internalised audience for both modes was made up of a combination of the consumer market and the extended electoral franchise, although the particular mix varies from country to country.

In the USA, for example, where commercial interests were particularly strong, the early broadcasting networks were federations of prime manufacturers, who had acquired production facilities as a secondary operation. These major networks, which began forming in 1926, became the defining institutions of both American radio and television. The finance for production itself was wholly drawn from advertising, in its two forms of sponsorship and insertion. Thus, manufacturing institutions, both directly in the sale of sets and indirectly in the sale of advertising money, determined the shape of broadcasting institutions in the USA more clearly than almost anywhere else. A public service ethos only developed later, within a structure already dominated by these commercial institutions. As this ethos eventually emerged it operated a classic kind of market regulatory control, into which notions of non-market interest were only gradually inserted. Thus, it was only after 1944 that the Federal Communications Commission (FCC) began to try to define the public interest in terms other than keeping the market open by means of the introduction of standards of social usefulness, of political fairness and of public morality. The audience for the American system of broadcasting has thus largely been that defined by the competitive broadcasting market alone, itself created through the channel of advertising.

In contrast, the relation between state and commercial interests in Britain was structured in terms of a limited separation of powers, owing to the relative success of the state in pressing for control of communications technology in the 'national' interest.[7] Hall (1986) explains the relative strength of the British state in terms of its ability to mediate the cultural and political leadership of the dominant groups at a time of social reconstruction. Certainly the period was more generally characterised by a number of new discourses about society and the state which were united, negatively, by their distance from the old ground of liberal individualism and *laissez-faire* and, positively, by their adherence to models of social collectivism, at the centre of which stood a new conception of the 'ethical' role of the state.

Under an Act dating from 1904, all radio transmitters and receivers had initially had to be licensed by the Post Office. By the 1920s, the GPO was faced with over a hundred demands for permission to broadcast from wireless manufacturers who had begun to see the large-scale distribution possibilities of radio. Rather than choosing between the companies, or granting them all permission to broadcast, the government decided to encourage the largest companies[8] to form a consortium.[9] This became the commercial–industrial base of the British Broadcasting Company: 'a broadcasting authority thinly disguised as an arm of private enterprise yet bearing a curious resemblance to an officially blessed monopoly' (Briggs, 1961, quoted in Hall, 1986: 42).

A guiding impetus behind the initial adoption of a public service model in broadcasting had been the fear among ruling groups of the perceived threat of 'Americanisation'. However, in time this was supplemented by a positive belief in the social and economic advantages of planning as a more 'ethical' means of managing broadcasting reproduction (Curran and Seaton, 1985; Hall, 1986; Hood, 1967). The BBC thus represented a reassertion of state interests in the regulation of cultural reproduction.

These interests were initially implemented through the granting of a monopoly to the Company and the agreement to finance broadcasting by the sale of licences for receivers, since, granted the elements of monopoly and guaranteed finance, the BBC acquired the necessary continuity and resources to become a producer as well as a transmitter of broadcasting. In 1925 the Crawford Committee, set up by the government to examine the future of broadcasting, rejected both free and unrestricted broadcasting for profit and a service directly controlled and operated by the state. It proposed that broadcasting be conducted by a public corporation acting as a trustee for the national interest, and consisting of a board of governors responsible for seeing that broadcasting was carried out as a public service. It further recommended that the British Broadcasting Company was a fit body for such a responsibility, and the Company duly became a Corporation in January 1927. Its then Managing Director, John Reith, became the first Director General.

Crucially, the agreement gave the BBC a limited degree of operational independence from the state as well as from commercial interests in the day-to-day production of broadcasting. As a consequence, the BBC was a cultural institution of a quite new type: it offered a kind of public service production linked to the effective internalisation of a *mass* audience, not as a market as in the case of the press or popular fiction, but *as a public*. However, this internalisation was shaped by the Corporation's indirect dependence upon the state, one consequence of which was an ambiguity about the relation between 'public' and 'national' interests. Furthermore, while on the one hand, the compactness of the ruling groups meant that although the BBC was a state sponsored system it was not subjected to detailed state control[10] since a dominant version of the national culture had already been established, on the other hand, the restrictive influence of the state was evident in a number of indirect practices. So, for example, the BBC has never had the right to broadcast in perpetuity; its licence has always been granted for strictly limited periods, and its performance has always been subject to review. Similarly, while the looseness and indefinition of some of its structures usually allow for some independence from immediate and short-term government interests, the state controls the governing body of the BBC, the Board of Governors, which it can fill as it chooses. It also controls the Corporation's purse strings since only it can increase the licence fee.

Nevertheless, the early BBC was a social institution with some cultural autonomy, not simply an arm of the state or the capitalist class. Most commentators agree that the flexibility which was latent in its constitution, though continually a matter of dispute, permitted the emergence of an independent corporate broadcasting policy, in which the independence was at once real, especially in relation to political parties, and qualified by its definition in terms of a pre-existing cultural hegemony. That is, while the BBC has always been active in its own definition, it depends finally on a consensus version of the 'public' interest which is assumed and then imposed through a voluntary system of corporate controls, rather than one which is openly arrived at and made subject to regular, open review. The potential problem of a technical medium of immense social and political power was thus settled by building the main editorial institution within a consenting and consensual grouping of the dominant political forces.

However, while the BBC's constitution meant that the assumption of this grouping's version of the 'public' was relatively secure, it was not clear how such understandings were to be given a specifically cultural expression in the BBC's programming policy, and there were a number of false starts. Although the Corporation's monopoly gave it an assured and increasing audience, it initially legitimated its model of public service broadcasting, not by popularity or audience appreciation, but in terms of the élite of 'The great and the good who trooped into studios to educate and inform on every subject from unemployment to the origin of the species' (Cardiff and Scannell, quoted in Curran and Seaton, 1985: 123). As a public service, it aimed to raise the general level of taste, information and understanding and so to make all members of society more actively responsive to what it saw as 'the nation's' culture and politics. To begin with then, the form of the internalised mass public which characterised public service broadcasting was defined by reference to the values of a specific, reforming fraction of the middle class: that is, the BBC saw its purpose in terms of giving authority to a specific set of cultural standards, and not the representation of listeners' interests.

In other words, the BBC did not aim to reflect public interests, but to educate, guide and shape the ordinary listener's tastes and values towards 'higher things'. This aspiration was reflected not only in certain kinds of programme content and specific standards for programmes, but also in a distinctive style of programming and an implied model of listening. In most communications systems before broadcasting, the conditions of distribution and reception ensured that cultural goods were perceived to be discrete, either spatially or temporally, often both: a book was taken and read as a specific item, a painting was seen in a particular place at a particular time, a play was performed in a particular building at a set time, and so on. As a result, most of the dominant vocabulary of aesthetic response and description was shaped by the experience of discrete events – texts: the general modes of aesthetic comprehension, judgement and taste were (and indeed still are) closely linked to specific kinds of local and isolated, temporary but reproducible forms of attention. These have been subject to public forms of authority, including the author-function, and contributed to experiences of reverence, ritual and respect for tradition. The BBC's early policy of programming and scheduling can be seen as an attempt to enforce similar conditions of reception.

In this respect, one of the striking features of the programming of this early period was the absence of routinisation. There were a few fixed points during the day when particular types of programme could be heard, but on the whole even these were not arranged in series, and had neither a regular presenter nor a settled format. Rather, listeners were enjoined to be selective in their choice of programmes: not to use the wireless to provide a continuous background of noise to punctuate domestic life, but to explore the range of programmes on offer as discrete texts. Indeed, programme continuity was so arranged as to inhibit what was contemptuously known as tap or 'lazy' non-stop listening:

> 'The BBC', the 1932 *Yearbook* claimed, 'definitely aims at having an interval of four or five minutes between programmes . . . it is obviously irritating for a listener who, switching on his set to hear, say, the news, finds himself listening to the last minute of an opera or vaudeville turn.'
> (Quoted in Curran and Seaton, 1985: 162)

As Curran and Seaton (1985) note, listening was obviously intended to be a serious business. Parallel with this was a policy of mixed programming, in which talks, light music, chamber music, quizzes, vaudeville and plays succeeded each other without respect for the listener's likely routine.

All this can be seen as part of an attempt by the BBC to impose the conventional cultural form on the new means of communication – the text. This aim was also evident in the associated model which the BBC had of the listener: 'Broadcasting is not a mass projection, though it seems to be so, it is an individual intimate business' (Hilda Matheson, the first Head of the Talks Department, quoted in Curran and Seaton, 1985: 162). This essentially personal relationship between listener and programme was elevated into a key principle of early public service broadcasting. Variety in programmes was justified in relation to the need for diversity of an individual listener rather than by reference to the interests of different groups. (In this way, even entertainment was seen to have its appropriate place in the broadcasting diet of the Reithian ideal listener.) Indeed, the tastes of groups of listeners were explicitly deemed irrelevant:

> It is something to bear in mind when we feel adversely critical towards those programmes [i.e. the BBC's]: were they not designed, we might pause and ask ourselves, as part of a scheme to please each of us as listeners [and allow us] to retain our separate entities as thinking men and women? A people's strength lies ultimately in its individuality. Individuality is the expression of spirit, and spirit lives in each of us separately – not as a crowd. Nothing must be allowed to swamp that individuality.
>
> (*Radio Times* editorial, 20 February 1931, quoted in
> Cardiff and Scannell, 1981: 69)

This model of public service broadcasting aimed to offer a mass audience access to cultural forms and experiences which had previously been largely confined to élite groups. Cardiff and Scannell (1981) argue that the policy was democratic, not in the sense that it sought to cater for the tastes and expectations of the ordinary listener, but in the way that it tried to bring within the reach of all people those cultural goods which had previously been restricted to the privileged. They suggest that, while this civilising policy was overtly prescriptive, with its roots in late nineteenth-century liberalism, it should not be simply dismissed as élitist, although it was this, since it provided a residual, but still ideologically powerful, oppositional space for the cultural producer to experiment. Not surprisingly, however, this original concept of public service broadcasting was gradually eroded as the BBC was forced to come to terms with the social and cultural conditions of its existence as a mass medium: the BBC had neither the necessary autonomy nor the external support to maintain such a prescriptive policy.

Consequently there was a gradual shift away from this early definition of public service broadcasting in relation to a public of individuals in need of education to a policy which took the already existing interests and tastes of a mass audience more seriously. This was part of an attempt to persuade the authorities of the integrity of the BBC as a national institution and involved the provision of an enduring sense of the moral and political order and a stable framework of knowledge. Cardiff and Scannell (1981) set out various reasons for this shift and various ways in which it was effected, but in general they summarise the new policy in terms of the development of an institutional voice speaking 'on behalf of' the nation. This was a complex process, but it can be illustrated through the history of news and current affairs production since this was a key sphere for the development of such an authoritative voice.

When it began broadcasting the new company was only allowed to transmit news bulletins written and supplied, for a flat annual fee, by Reuters (incorporating material from other agencies).[11] Indeed, the BBC was largely dependent on agency material for its news output throughout the first decade of its existence. However, particularly after 1927 when the Corporation's charter recognised the BBC's right to establish its own broadcasting facilities, it made efforts either to supplement or by-pass this material by obtaining information direct from official sources on the grounds that, as a Corporation official wrote, 'We ought to be the arbiters of what Government news goes out . . . not a commercial company like Reuters' (BBC Written Archives, quoted in Curran and Seaton, 1985: 129). At the same time as struggling to establish its independence from existing information-gathering agencies, however, the BBC had to face continual government interference, both direct and indirect, in the broadcasting of social and political issues: indeed, it was sometimes forced to pass off government intervention as its own decision.[12]

Nevertheless by 1930, after protracted negotiations with Reuters, the BBC had secured the right to edit and write its own news bulletins. Even then, however, it only gradually recognised that broadcast news was potentially other than newspaper news distributed in a new way, and it was not until 1938 that a coherent internal approach to radio news began to develop. This process was aided by a more general development of a new ethic in news reporting which was part of a shift in the social function of journalism. Rather than seeing themselves as passionate advocates, journalists at this time began to see themselves more self-consciously as independent professionals, and their writing as a negotiated product of conflict between partisan views; occupying a new position between government and the governed, the new journalist acted as a broker of information, exercising the specialised skill of journalistic writing (Smith, 1976). The development of this new code of professional responsibility was related to the contemporary understanding of mass society which gave the journalist as an individual a new status and an entirely new role to play. This new role of 'professional communicator' was adopted and developed by the journalists at the BBC and contributed to the emerging codes and conventions of broadcast news and current affairs.

By the 1950s new televisual formats for documentary and current affairs coverage had been established, both of which involved the use of some kind of programme presenter:

> '[we] were using film, but we were not trying to make films. We wanted the programmes to be dominated by the personality of the commentator. . . . We were all feeling our way but when the series finished we felt that we had hit on a new form that had come to stay in television. The key to the new form is the use of film to illustrate a personal experience.'
>
> (Goldie, quoted in Curran and Seaton, 1985: 183)

This form of televised politics, which combined 'objectivity' with personalisation to dramatise public events, was quite opposed to the style of the existing British cinema documentary movement, in which the film purported to represent an authoritative reality rather than any personal view. As such, it represented the beginnings of a cultural form – in the sense of a relationship between broadcaster and listener – specific to broadcasting and provided a symbolic means of 'representing' the mass audience as a public. Smith writes,

> In creating a new genre specifically for television the newsmen were setting the seal on a new relationship

between broadcasting and the mass audience ... in constructing a new genre, they were involved in the making of a new type of reporter's personality, a different system for dividing up and arranging the facts of news, a new stance towards political interviewees (and hence towards authority), and a restatement of the inherited professional canons of journalism. The reporters and producers were impliedly working now for a completely new client.

(Smith, 1976: 153)

What is significant here is the emergence of the notion of the audience as a client as a structuring principle in the relation between cultural producers and audiences since it is this understanding which characterised the new form of public service broadcasting.

The BBC's ordering of the conditions of cultural distribution and its work of putting together a new sort of national mass audience was not confined to its coverage of politics and public affairs: the development of 'normal standards of entertainment' was equally important (Frith, 1988). As with news, radio was initially dependent on existing cultural forms for variety and entertainment, transmitting acts from existing stage performers and writers.13 Even when a separate Variety Department was formed at the BBC in 1933, it still partly relied on the recruit- ment of the stars of musical comedy and concert party, a type of variety which had first made its appearance at seaside resorts in the 1890s. However, the Department's director, Maschwitz, began to introduce a number of regular series[14] which were not dependent on the stage conventions of the variety theatre and developed the potential of radio to evoke scenes in the listeners' imaginations through sound. At the same time, as with news and current affairs production, entertainment was organised in such a way as to position the listener as private and domestic; it contributed to the resonance of notions of democracy, neighbourliness, and the community through its assumption of family life and domestic routine as the preferred context of listening (Frith, 1988).

More generally, this was the period when Listener Research, which had begun in 1936, revealed that the policy of mixed programming had not achieved its aim of cultural amelioration. As the examples of news and entertainment suggest, the BBC's response was to begin to make new kinds of programme specifically for radio, often with a weekly serial or series format, and the gradual development of a new programming policy, an important aspect of which was the increased routinisation of schedules. Increasingly, too, series were divided into successions of short segments, a strategy which emerged in contradistinction to the earlier use of the discrete text (Ellis, 1982). New styles of presentation were also implemented, with a systematic separation out of 'serious' and 'popular' styles of presentation and production,[15] suggesting that there was a growing recognition of different audiences with specific kinds of tastes and levels of education.[16] Radio thus gradually began to cater more proportionately to different taste constituencies (and in this sense drew closer to other, more market-oriented producers of culture) at the same time as it began producing forms which were more specific to the medium.

All these changes can be seen as a consequence of the BBC's adaptation of its own image of the mass as it was gradually forced to take the differentiation of audience tastes and needs more seriously. As Frith remarks,

> the BBC's production staff found themselves in an odd position. Working in a mass medium with explicitly anti-mass principles, they had daily to answer the questions that other intellectuals avoided. What did it mean to construct a national culture? Who were 'the people'? What did it mean to 'please' the public? If market measures (listening figures, advertising revenue, profits) were rejected, how could the 'success' of a programme be defined?
>
> (Frith, 1988: 27)

The solution, it seems, was to understand 'the people', not in terms of the individual Reithian listener, but as a socially differentiated audience, united through a particular conception of the family at home:[17] as Leonard Henry, one of Britain's successful radio comics of the time, wrote, 'it is one of the great charms of broadcasting that we manage to get this intimate family kind of atmosphere through the mike and out of your loudspeakers' (quoted in Frith, 1988: 36). In this way, the BBC began to construct a mass 'middle-brow', through their organisation of a new home-based public.[18]

The separation out of streams of broadcasting was formalised after the Second World War via the use of three channels with distinct programming policies: the Third Programme, the Home Service and the Light Programme. This represented the completion of a move away from the internalisation of an image of the mass as an aggregate of individuals towards an image in terms of particular groupings with separate interests which the BBC was obliged to identify rather than to change. These changes meant that competition was introduced between various parts of the Corporation, and provided the impetus for an internal reform which in many ways was more important for the development of broadcasting than the competition later offered by commercial radio and television since it meant that providing the audience with 'what it wanted' had become central to the Corporation's plans (Curran and Seaton, 1985).

In general terms, the early development of British television in the 1940s echoed that of radio. There was a similar restraint on television news and current affairs, imposed not by the press this time but by the hostile senior service of radio who still dominated the BBC. There was the same inability, for financial, technical and programmatic reasons, to offer popular entertainment. In programming there was the same absence of continuity between items and an almost equally determined avoidance of serial forms, accompanied by a return to the old pleas to the audience to use the service selectively. However, the arrival of commercial broadcasting in 1955 provided the impetus for a similar process of redefinition to that which had shaped the 'popularisation' of radio, with the development of new cultural forms specifically for television and the systematic adoption of the strategies of segmenting, serialisation, sequencing and scheduling.

The model of public service broadcasting which had emerged by the middle of the twentieth century can thus be seen to have defined a form of asymmetry between cultural and social reproduction that was reliant upon both the professional practices of autonomy and impartiality and, linked to these practices, a form of public representation. However, there was a tension between these two elements; professionalism both justifies the weight given to the judgement of the colleague group and provides a reason for rejecting the twin goals of audience satisfaction and commercial success (Elliott, 1977). Moreover, the limited autonomy which the ideology of professionalism allowed was, in practice, often constrained through the operation of the principles of 'voluntary censorship' and self-regulation which were implemented via a whole range of guidelines and practices, including 'referral upwards', in which problematic decisions were referred to superiors in the institutional hierarchy. Institutional screening and selection procedures ensured that only those of 'acceptable' background and views were able to hold such positions of authority. This meant that serious attempts to reflect, for example, the experience and opinions of members of the working class tended to provoke strong critical reactions, especially when these representations conflicted with dominant definitions of the condition of the people (Cardiff and Scannell, 1981, 1991).

Moreover, domestic reception was clearly a severely restricted form of participation, and the decisive role in the form of public representation which was adopted in this form of public broadcasting was that of the commentator whose job often seemed to be to teach the audience how to join in a broadcasting event. The experience of broadcasting was thus very clearly regulated through the hierarchical relations of re-presentation in which the listener was regularly fixed at the bottom of a chain of mediation that ran through the presenters into the home: as Frith notes, 'Access was available, [but] through an authority' (1988: 42). Ellis (1982) develops this point when he argues that the process of delegation of the look to television leaves the viewer in a position of isolation or insulation from, rather than involvement with, the events shown. He suggests that television confirms the domestic isolation of the viewer, and invites the viewer to regard the world from that position. The viewer is confirmed in a basic division of the world between the 'inside' of the home, the family and the domestic, and the 'outside' of paid work, politics, public life, the city and the crowd.

The particular definition of public service broadcasting which finally emerged was thus closely tied in with a form of professionalism which secured privileges for broadcasters as cultural producers. It was, in part, able to do this by drawing on the traditional view that creative labour must be distinguished from other forms of labour in terms of a necessary autonomy, but this strategy was extended and transformed in the principles and practices of 'impartiality', 'balance' and 'quality' as they came to define professional broadcasting. However, as noted earlier, there were new institutional limits to this autonomy.

First, it was located within an institutional, bureaucratic context, in which those responsible for commissioning, planning and programming functions – broadly speaking, editorial and management functions – had a decisive importance in the origination of cultural goods. On the one hand, this marked an erosion of one of the key principles of the privileges and authority of the cultural producer as author – the fixing of meaning in a unitary origin or autonomous intention.[19] (It is also related to the decline in the significance of the text in cultural reproduction.) On the other hand, in so far as it allowed an author-isation of administrative and organisational activities,[20] it represented an acknowledgement of the social character of cultural production.

Second, this autonomy was both limited by and defined in relation to a notion of social responsibility. Thus, while audience appreciation itself was not used as an index for the evaluation of broadcasting, cultural producers' own sense of the quality of cultural production now included some acknowledgement of a need to represent the public: it was seen as part of broadcasters' responsibilities to attempt to develop, in ways they thought creative and constructive, aspects of popular taste or represent-ations of popular interests. The privileges of cultural producers (Abercrombie, 1991) were thus no longer only legitimated by reference to the specificity of creative labour and autonomous intention, but were supplemented by the claims of social responsibility. This, it has been suggested here, was linked to the internalisation of a specific form of mass distribution in the development of broadcasting as a technology of cultural reproduction.

To sum up, this concept of public service broadcasting thus assumed (or perhaps it should be imposed) a responsible élite who were to be trusted to act 'on behalf of' public opinion. It was simultaneously a form of paternalism, which rested on a com-bination of trust and privilege for an administrative and creative élite, and a significant form of asymmetry in so far as it provided an institutional defence of authorship and creativity. Significantly though, this defence was, in part, legitimated by reference to the needs of the audience, and, in this way, included a mediated representation of public interests.

In the mid-1950s, however, the BBC's 'public service' mode of broadcasting was challenged by, and made competitive with, a new network – the Independent Television Authority (later the Independent Broadcasting Authority, following the addition of commercial radio stations). The new network was financed not through a public licence, but through the sale of advertising time. It can thus be seen to mark an initially tentative, but increasingly definite, shift away from the internalisation of the audience-as-mass public as the dominant method of regulating the reproduction of cultural goods in broadcasting. From the beginning, the new network was of a commercial type: that is, it was a channel for advertising in which programmmes were made for profit in a known market. While the IBA, which owned its own means of transmission, was public in legal status and in the character of its constitution, it was commercial in its dependence for income on regional contracted companies. These, in turn, obtained their funds from selling insertion-advertisement time, and, in this way, a national network of programming, dominated by the larger companies from the richer regions, was built up, with some regional variation.

Since the capital cost of developing commercial television was initially so great, franchises were given to syndicates which had the resources to undertake the necessary investment. This brought an important change in the group of people who controlled broadcasting. Hitherto, in the BBC, responsibility had been vested in professional administrators whose social origins, training and attitudes contributed to and reflected the public service ethos of the Corporation. Independent television introduced a new type of executive, who was business-oriented and entre-preneurial, geared to the commercial criteria of the advertisers.

However, the new network was not only a product of market forces since a framework of public service broadcasting was also extended to the new authority. While 'independently' organised and financed, ITV, like the BBC, was only licensed for a limited period, and in the IBA had a publicly appointed controlling body which moderated the allocation of franchises. In addition, the IBA was explicitly required to ensure 'balanced programming', 'due impartiality' in the treatment of controversial issues, and a high quality in programme production as a whole,[21] duties which were assumed to be part of the BBC's unwritten ethical code (Hood, 1967). As a result, programme making and scheduling by the regional companies had an important secondary goal, that of securing the reallocation of franchises. In this way, the established tradition of public service broadcasting proved an influential, although indirect, example of cultural asymmetry whose practices of professional authority and standards of quality commercial interests were obliged to concede.

However, the IBA's statutory obligations were imprecise in many areas, and its implementation of them was constrained by a highly organised and politically effective lobby for commercial television.[22] Thus, for example, early claims that commercial television would promote regional cultures, and thus counteract the BBC's metropolitan bias, were not justified. The allocation of franchise areas, in which selected commercial companies were given the right to broadcast, produced a system in which four (later five) of the largest and wealthiest regional companies came to make most of the programmes for the national network.[23] The smaller companies made most of their programmes for local consumption: only a few of their products were ever shown nationally. Even decisions about which programmes should be networked were quickly centralised when in 1971 the ITCA (Independent Television Companies Association), itself dominated by the major companies, was set up to administer this process. As a result, although regional commercial broadcasting survived, it did so in a form that made little sense in political or cultural terms, since most of the broadcasting regions had no real justification except in marketing terms.[24] A television network that was supposed to be pluralistic and devolved developed into a system that was homogenous and highly centralised.

By the 1960s and 1970s the distinctions between commercial and public service broadcasting institutions were not as sharp or as uniform as had initially been forecast. Indeed, there was a convergence between public service and commercial broadcasting, as the two systems came to influence each other:[25]

> The effects of competition were . . . complex. The BBC was obliged to become more populist, more democratic, more calculatingly competitive in its struggle to secure a majority of the audience. But ITV also broadened and varied its output over time, producing a higher proportion of 'quality' material, in the face of public criticism.
>
> (Hall, 1986: 46)

Channel 4 can be seen as the culmination of this convergence. This channel, established in 1982, was initially a wholly owned subsidiary of the IBA, which publishes programmes made by both independent production and existing ITV companies, and is financed by advertising revenue.[26] It makes very few programmes of its own, although it does commission them, but is obliged by its charter to screen programmes for the various 'minority' interests not served elsewhere in the television system. In addition, the channel was given the opportunity to create new conventions for dealing with controversial and political issues: it was not obliged to balance views within a programme (the final decline of the assumption of the text as the locus of cultural reproduction), but only over the schedule and over time. It can therefore, in principle, broadcast more clearly partisan material than the other channels.

The minority-based rationale of Channel 4 had a number of origins, including the pressure of the new social movements of the 1970s, including second wave feminism and black politics. However, according to Curran and Seaton (1985), the most important was the view of television producers and directors, who argued that any innovation in television services ought to make it possible for 'independent' producers to explore the interests of those minorities not represented elsewhere in broadcasting. Channel 4 can thus be seen as a reinterpretation and extension of the public service principle, in which cultural producers assume the power to represent the interest of others through the codes and conventions of professional broadcasting forms. However, it is unlikely that this principle would have been adopted for the new channel if it had not been for the support of commercial interests.[27] As a result of this alliance, the channel's interpretation of its public service role has been mediated by the revenue of the advertising industry in a quite new way.

More generally, however, the implications of commercial mediation, both in relation to Channel 4 and the commercial mode of broadcasting are not clear. Williams (1974) argues that the 'commercial' character of television has to be seen at several levels including: the making of programmes for profit; its use as a channel for advertising; and, lastly, its dependence on the norms of a capitalist society, selling both consumer goods and a 'way of life' based on them. Yet this still leaves open the extent to which commercial broadcasting's dependence on advertising means that its characteristic forms of cultural reproduction are symmetrical, or integrated, with dominant social relations.

In order to pursue this question, an initial distinction can be made between two broad sets of relations which defined the commercial character of broadcasting in Britain in the early stages of its development. The first comprise the economic and social relations of programme production itself; the second consist in the complex of relations which surround the financing of such production through advertising revenue and structure the form of the consumer market with which commercial broadcasting production is articulated. In relation to the first of these, it is recognised that, in the main, public service broadcasting has been subject to many of the same economic pressures which have shaped what is known as commercial broadcasting. Thus, for example, both modes are characterised by an industrial organisation of labour for the production of programmes, and the adoption of the series has been the characteristic formal response to these relations of cultural production and distribution for both (as it was for many other, earlier industrialised forms of cultural production).[28] In both modes of broadcasting, programmes are produced within a defined hierarchy of labour which is subordinated to a management structure which plans production, including the overall scheduling of programmes, their budgetary levels and general aims. This organisation of labour (including the de-moting of creative labour from its traditionally privileged position) was a consequence of the development of broadcasting, regulated, at the most general level, by the socialised technology of centralised transmission for privatised reception, rather than financing through advertising or the licence fee, since it was this decision which ensured that the effective locus for cultural production was the large corporate institution.

However, there has been a difference between commercial and public service broadcasting in the intensity of economic pressure applied at the level of decision-making within the management structure. Put starkly, one key element of 'commercial' television is the presence of a profit motive. However, as discussed earlier, financing, from whatever source, has been linked to the total output of the broadcasting institution rather than to any specific programme or series as a consequence of the mediated exchange relations which financed all broadcasting until recently. This meant that the primary site of calculation of finance (and profit) was over the whole output of a production company rather than being located in any particular programme. It was thus the structure and operation of the calculus of legitimation (Murdock, 1980) at this level which determined, for example, the relationship between cultural producers and organisational imperatives such as profitability, public service and industry prestige, through the operation of processes such as cross-subsidy between different programmes and channels.[29] The presence of this 'economic slack in the system', allowing organisations some leeway in applying judgements about the cost-effectiveness of particular items of output, has thus been a source of diversity in both commercial and public service broadcasting.

In addition, it is not possible to establish, in absolute terms, the relative balance in strength of public bodies, trade unions, advertisers and cultural producers (a breakdown of the key agents according to Tunstall, 1983) within broadcasting institutions, since this is the outcome of historically specific relations between each of these groups. However, there is one general point which has had a relatively persistent bearing on the significance of the different parties in the estimation of this calculus of legitimation. This is that, until recently, ITV has had a monopoly on the sale of broadcasting time for advertisers, which, given the importance attached to television as a medium for advertising, meant that ITV had the upper hand in its bargaining relations with advertisers.

This not only meant that the regional companies had a reliable source of income for programme production, but that it was not hard to justify employing the principle of cross-subsidy to fund a diversity of programmes according to different orderings of commercial, political and aesthetic criteria. There was thus the possibility of sustaining differences between the company's standards of evaluation of a particular programme and its market value for advertisers. In short, there was, historically, a systematic divergence in the criteria of quality adopted by a programme's producers and its funders. The sources of this divergence were relatively mixed in origin; they included the traditional privilege of the cultural producer, public service credibility and responsibilities, and industry prestige.

Another crucial way in which broadcasting as a whole has been influenced by commercial factors is in its adoption of the already existing understanding of the audience in terms of the family in a domestic setting. It is difficult to weigh up the precise balance between commercial, political and ideological interests in this decision, but some have argued that the internalisation of the family as the preferred target audience would have happened independently of the role of advertising as the source of finance for commercial broadcasting. Indeed, Ellis (1982) argues that it is the domestic circumstances within which broadcasting is received – which mean that it is likely to have a relatively low degree of sustained concentration from its viewers, but an extended period of watching and frequent use – which have decisively shaped its characteristic forms of production: 'broadcast tv has developed distinctive aesthetic forms to suit the circumstances within which it is used' (1982: 111). According to Ellis, these forms include: a massive concentration of fictional representations around the family; the frequent use of direct address and a framework of presence and immediacy; the engagement of the look or the glance rather than the gaze; and a specific balance between sound and image. All these aspects are seen by Ellis to be characteristic of both commercial and public modes of broadcasting. He argues that the use of a succession of segments, in either cumulative or sequential order rather than a single coherent text, is characteristic of broadcasting as a whole, and that, 'The major difference between BBC television service without advertising and ITV with advertising lies only in the size of the conglomeration of segments' (1982: 122).

The second set of relations isolated above are those that surround the financing of programme production through advertising. The particular issue to be considered is whether a dependence upon advertising reduces the possibility of divergence or asymmetry between forms of social and cultural reproduction in broadcasting. Clearly, this is a complex question. However, one view, put forward by Williams (1974, 1981), is that, in general terms, the degree of possible asymmetry depends on the balance between the use of advertising as a support system to a primary communicative function and its use in the extension and transformation of the internalised audience. The example discussed by Williams is that of the press; he argues that while newspapers were financed primarily through the direct proceeds of their sale, they were able to retain certain necessary elements of their original purpose, but that since their production came to be dependent on advertising there have been increasingly open definitions of the success or failure of a newspaper in terms of the condition required by advertisers, that is, the reliable delivery of a body of consumers. He further argues that newspapers have been sharply reduced in number and variety in a period of expanding readership and increasing importance of public opinion as a result of their increasing dependence upon advertising.

The question that arises here then is the extent of the influence which advertising has historically had on the form of the internalisation of this distribution. In this respect, it is clear that on its introduction to broadcasting advertising generated a strong pressure for commercial television companies to produce audiences in 'a consumer form'. In other words, it is not simply the ability to create audiences, but the ability reliably to produce audiences to which advertisers are willing to purchase access, that has been a crucial drive in the determination of standards of commercial broadcasting. The suggestion here then is that the audience internalised in commercial broadcasting is the audience-as-consumer rather than the audience-as-market (see Chapter 2).

Dallas Smythe (1981) argues that this transformation in the internalised audience has resulted in the creation of what he calls 'audience power' as the audience is constructed in a commodity form through the consumer market. Like Williams, he argues that until the 1880s the principal product of the press was news and other non-advertising content, but that since then the ostensibly non-advertising content of the mass media has been produced – not as the principal product – but as the lure with which to create an audience whose power is sold by the mass media to the advertiser. Although Smythe compares audience-power (which includes audience loyalty to particular products and the power of audiences to market products to themselves) directly with labour-power, he highlights a significant difference: audiences do not sell their own labour, but the media operators do. More generally, the historically changing relations between cultural production, the consumer market and advertising have been fundamental to the construction of the sale of 'audience power'.[30]

One consequence of the need to create and exploit audience power has been a drive to produce maximum audiences on a predictable and regular basis. Scheduling, for example, was developed to expand and consolidate the audience throughout the evening. However, size has never been the only significant variable for the advertiser;[31] in recent years especially there has been noticeably less interest in absolute numbers, and an increasingly greater emphasis on consumer behaviour. This has meant that broadcasting production has begun to target specific audience groups within the mass audience. Thus, for example, the crucial demographic variables for advertisers on television in recent years have been gender, age and locality since it is believed that young, urban adults, especially women, aged 18–49, are the prime consumers of the types of goods advertised on television. There has also been growing attention not simply to the size and composition of the audience, but also to the quality of their attention.

It seems, then, that, to the extent that production is oriented towards the creation of audiences as consumers, commercial broadcasting can be seen in terms of a convergence between cultural and social reproduction. However, the force of this tendency is constrained by the difficulties involved in translating the aims of marketing strategies into buying broadcasting time. Thus, for example, current research by broadcasting authorities themselves indicates that different categories of programmes do not, in general, divide audiences into conveniently specialised consumer groups.[32] Selectivity of different target groups within the total audience is possible to a small extent, in terms of time of day and day of week, but hardly at all by type of programme (Barwise and Ehrenberg, 1988).

More significantly, divergences between the social and cultural construction of 'audiences' and 'consumers' and the differences in their organisation of viewing represent a significant source of diversity within the reactivation patterns of the viewers for commercial broadcasting. The fact that individuals do not become audiences and consumers in directly parallel ways poses a real problem for broadcasters seeking to produce audiences in a consumer form. Moreover, the extent of diversity in reactivation within commercial broadcasting is increased by the potentially universal distribution and relatively direct character of broadcasting as a means of communication.

As Ien Ang (1991) has convincingly argued, the predilection within television institutions, commercial or public service, to think about audiences as a knowable object is misleading; the ascription of stability and objectivity to the television audience is only possible by purging from it the unpredictable, the capricious and the erratic that characterise the social world of actual audiences. As Ellis writes,

> For 'audiences' is a profoundly ideological concept, that has very little to do with what viewers are doing or how they are interpellated. Broadcasting institutions are not concerned with 'viewers', but they are with the 'audience'. Viewers are individuals who use television within their domestic and group social contexts. . . . Audiences are bulk agglomerations created by statistical research. They have no voices and the most basic of characteristics, they 'belong' to income groups and are endowed with a few broad educational and cultural features. Audiences do not use television, they watch and consume it. Broadcasting institutions do not seek viewers, they seek audiences.
>
> (Ellis, 1983: 49, quoted in Ang, 1991)

The suggestion here is that the solidity of the category of audience is a precondition for effective broadcasting reproduction. This is bolstered by the taxonomic activities of the audience measurement industry, but while television institutions do have the power to determine the formal boundaries of television culture these are never equivalent, in the last instance, to the social world of actual audiences.

Despite these countervailing forces, however, it seems that in recent years broadcasting has undergone a shift in the character of its internalised audience. This has been accelerated by recent modifications in state regulation which have facilitated the shift towards the internalisation of the audience in a commodity form by strengthening the position of commercial forces within the calculus of legitimation structuring broadcasting networks. At the same time, however, it is important to recognise changes within the audience itself, including changes within households relating to the increasing diversity of forms of family life and relations between the domestic and the public since such changes may undermine the ability of broadcasters to sell audience power (Berland, 1992).

This chapter has been restricted to a consideration of the organisation of broadcasting during a time when technologies were such that there could be no direct exchange relation

147

between audiences and broadcasters. Audiences have paid for programmes through forms of taxation or through increased costs of goods advertised, but they have not directly paid for programmes. Recent technological advances have transformed this situation, and it is with the position and significance of cultural reproduction in the push towards a more direct market economy in communication that the next chapter is concerned. The primary focus will be on the implications of micro-electronic technologies for cultural reproduction and their position in relation to, and significance for, social and economic reproduction.

NOTES

1 This chapter does not consider the implications of the technologies of video, cable or satellite for broadcasting; see Chapter 7 for a discussion of the convergence between computing and telecommunications.

2 As the general market has been extended, the level of viability has also risen.

3 Thus, for example, it was (and is) possible, in technical terms, that broadcasting should have been conceived as a medium for communal reception in public centres.

4 Williams (1974) argues that, as a result, autonomous production was relatively unimportant for both radio and television in the early stages of their development: thus, he suggests that specific content was initially a by-product of the socialised technology rather than an independent enterprise.

5 Although Ellis develops this argument specifically in relation to television, it has implications for the analysis of broadcasting as a whole during this period.

6 For this to happen, it was necessary for the wavelength to become a national possession by international agreement.

7 A more common solution in Western European societies of a similar size was direct state regulation of broadcasting at the level of its early technical organisation, leading to direct state control of broadcasting production.

8 These included Marconi, Metropolitan Vickers, General Electric, Radio Communications, Hotpoint and Western Electric.

9 The official reason given for this was that only a few frequencies were available to be shared out, but clearly things could have been organised differently – for example, on a decentralised basis.

10 In general terms, very few restrictive injunctions occur in the BBC Charter: for example,

The BBC has never been required or directed in any Charter

or Licence to observe impartiality. What has happened is that the Postmaster-General has *desired* the Corporation 'as in the past' to refrain from broadcasting any expression of its own opinion on current affairs or on matters of public policy. The situation is therefore based on *trust* – on the belief, to quote the White Paper on Broadcasting Policy published in 1946, 'that the Corporation would ensure that such subjects would be treated with complete impartiality'.

(Hood, 1967: 19)

11 Before it even came into being, the Post Office, the press barons and the news agencies had arranged that radio would not develop its own news service in competition with the newspapers, or in any other way threaten their interests.

12 This interference is still clearly evident in contemporary broadcasting.

13 There were a number of practical limitations in this policy: many top variety stars could not switch from the footlights to the microphone, and even those who could feared they would quickly exhaust their material on radio. In addition, there were recurring disagreements with the leading theatrical agencies, which periodically banned their contracted artists from the microphone, or refused permission for relays from their stages. Even when such relays were allowed, they often made awkward broadcasting: 'loud applause might overpower the microphone and purely visual acts, like juggling or conjuring, were incomprehensible to listeners unless the clumsy expedient of using a commentator was adopted' (Cardiff and Scannell, 1981: 178).

14 Frith suggests that by the end of the 1930s the BBC was no longer getting its entertainers from the stage: rather, the relation was structured in the reverse direction – the stage was getting its entertainers from the BBC. In this way, he argues, the BBC's public service principles of entertainment-as-relaxation came, from this point on, to be an important influence on what commercial entertainment itself was like.

15 Cardiff writes, 'The stylistic innovation in talks reflects the problems faced by broadcasters who were committed to an ideal of public service but were becoming increasingly aware of the differentiated structure of their public' (1986: 246).

16 One symptom of this change was the increase in the number of programmes directed at specific sections of the audience, such as women and youth, or covering particular interests, such as sport. These took items which had earlier been scattered among individual programmes and packaged them together, often in a magazine format, in a style appropriate to the target audience.

17 As noted above, Ellis (1982) makes this argument on the basis that the domestic setting for reception placed limits on the kinds of attention that could be expected from listeners/viewers.

18 Frith makes the important point that 'mass' does not always mean American, Hollywood or popular.

19 However, as Murdock (1980) notes, there is still a degree of latitude in the positioning of, for example, the author-as-writer within the overall output of any broadcasting institution:

> The 'primary' sector of series and serial production is geared to audience maximisation and confines the writer primarily to the role of craftsman, turning out scripts to other people's specifications; whereas the 'secondary' sector of single play production operates with an ideology of authorship which nominates authors as the main originators of the text and accords them a good deal of expressive autonomy.
>
> (Murdock, 1980: 25)

20 Ellis writes, 'Television management structures are ... equally creative structures, ... in the sense that they take the major decisions that determine the general aesthetic features of a particular television output' (1982: 220). An interesting extrapolation of this argument is to be found in Jane Feuer's discussion of the American television production company, MTM, which explains its commercial success partly in terms of the construction and maintenance of a corporate authorial status (Feuer *et al.*, 1984).

21 As Hood (1967) notes, the generally restrictive nature of the Television Act of 1954 is in marked contrast to the generally permissive character of the BBC's Charter which has very few restrictive injunctions.

22 This lobby was made up of an extensive network of contacts based on the interlocking directorships linking commercial television companies to banking and industrial organisations (Murdock and Golding, 1982).

23 Between them the top five companies produced 49.5 per cent of all programmes transmitted by ITV companies in 1978–9 (Curran, 1986: 330).

24 For example, the Central region has been promoted to advertisers as one which is characterised by a particularly high proportion of margarine buyers. Indeed, apart from London, television regions do not even approximately coincide with local authority areas, inhibiting the discussion of local political issues. Similarly, Harlech caters for a mixed Welsh and English audience.

25 So, for example, according to Curran,

> When in 1958 its audience share slipped to below 30%, senior BBC executives became convinced that the BBC had to imitate, to some extent, the programme and scheduling policy of ITV. Increasingly, the output and schedules of BBC1 have come to resemble those of its principal rival.
>
> (Curran, 1986: 327)

26 In the early period, while Channel 4 sought to establish its audience this finance was drawn from the advertising income of the existing commercial companies. However, it is now required to fund its own programming.

150

27 This support is, more or less cynically, understood either in terms of the view that advertisers believed they would be able to make use of the more accurate targeting that market research suggested minority programming would supply, or that advertisers saw the setting-up of a second advertising-funded channel as a lever with which to break ITV's monopoly of broadcasting advertising time.

28 As the last chapter suggested, the adoption and elaboration of the series or serial form are not specific to commercial broadcasting, or even broadcasting more generally, but, historically, have been a characteristic means of determining aesthetic standards in industrial cultural production.

29 For example, it was the operation of this level of management which determined the ratio of low-budget programmes such as quiz shows and soap operas to the relatively more expensive current affairs programmes or one-off dramas. It also affected decisions about co-production or the development of programmes for non-British markets.

30 Dallas Smythe (1981) extends his analysis of the sale of audience-power to include not only the commercial media, but public service organisations, such as the BBC, through a consideration of the significance of media audiences to the contemporary organisation of politics.

31 Small audiences which are attractive to advertisers have always been of greater significance than larger audiences with lower socio-economic profiles.

32 This mismatch or divergence may reduce the potential for new forms of commercial broadcasting to create new forms of programme and patterns of programming, although the commercial plans for cable and satellite television depend on the development of a form of 'narrow-casting' which is able to co-ordinate these two sets of evaluation more accurately.

7

MICRO-ELECTRONIC REPRODUCTION: COMMUNICATION, THE FLOW OF INFORMATION AND USERS

This chapter will focus on the introduction and early stages of the development of a key contemporary technology of culture – the emerging communication and information technologies based on the use of micro-electronics. It will consider the extent to which this technology is a cause and consequence of a convergence between the processes of cultural and social, including economic, reproduction. In short, it will use a study of communication technology as a point of entry to consider the question of whether or not there has been a qualitative transformation in the significance and functioning of the cultural sphere in contemporary society (Castells, 1983; Harvey, 1989; Jameson, 1984; Lash and Urry, 1987; Mulgan, 1991).

This question has been raised by a number of analyses which have considered the ways in which cultural reproduction has been progressively commodified. This process of commodification has been explored in relation to processes as various as genetic engineering (Stanworth, 1987; Spallone and Steinberg, 1987; Franklin, 1990); tourism (Urry, 1990); gentrification (Zukin, 1988); cultural policy and planning (Bianchini, 1987; Lewis, 1990); and advertising and promotional culture (Leiss *et al.*, 1986; Baudrillard, 1983a, 1988, 1990; Haug, 1986; Wernick, 1991). The focus here, however, will be on communication technology and the processes through which information has acquired a new significance as a resource for capital accumulation.

The view that the collection, manipulation and regulation of information is increasingly central to the organisation of capital accumulation has been developed from a number of different perspectives. In general terms, it is argued that information processes have become a significant part of economic

152

organisation, the modern administrative state and modern political systems. Indeed, it is suggested that they have become so central that the general character of these operations has qualitatively changed. In this way, it is implied, a major part of the whole modern labour process can now be defined in terms which are not easily separable from what would conventionally have been described as 'cultural' activities.

It is further suggested that while information previously existed outside generalised commodity production, in the sense that there were distinct fields and standards for its realisation, it is becoming increasingly commodified through a variety of mechanisms. Hepworth and Robins, for example, argue that, 'The "information revolution" centres on the commodification of information; not only information but also information about information costs money' (1988: 335). Furthermore, information is seen to be characterised by a transition from open 'library' systems to a closed system of private ownership. In this sense, the 'information society' is viewed as a society within and for which information is progressively privatised and commodified.

However, there has been some disagreement about how best to understand the process of convergence between social and cultural reproduction implied by the term information society. On the one hand, social scientists such as Bell (1974), Castells (1983, 1989) and Harvey (1989) have argued that new communications systems and information technologies are shaping the regime of capital accumulation through what has been variously called an informational mode of development or informatics. The basic idea here is that knowledge and information are becoming the strategic resources and transforming agents in a 'post-industrial' society. Bell (1974), for example, suggests that in modern societies, theoretical knowledge forms the 'axial principle' of society and is the source of innovation and policy formulation. In the economy this is reflected in the decline of goods-producing and manufacturing as the main form of economic activity, and the growth of services. He writes,

> the post-industrial society means the rise of new axial structures and axial principles: a change-over from a goods-producing society to an information or knowledge society; and, in the modes of knowledge, a change in the axis of abstraction from empiricism or trial-and-error

tinkering to theory and the codification of theoretical knowledge for directing innovation and the formulation of policy.

(Bell, 1974: 487)

With regard to the class structure, the new axial principle fosters the supremacy of professional and technical occupations which constitute a new class. In all spheres – economic, political and social – decision-making is crucially influenced by new intellectual technologies and the new intellectual class.

Similarly, Castells (1983) suggests that communication and information technologies have radically re-ordered the processes of capital accumulation; more specifically, he suggests that we are moving towards a fundamentally delocalised world order articulated around a small number of 'concentrated centres for production of knowledge and storage of information, as well as centres for emission of images and information' (1983: 6). These nerve centres, organised through cybernetic grids, act as command and control headquarters of the world financial and industrial system. He thus argues that corporate information networks are underpinning the expansion and integration of the capitalist world system, realising the possibility of a world assembly line, and opening up truly global markets: 'The new space of a world capitalist system is a space of variable geometry, formed by locations hierarchically ordered in a continuously changing network of flows' (1983: 7). The consequence, Castells believes, is the formation of a new historical relationship between space and society, since communication and information technologies are bringing about the transformation of spatial places into flows and channels through what amounts to the delocalisation of the processes of production and consumption.

These arguments have been criticised for exaggerating the power and influence of the new professional and technical occupations: there is no agreement that these occupations constitute a discrete social group, that they effectively control corporations, or that they exercise significant political power. In short, while it is generally acknowledged that knowledge and information have become steadily more visible as resources of economic production throughout this century, this is not always seen to imply any necessary change in the locus of power.[1] Rather, it is suggested that information technologies should be seen as manifestations of prevailing social relations, and that the 'information revolution' builds on, rather than supersedes or dissolves, existing class and regional inequalities (Hepworth and Robins, 1988). Either way, however, this approach tends to suggest that cultural reproduction is increasingly defined in relation to, and subsumed by, the processes of economic and social reproduction, specifically commodification and the regime of capital accumulation.

On the other hand, cultural theorists, such as Bataille (1982), Debord (1983), Baudrillard (1983a; 1988; 1990) and Kroker and Cook (1986), argue that the newly visible significance of information, knowledge and aesthetics as resources of production should lead to a reconsideration of the very nature of the commodity and thus a rethinking of contemporary industrial society and its history. For example, in Baudrillard's work, production as the dominant material scheme of the industrial order is argued to be giving way to simulation as the dominant scheme of an order regulated by the 'code'. In general terms, capitalism, and stages in its organisation, are theorised as an aspect of the history of signification, since the commodity form is understood in terms of the fetishism of the value form of the sign which is seen as inherently random, abstract and tautological. Similarly, Kroker and Cook write, 'capitalism may now be described as entering its last, purely artistic, phase under the sign of aestheticised recommodification' (1986: 19). In short, such analysts propose that the social is imploding into the cultural.

Such ideas have gained only limited credibility among social theorists; nevertheless, they are important in that they have encouraged a discussion of the specificity of cultural reproduction as a medium of value creation. However, rather than analyse this specificity in terms of a general, universal, theory of the value form of the sign, the approach adopted so far here has been to explore the ways in which this specificity is produced within particular processes of reproduction. Through an examination of the history of the development of information technologies, this chapter will take as its double focus the impact of the commodification of information on cultural reproduction, and the ways in which information reproduction transforms social and economic reproduction.

On the one hand, as the primary technical means through which information is being redefined, information and communication technologies should be seen as part of a qualitative reorganisation of the determinants of cultural reproduction. It is therefore important to consider the social and economic decisions which have shaped its development, including the desire to tap commercial organisations as a market for cultural works. On the other hand, it is also important to consider the limits to this process presented by the specificities of cultural reproduction, including its constitution as intellectual property and the difficulties of constraining the activities of reactivation.

In order to develop this analysis, it is first necessary to consider what is meant by communication and information technologies (or IT). The general literature about the 'information society' suggests that 80 per cent of the members of the 'information' workforce collect, arrange, co-ordinate, monitor and disseminate information about activities taking place within the production economy (Smith, 1987). Thus, they are mainly servicing production as accountants and managers, advertisers and brokers, clerks and administrators, buyers and sellers of goods and services.[2] Much of the phenomenon which is labelled information, such as banking data, is thus an emanation of economic activities, and refers to kinds of value which were not previously thought to have anything to do with a differentiated cultural sphere.

The absolute and relative size of the information sector has grown as a consequence of the rapid multiplication in the quantity of transactions internal to the economy which has followed in the wake of increased technical efficiency in production and distribution.[3] In the first instance, then, IT refers to those technologies for the mechanisation and rationalisation of informational activities within production which result from the commercial attempt to increase efficiency and control[4] in a sector which had been relatively untouched by automation since the development of the typewriter; and the 'information economy' results from the task of refocusing investment into this area.[5]

IT itself is commonly taken to include micro-electronic technologies for the manipulation, storage and transmission, and retrieval of the spoken and written word as well as of drawings and images.[6] At the heart of these technologies is the impact of the computer and the semiconductor, and of the digital languages and codes with which they operate. A significant advantage of digital forms is that any signal, whether a sound or an image, can be transmitted or manipulated in similar ways. These technologies thus provide, for the first time, the possibility of a closed system for handling information in terms of the single medium of electronic signals: 'for the first time we have a coherent technology to handle information' (Barron and Currow, 1979: 28); 'Pulses of electromagnetic energy embody and convey messages that up to now have been sent by sound, pictures and text. All media are becoming electronic' (Sola Pool, 1987: 20); 'Material which was once associated with different arts and industries, even with different physical senses (music, film, novels, magazines), has come to depend upon the same branches of electronics for reaching the public' (Smith, 1987: 332). The radically democratising potential of these new technologies is thus that all signals, previously confined within specialised means of production, can now be transmitted to the audience within one common means of distribution.

The impetus for this convergence between communications and computing was initially fuelled by the dependence of the computing industries upon telecommunications for the creation of new markets,[7] that is, for an extension of reach to new audiences. Until recently, telecommunications had been one of the most protected, insulated and monopolised industries in the economies of virtually all nations. These restrictions applied not only to participation in production but also to access and reception; for example, state policy often prohibited the interconnection to the telecommunication network of terminal devices (even telephones, let alone computers) that were not owned and controlled by a telecommunications monopoly. However, Melody (1987) and others argue that from the 1960s onwards there were significant moves towards the integration of computing and telecommunications functions.

The pace and direction of this development were set, not only by technological developments in the computing industries, but by state policies in the telecommunications sector. Or rather, the technological developments themselves were made and developed in a state-supported market environment; for example, many national governments, especially the US through its military and space programmes, provided large subsidies for research and development and experimental service applications[8] and stimulated a large market through government purchases of the industries' products and services. State intervention has also been responsible for the breakdown of numerous political and legal separations between telecommunications and computing in most Western countries over the last twenty or so years, including those between control of voice and text transmission, and between domestic and international carriers.[9] In this way, the technical possibility of a closed production system for the transmission of signals was brought into being through a particular alliance of state and commercial interests.

In the UK, Garnham (1985) suggests that in the five years from 1979 to 1984 the telecommunications industry was forced through a process which it took the US twenty-five years to complete. He writes that,

> ... BT has been transformed from a state-owned and controlled monopoly supplier of all telecommunication goods and services ... into a limited public company operating under licence.... The terminal market has been completely liberalised.... A competitive company, Mercury, a wholly owned subsidiary of Cable and Wireless, has been licensed to offer switched telecommunications services on its own network across the whole range from local loop through trunk to international.... In addition a ... license has been offered to operators of Value Added Network Services.
>
> (Garnham, 1985: 10–11)

He notes that while this process is often described, using the example of the US, as one of deregulation, it is more accurately described as a move from a public monopoly to a regime of regulated market competition.

This competition was intended by the government to support the development of new IT-related telecommunication services, the majority of which were designed for business use. It was thus a consequence of a new factor in the commercialisation of information, that is, the concern of commercial interests not only in the production of hardware for information manipulation, but also in software – in information itself as a commodity. This, in turn, arises from the increasing significance of information as a resource for commodity production, in short, from a recognition and commercial exploitation of a market among businesses[10] as well as the general public for information goods and services.

Thus, for example, the value added network and data services (VADS) which Garnham mentions are currently a major growth area:[11] these are anything other than traditional voice communications, usually 'intelligent' access to databases, over networks based on private circuits hired from BT or Mercury. Leading companies, including IBM, Intel, ICL and the Midland Bank subsidiary Fastrak, offer VADS which are targeted at specific industry sectors. They thus offer a prime example of the way in which information is now not only a commodity, but reinforces the general conditions of commodity production (Locksley, 1986). IT is the technical facility that has allowed the resource of information to be developed and gain ascendancy in this way.

The mechanisation of information production can thus be seen in terms of a new commercial significance of cultural reproduction and its restructuring in relation to the priorities of economic and social reproduction. The preceding two chapters looked at the ways in which the relation between producers and audiences has been structured through an internalisation of the concepts of the audience-as-market, the audience-as-public and the audience-as-consumer in the development of print and broadcasting technologies. This internalisation was seen as one of the key mechanisms by which the indeterminacy of the relation between producers and audiences characteristic of modern technologies of culture has been limited. What is being suggested here is that this indeterminacy is not as severe for the communication and information technologies described above. This is because the 'audience' is made up of commercial organisations, and their activities of reactivation are motivated by commercial, not expressive, purposes. Their demand for cultural works is therefore more predictable, constrained as it is by the impetus for economic growth. It is in this sense that the development of telecommunication and information technologies can be seen to be both a cause and consequence of a convergence between cultural and social, specifically economic, reproduction.

However, it is important to recognise that while the 'audience' is principally businesses, it is by no means solely made up of commercial organisations, but also contains other kinds of groupings and private individuals. Moreover, the process of convergence is not without its own internal contradictions. These contradictions derive from a number of sources, including conflicts between different sectors of the information economy over which market to target (between, for example, the market for information hardware and that for information software), and disputes over rights in information as intellectual property and its circulation in the public sphere. In addition, while it has been suggested that the selection and use of information by businesses is motivated by commercial purposes, such decisions are continually undercut by the radical instability of information, even when constituted as a commodity, and the difficulties of employing information in the pursuit of economic growth. These problems are exacerbated by the increasing power of users, or the audience, in relation to producers within this mode of cultural reproduction.

The first set of contradictions is evident in the previously mentioned example of telecommunications-related consumer services. Business subscribers to the new telecommunications services increasingly demand advanced digital network capacity and sophisticated terminal apparatus, while residential sub-scribers generally only require standard telephone service. It is not yet clear how these conflicting demands will be met, not only because of the difficulties of costing the economics of network provision, but also because business requires access to and from residential subscribers for a growing range of marketing initiatives and for the range of new value added services such as home banking, electronic funds transfer, and remote booking and billing. However, while the clash of interests between business and residential subscribers is the most usually discussed, Garnham suggests that it is underpinned by a more fundamental tension: that between an industrial and a service-based policy at a national level:

> Here we face one of the central contradictions of UK policy. On the one hand, here is an industrial policy that aims to use BT as the engine for the development of a UK electronic and IT equipment industry capable of competing on a world scale and that therefore requires a powerful, fully integrated BT. On the other hand, there is a policy that favours competition in network provision and apparatus supply in the interest of users of telecom-munications goods and services and of the development of an information services industry.
>
> (Garnham, 1985: 26)

He suggests that the whole question of the proper relationship between BT as a developer, manufacturer and seller of equipment and BT as a network operator has yet to be resolved. But it is clear that the previously existing close monopsonic relationship between the national monopoly equipment supply industry and the national monopoly network provider has come under pressure. More generally, Collins argues that while the information society thesis has been embraced and consciously promulgated as state policy, 'nowhere has national policy considered and successfully articulated the hardware and software elements of the information industries' (Collins, 1986: 291).[12] This problem is further exacerbated because of the paranational level at which industrialisation is occurring, and the difficulties this produces for national governments attempting to develop competitive policies.

Both kinds of conflict – between hardware and software producers, national and international priorities – are also increasingly evident in other means of cultural production, such as, for example, broadcasting.[13] In this case, these conflicts derive, in part, from the newly possible commercial exploitation of shared transmission technologies which make feasible novel scales of distribution. In the past a limitation of distribution capacity (and the imposition of an 86 per cent British quota) enabled broadcast production to amortise its costs at home and compete on the world market on the same basis as US producers. This limitation was not technical (the limit of the spectrum capacity was not used), but was rather the result of a series of political and cultural judgements that the 'national interest' was best served by restricting supply of programming to an amount that could be financed and produced indigenously.[14] However, the recent political decision to allow the introduction of new distribution technologies such as cable and direct broadcast satellites will expand distribution channels and thus transmission potential at a speed which is likely to upset this balance by creating a demand for 'software' that cannot be met by the national production industry.[15] Many commentators have made gloomy predictions about the consequences of this decision: Collins, for example, argues that,

> The consequential importation of software from overseas will attract audiences away from existing services (whether

by having smaller audiences to sell to advertisers or by
reducing the political acceptability of expenditure from the
state budget or the levying of broadcast receiving licence
fees), thus reducing the quality of indigenously produced
software and initiating a spiral of decline.

(Collins, 1986: 295)

This prognosis follows from the judgement that current
developments in broadcasting relate primarily to what Collins
describes as industrial (by which he means commercial hardware)
rather than cultural (commercial or public service software)
intentions. However, while the new systems of communication
are clearly being installed as forms of distribution with little
thought of corresponding forms of production, as Williams
(1981) and others have pointed out, so were the very first
developments in broadcasting. In fact, it is unclear what the
implications of implementing either set of intentions will be for
cultural reproduction. The social and political restraints to be
placed on the commercial exploitation of the possibilities of
production and distribution offered by micro-electronic technologies are still in the process of being settled, and it is not
certain whether or not they will result in the form of distinctively
cultural asymmetries. Nevertheless, it is likely that political and
cultural interests will continue to limit the commercial
exploitation of the processes of cultural reproduction in some
way or other.

The projected internationalisation of television audiences
provides a case in point. One of the fears expressed by Collins
among others is that the new technology will be used to override
political and cultural boundaries in order to create new international commercial audiences, and certainly one of the key
distinguishing characteristics of the new media order will be that
television will no longer be a national medium, but an
international one.[16] IT and the associated business initiatives
have created a substantially different spatial order for broadcasting in which public service broadcasters are required, more
or less for the first time, to compete seriously with a large number
of other channels, including national private channels, public
service broadcasters from other countries and private
pan-European channels. Yet, as Porter notes, despite the
pervasiveness of the ideology of the free market, no country has

adopted the concept of allocating all spectrum frequencies by price alone:

> Each country has continued to reserve certain frequencies for television broadcasting while others have been allocated to the military, the police and other privileged users. There are proposals for the allocation of radio [and television] frequencies by competitive tendering in the UK, but even here, the government proposes to require certain minimum undertakings from those tendering to use the frequency.
>
> (Porter 1989: 23)

He argues that resistance to the process of globalisation is evident in legal debates about the regulation of broadcasting which oppose the citizen's right to impart information freely with the citizen's right to receive a plurality of information. He shows that a number of constitutional courts (including those of the USA, West Germany and France) have asserted that pluralism is an essential criterion for which governments have to legislate when regulating broadcasting: 'Nowhere have the courts accepted that the right to communicate should take precedence over the political need for pluralism' (Porter, 1989: 24). However, he further notes that the concept of pluralism has been defended at an economic level, frequently in terms of the need for a diversity of ownership of broadcasting organisations, rather than at a directly political or cultural level:

> Nowhere has there been any consideration of the relationship in the private sector between ownership of a channel of communication and the pluralism, or the lack of it, in the programmes it broadcasts. The tendency rather has been to look either to regulatory provision or to anti-trust bodies to break up large-scale organisations.
>
> (Porter, 1989: 25)

Further conflicts arise in relation to copying rights: indeed, as the economic importance of the control of information has increased, so have the stakes in its ownership and protection. As Locksley argues, 'Information has been held in common ownership but the purveyors of IT services need private rights of ownership if a surplus is to be realised' (Locksley, 1986: 83). While Locksley may overstate the extent to which information has in the past actually been held in common ownership, it is clear that private firms depend upon the containment of free flow to protect copyrights, patents and trade secrets. Without laws and enforcement agencies to protect exclusive rights of this kind markets in information could not function. However, these rights of ownership are not easy to define let alone protect, particularly since the possibilities of computer crime – embezzlement, piracy of software and data, theft of computer time and sabotage – have vastly increased,[17] and in ways that existing intellectual property law is not fully adequate to prevent.

To give just one example of the problems which arise as a consequence of the relative increase in access to cultural production (as opposed simply to consumption) made possible by IT, it has been estimated that the number of programmes written daily in the US is 15,000 (quoted in Frow, 1988). More generally, the problem of control is exacerbated in the international marketplace, and it is with the question of transnational data flows that some of the severest contradictions in the commercial realisation of information come to light. For example, until recently China did not acknowledge the legitimacy of copyright, since copying was traditionally seen as a means of adding value to a work, and thus Chinese publishers were allowed to publish reprints or translations of imported works without penalty.

At another level, even within the UK, legal support for a commercial right of ownership, as represented by the laws of copyright, has been rendered problematic as a consequence of the ease of copying made possible through the increasing availability of technologies of copying such as photocopiers, video and cassette recorders and personal computers. And such copying has already inflicted considerable damage on the culture industry; thus, for example, in 1986 sector estimates (necessarily rather approximate) were £1 billion in losses each for book and film, and £1.5 billion for the music sector (Mulgan, 1991) – it has been estimated that six times more music is copied than is bought.

In addition, the extent of piracy has contributed to a number of disputes between cultural hardware and cultural software producers. Thus, for example, DAT (digital audio tape) machines were repeatedly held back from the British electronics mass market by the efforts of record companies who were worried about the capacity they offered for high-quality copying from CDs; they have now become obsolete before having seen the light of day as new technologies are developed. However, the conflict between hardware and software manufacturers is not clear-cut since the success of any particular piece of hardware equipment is obviously dependent upon the availability of software, and there is currently some evidence of vertical integration among such manufacturers, perhaps driven, at least in part, by an attempt to capitalise on such dependence. So, for example, Philips, the inventor of the CD, is the parent group of the giant Polygram music group, and Sony, the world's biggest producer of hi-fi equipment and one of the major companies behind the development of DAT, recently acquired CBS records.

In short, conflicts over the constitution and exploitation of information as intellectual property are not simply confined to the issue of copying at the point of production, but also arise in relation to the second dimension of reproduction, that is, relations between producers and audiences. As discussed in Chapter 2, Anglo-American law originally defined copyright as a right to copy, and in this sense it was always a publisher's right rather than that of an author, since it vested the right of reproduction in the copyright holder rather than the author. Successive mechanical and electronic developments have posed a number of problems for this principle in so far as they complicate existing distinctions between 'work' and 'copy', between original research and 'mere' compilation, and thus blur the primary distinction between origination and copying; however, the most recent developments in cultural technology additionally confuse the distinction between production and reception.

Both dimensions of reproduction are therefore no longer easily regulated through the regime of rights associated with copyright. Indeed, the computer, as a machine expressly designed for the purpose of copying any other, is intrinsically at odds with copyright law. At the most basic level, a computer must write, or at least copy, before it can either read a piece of incoming information or be read by a user; this means that, as Mulgan (1991) notes, a basic principle of copyright, that copying is prohibited and reading is facilitated, is perforce turned on its head.

IT thus further intensifies the complications relating to the implementation of copyright law by multiplying the possibilities of deployment of complex bodies of information. The distinction between idea and expression has always been arbitrary, but when ideas can be expressed and reworked in multiple forms, in software, CD-ROMs or digital communications, the distinction breaks down. Other complications relate to the routine blurring of artificial and human agency in the use of IT, and the removal of a fixed physical substrate for an idea's expression. While in the past, a form of control was structured into the technologies used to make and copy information through the technical fixing of expression in a physical substrate, control in this sense is less possible with the flow of information through networks. Temporary solutions to these problems of copyright under these new conditions of cultural reproduction include: the spread of compulsory licensing schemes, of unified collection agencies sharing earnings in a pool, of governing tribunals, of special taxes on hardware, and the production of immediate information, such as news and financial information, which loses its value very quickly, before copying can infringe on the rights of its owners.

At the same time, commercial organisations are pressing for further revisions to the traditional terms of ownership of rights in intellectual property in ways which will contain the free flow of ideas. This is evident in, for example, new interpretations of authorship. As noted earlier, this is often seen as the most fundamental category of copyright law, in relation to which all other categories are secondary. It has been the principle that founds both the work and the copy in their respective acts, both the idea and its expression. In turn, copyright law has, historically, been used to protect authoring as a special form of labour through the definition of the right to copy (or not) in relation to the notion of originality, located either in the work itself in the form of 'distinguishable variation' in the expression of ideas or 'the causal relationship between an author and the material form in which a work is embodied'. However, recent American interpretations of copyright law in relation to works such as computer databases and compilations, where there is no 'organisation of ideas' to protect, have taken the approach of directly protecting the investment of labour rather than the creative work which is the ostensibly protected object:[18]

> Thus the Court in National Business Lists v Dun and Bradstreet, Inc (1982) decided that, 'compilations such as

Dun and Bradstreet's have value because the compiler has collected data which otherwise would not be available. The compiler's contribution to knowledge is normally the collection of the information, not its arrangement. If his protection is limited solely to the form of expression, the economic incentives underlying the copyright law are largely swept away.'

(Frow, 1988: 11)

In this way, the legally privileged concept of originality, and the associated ideology of creativity, are being redrawn in line with current commercial imperatives. Frow (1988) concludes that the legal and commercial conditions for dropping the insistence on individual human creativity as the source of copyright are fully in place.

In addition, there is pressure in the US from some jurists for a

fuller integration of copyright law into the services of the market, through a dismantling of the doctrinal distinction between ideas and expressions. Hopkins argues, for example, that the law at present provides no protection for such things as 'a game concept, the system that goes into legal papers, or the ideas comprising the methodology or processes adopted within a computer program', and, more generally, that 'the very fact that ideas are free creates a disincentive to the development of ideas. It is only when people can fully exploit the benefits of their ideas and receive protection in these endeavours that they will donate the product of their work process to the public domain.'

(Frow, 1988: 4–5)

Such a move would undermine the legal tradition which has historically attempted to balance a commercial right of ownership against a public right to the free circulation of ideas, and as such can be seen as an indication of commercial support for a complete convergence between cultural and social reproduction.

At the same time, however, the implications of allowing the 'free' circulation of ideas are also changing, in part as a result of the uses of IT to expand the sphere of information or ideas which is realisable through commodification, and in part as a consequence of transformations in the operation of the public sphere. Such changes must also be examined before judgements about the implications of such a convergence for the circulation of cultural value can be made. One example of the expanded sphere of cultural value subject to commodification is provided by the development of firms gathering the information which arises in vast quantity from the total activity of a society, not just economic activities. Details not only about the income, but also the interests, attitudes, purchases, travel and leisure pursuits of households and groups are regularly amassed, collected and traded as commodities in ways made newly possible by IT. Thus, for example, CACI, an international market analysis consultancy, organises such information in the form of ACORN, a census-based system which comprises 43 million names and addresses from the electoral roll. The data are cross-referenced to market research, such as the National Readership Survey, the Target Group Index and to unemployment data and sold to direct marketing agencies, list brokers and manufacturing clients. For example, a new service, ACORN Lifestyle analyses first names:

> Given that my name is Clive you know there is a probability of 0.72 that I am aged between 27 and 44. . . . If I find a Kevin and Sharon I am going to put money on them being under 30. If I find Percy and Ethel I'll put money on them being retired. . . .
> For mailings by charities, the best responses came from elderly, well-off women, preferably single. In a test mailing of a list selected through ACORN Lifestyle the positive results doubled from 1.5%.
>
> (*Campaign*, 3 March 1989: 71)

In 1988 Britain's largest list manager and broker was Nationwide Direct Marketing; it rented out 130 million names and addresses (Novek *et al.*, 1990).

The collection and manipulation of information deriving from the everyday activities, beliefs and attitudes of 'the public' made possible by IT is not only organised to be sold as a commodity: it also has specific social and political effects, both in terms of the creation of new techniques of surveillance and the construction of public opinion. In relation to the first of these, the use of IT to rationalise the conditions of economic information processing has produced a new kind of information, 'transactional information', which is generated through the use of electronic terminals in the home, on the phone, in banks, shops and restaurants. One potential consequence of the collection of this information is that the individual becomes constantly and routinely subject to monitoring and study. In these ways, IT can constitute an indispensable 'tool to burrow into the psyches of unsuspecting customers and citizens' (Robins and Webster, 1987: 155). Networks of information flow thus themselves produce information about consumer behaviour that in turn aids producer control. The development and implementation of IT may therefore require new kinds of political control if the 'free circulation' of cultural value in the form of information flows is not to lead to new forms of power and control.

In terms of the construction of public opinion, Williams (1985b) has argued that IT has been used to create an electoral market, which can be distinguished from earlier, more active forms of democracy in terms of a shift from a system of representation operating through the creation and circulation of opinion to one dependent upon information. In making this distinction, he makes the suggestion that the process of representation is always both political and cultural, and that the social and technical organisation of the processes comprising the latter structures the former. Williams argues that in contrast to representation which relies upon the active formulation of opinion, an informational mode of representation relies upon aggregations of information; these run through polling and voting systems, flattening differences, stabilising the range of choices. Such aggregations themselves become persuasive forms of apparent opinion, not only indicating but at some levels forming 'public opinion'. Similarly, Baudrillard (1988) argues that public opinion polling can be seen as an example of the process of virtual inclusion discussed in Chapter 4 in the context of the emergence of branding within the culture industry; he writes that it is,

> An operational system which is statistical, information-based, and simulational [which] is projected onto a traditional values system, onto a system of representation, will and opinion. This collage, this collusion between the two, gives rise to an indefinite and useless polemic. . . . Publicity and opinion polls and the media in general can

only be imagined; they only 'exist' on the basis of a disappearance, the disappearance from the public space, from the scene of politics, of public opinion in a form at once theatrical and representative as it was enacted in earlier epochs.

(Baudrillard, 1988: 209)

What is being suggested here is that opinion polling can be seen to display, in common with the so-called 'interactive' uses which characterise other examples of virtual inclusion, simple and determined choices which undercut the process of representation.

This process of virtual inclusion does not operate in a vacuum, however, and a consideration of other factors, including the independent forces underpinning reactivation, is a necessary part of the analysis of the availability and use of rights of cultural reproduction. Such forces include the contemporary reorganisation of the public sphere. Habermas (1989) provides a useful framework for an investigation of this process of change at a general level. In his work, the concept of the public sphere is used to refer to a realm of the social life in which 'public opinion' can be formed. Citizens meet as part of the public sphere when they come together not as subjects of the state or as private economic actors concerned with matters of individual interest, but rather as a free and open public body to discuss matters of general interest. Public opinion refers to the tasks of criticism, influence, oversight and control which such a body practises over the state, usually informally except for periodic elections. The central principle of the public sphere Habermas calls 'discursive will-formation', by which he means equal, open and constraint-free discussion. Within the public sphere, the 'reasoning public' attempts to achieve a consensus on political questions under conditions of the open and free discussion of all issues without dogmatic appeal to authority or tradition. Under such conditions, 'public opinion' is seen to possess legitimate authority as an expression of 'the rule of reason' and, thus, is capable in principle of truly articulating the general interest.

Habermas' historical account revealed, however, the social basis of the public sphere which effectively limited the 'reasoning public' to the (male) bourgeoisie and meant that the commitment to 'rational formation of the public will' was never actualised. He also argued that the commercialisation of the public media, the increase in state intervention in the economy, the increase in large economic enterprises and the expanding influence of science and technology all furthered the process of the 'depoliticisation of the public sphere'. For Habermas, too, then, public opinion has increasingly become a matter of the technically sophisticated manipulation of the public which forecloses its practical and political function. Although Habermas locates counter-tendencies in contemporary societies (such as the demand for open information on all public matters), he concludes that under the influence of 'technocratic conscious-ness', and the institutions which support it, a 'repoliticisation' of the public sphere is unlikely.

Similarly, Elliott (1986) argues that the new information and communications technologies are contributing to the continuation of a shift away from involving people in society as political citizens of nation states towards involving them as consumption units in a corporate world. He analyses this shift by taking up Habermas' notion of the historical importance of communicatively generated rationality for contests between politically expressed demands based on knowledge, information and association in democratic nation states. He argues that the concept of information was initially developed by intellectuals as a social resource in the development of a public sphere as part of the promulgation of society as a rational, democratic polity. Thus, for example, he argues as was suggested in Chapter 5, that the emergence of newspapers was based on two processes, the provision of useful information, mainly commercial and financial intelligence to interested parties, and political controversy, but, over time, these functions have withered away.

Similarly, he argues, as was suggested in Chapter 6, that broadcasting was influential in developing a general notion of public or national interest through the operation of professional codes of balance and objectivity and the internalisation of a mass public audience. Thus, while the coalition of interests that set up public service broadcasting – intellectual and cultural élites, politicians anxious to lay down rules of debate, and new professionals skilled in the techniques of the new media – may have been paternalist, the concept of the public good allowed broadcasters to step outside a straightforward technical rationality of means to take on questions of ends as well. In this way, Elliott suggests, through the medium of the nation state and the attempt to use its political power, intellectuals were able to find a basis for a significant form of asymmetry in the form of public service. However, he goes on to suggest that the development of new distributive systems for communication puts public service broadcasting under severe threat as two of the conditions which were necessary historically to enable public service broadcasting to develop are removed. Firstly, the framework of government regulation which required a non-partisan approach has been dismantled. Secondly, and more significantly, the national boundaries of distribution which meant that 'the public' audience was coterminous with the citizenry of the nation state have been transgressed. Even when given the political will, national power is no longer adequate to regulate supra-national bodies.

This chapter has presented some arguments which support this view; thus, it has been suggested that the development and implementation of communication and information technologies have facilitated the targeting of commercial organisations as the audience for cultural reproduction; this has meant that the activities of reactivation are increasingly motivated by commercial rather than by expressive purposes. In other words, cultural reproduction has been reorganised in relation to a market constituted as an audience (rather than, as had been the case with previous cultural technologies, in relation to an audience addressed as a market). Furthermore, the use of these technologies has led to the virtual inclusion of the public-as-audience in the constitution of public opinion in ways which have contributed to a decline in the autonomy of the public sphere. In these two ways, then, that is, through the actual inclusion of a market as an audience, and through the virtual inclusion of the public as an audience, communication and information technologies have contributed to a convergence between cultural and social reproduction.

However, against this, and other pessimistic accounts of the implications of the implementation of communication and information technologies, some limitations to the contemporary convergence between cultural and social reproduction can be suggested. Possible sources of such limitation are sometimes seen to reside in the very nature of information reproduction as a value-creating activity. One such suggestion is that cultural goods are characterised by a 'public good' status; this, in turn, is explained in terms of the 'almost limitless' nature of their use value (Garnham, 1979). It is also suggested that the use value of cultural goods cannot be destroyed or consumed in reception; for this reason, it is seen to be particularly difficult to attach an exchange value to them. Cultural works are said never to be consumed as other goods are; they are added to by those who purchase and reactivate them (Smith, 1972).

However, one of the assumptions underpinning this study is that such arguments are not absolute; the public good status of cultural works is produced within historically specific modes of cultural reproduction. So, for example, as Benjamin notes, 'the value of information does not survive the moment it is new' (1970: 90). It is thus necessary to provide more detailed, historically specific, accounts of the ways in which cultural goods have (or have not) been given the status of public goods. Nevertheless, the technologies of culture, although always a product of particular social systems, developed with reproductive intent and for uses which are known, are 'open' to the extent that their uses are not completely predetermined by their forms, nor unalterable. As Williams writes,

> There are contradictory factors, in the whole social development, which may make it possible to use some or all of the new technology for purposes quite different from those of the existing social order . . . the choices and uses actually made will in any case be part of a more general process of social development, social growth and social struggle.
>
> (Williams, 1974: 135)

In other words, the diversity of contexts in which information is necessarily put to use disrupts and disturbs the trajectory of convergence between social and cultural reproduction. However, such contexts, in part because of their very diversity, provide a very different, altogether more amorphous, alternative to the bourgeois public sphere.

When recognised at all, the amorphous character of such practices of reactivation is sometimes seen to weaken the power of individuals as citizens; it is suggested that, by privatising activities, IT sets up a type of social grouping which has no other connection with any other apart from their common use of the same service. This process of privatisation is seen to deprive people of the possibility of answering back because it deprives them of the opportunities for association in which common needs might be recognised and demands formulated. However, this implicitly ignores the exclusivity of previous forms of association, and downplays the ways in which previously excluded groups may benefit from the breakdown of earlier forms of the public sphere which assume a representational norm (see Chapter 9). In addition, such arguments ignore the potential challenge to the presentation of opinion as information which is provided by its use in non-calculative ways. In short, it is not simply the amorphous distribution of practices of reactivation which disturbs the convergence between cultural and social reproduction, but also the potential for such practices to deconstruct information itself as a cultural form.

NOTES

1. It has, for example, been pointed out that, despite their control of another means of production, labour, the power of the working class has been relatively limited.
2 Porat (1973, in Arriaga, 1985) defined information labour as all labour related to information activities. Thus, he included the following groups of workers: (i) workers whose output or primary activity is the production and selling of knowledge, like scientists, teachers, librarians and journalists; (ii) workers who handle information within firms such as secretaries, messengers, managers, clerks and typists; and (iii) workers who operate information machines and information technology that support the two previous categories, such as telephone operators and drivers.
3 The 'information' workforce has beeen aggregated at more than 50 per cent of all employment in many of the 'most developed' industrial societies, including the US and Britain.
4 According to Robins and Webster IT stands in a 'tradition of technological domination and deskilling ... as IT, finding application in white-collar work, is initiating the era of Taylorism/Fordism in the office' (1987: 149–50).
5 See Arriaga (1985) for a political economy perspective on information labour and the economic importance of information activities for capital accumulation.
6 Most previous technologies of culture used analog techniques: the grooves on a record, the magnetic patterns on tape, the waves broadcast for television or radio, all used techniques which replicated in analog form the wave patterns of sound or image. In contrast, digital techniques mean that any signal can in principle be

coded into a sequence of digital numbers. In the case of music stored on compact disc, for example, sounds are sampled 44,000 times each second, stored in digital form in the 'pits' of the disc, from which the numerical sequences are read by laser, and then reproduced by the player in a wave form.

7 The computing industry argued that the constraints of stand-alone data processing were limiting growth, and that access to data processing from a distance through telecommunications connections could extend the spatial boundaries of the market and open new market opportunities.

8 The perceived needs of the military have played a major role in the research and development of both computing and telecommunications, and in the possibility of their convergence. This line of development was reinforced by the broadly similar information and communications needs of globalised capital.

9 Key decisions in the US meant that while in 1960 Western Union was compelled to divest itself of Western Union International and was given a monopoly in domestic telegraphy by the FCC, in 1981 the Record Carrier Competition Act allowed Western Union and international record carriers to compete both domestically and internationally. Similarly, AT&T, which handled domestic and international voice traffic, was not permitted to use telephone lines for international data traffic until the 1980s when technological developments made this restriction impossible to enforce. At the same time, the FCC's 'Computer II' decision caused the break-up of AT&T into seven regional telephone companies, and the development of a new AT&T which is allowed to enter markets from which it was previously banned, including hardware sales, and new service provisions, such as data communication, electronic information processing and office automation. (Garnham [1985] suggests that this decision was designed to release AT&T to play a key role as a world market leader in competition with the Japanese.) The 'Computer II' decision also lifted the restriction on IBM entering the telecommunications market and, at about the same time, a long anti-trust case against IBM in the US was dropped as having 'no merit'.

10 As suggested earlier, changes in business practice, in particular the development of transnational, multi-plant operations, and the development of the service sector, especially international financial services, have meant that information activities have become, for many corporations, a major business cost and therefore control of these costs has become a high management priority.

11 It is predicted that the European market for these services will be worth over £1,000 million by 1992 (Mary Fagan, *The Independent*, 8 February 1989). Firms like the *Financial Times* and Reuters, which had already established markets for the sale of information, now run these on IT. Others like *Reader's Digest* have moved into the market for the sale of information through its service called 'The Source'.

12 Collins cites the case of Canada to exemplify,

> the contradictions of national policy directed to securing an advantageous position in the international communications hardware business ... but which in using the domestic information economy as a base for hardware manufacturers from which international markets may be colonized open the domestic software market to very serious international competition.
>
> (Collins, 1986: 291)

13 As Collins (1986) notes, although in the UK broadcasting and telecommunications historically developed as largely distinct technologies and institutions, this is, to some extent, an arbitrary separation in technical terms.

14 In 1985, Varis found that 50–90 per cent of the hours broadcast by West European public channels were 'national' productions (in Sepstrup, 1989).

15 Recent years have seen a growing number of channels: the Varis study from 1983 covered 31 channels from West Europe with an accumulated output of 110,000 hours, whereas in 1985 there were 51 channels with 186,000 hours of output, and in 1986 61 channels and 234,000 hours of supply. The growth from 1983 to 1986 comprised 21 private channels and 3 public service channels (in Sepstrup, 1989).

16 This process is usually referred to as transnationalisation, which is often inaccurately reduced to Americanisation. Yet Sepstrup (1989) provides figures to show that 73 per cent of total national supply in all of West Europe was domestically produced, 13 per cent from the USA and 12 per cent from West European countries and 4 per cent from co-productions with other countries. However, he goes on to argue that both the total transnationalisation and especially the share of US-produced supply are strongly correlated to the dimensions of commercialisation.

17 The International Data Corporation estimated that in 1980 there were more than 4,300 companies in the software industry, with total revenues of $13.14 billion rising to $33.8 billion in 1984, although this market is becoming increasingly dominated by large corporations.

18 This directly parallels the shifts discussed in Chapter 4 in cases concerning cartography.

8

TECHNOLOGIES OF CULTURE
AND GENDER

This chapter is intended to provide a provisional investigation of the ways in which technologies of culture are both themselves produced by and in turn are productive of the social category 'woman' (Riley, 1988; Nicholson, 1990). It will include a consideration of both the gendered relations of cultural reproduction and the implications of such relations for the constitution of gender; that is, it will investigate both the ways in which gender has shaped the ordering of cultural reproduction and the significance of cultural reproduction for the organisation of gender relations. In particular, this chapter will argue that the emergence and development of modern cultural technologies have been a key factor in the shaping of femininity; the role they play will be analysed in terms of changes in the social organisation of the two axes of reproduction, that is, first, the capacity for copying at the moment of production, and, second, the relation between production and reception or the audience. It will further be argued that the social category of women has influenced the deployment of cultural technologies themselves, including the distinction between high and popular culture.

This analysis is thus intended to add to recent feminist discussions of the ways in which the category of 'woman' is both the product and process of its representation and self-representation (de Lauretis, 1987). More specifically, it will be argued that this process has been characterised by a transition from the representation of woman as sign within modernism to the simulation of femininity in what has been called postmodern culture. Clearly, such a sweeping interpretation can only be made schematically here, and examples from visual arts,

177

literature and popular culture will be used merely to suggest more general processes.

At the most general level, the shift from the mode of repetition to that of replication identified in Chapter 2 can be seen to have had a number of consequences for the participation of women in cultural reproduction. In relation to the visual arts, for instance, the result of this shift was their gradual exclusion from production. So, for example, it is clear that while women's participation in the varied forms of medieval art was limited, their contribution was not insignificant: for example, illumination was carried out in religious institutions by not only the male but also the female members; similarly, guild and parish records indicate that women sculptors and illuminators worked alone or as heads of households as well as members of a family production unit. Significantly, such activity commonly took the form of production of tokens or occurrences of the same type or model; that is, the women painters of the fifteenth century were essentially craftspeople working within the conventions of an established style (Parker and Pollock, 1981).

However, the social conditions of art practice changed with the Renaissance, contributing to a new identity and social position for the artist and the emergence of originality as the key criterion for the evaluation of cultural goods (see Chapter 2). This shift and the growing professionalisation of the artist in the later Middle Ages and early Renaissance had far-reaching implications for women:

> they have become not merely unnamed, but anonymous, without the individual immediacy of their earlier medieval counterparts. . . . The amateur monastic workshop was giving way to the highly trained professional one. . . . Art itself was changing. And with it, not surprisingly, the context of medieval women's art was being swept away.
>
> (Weyl Carr, quoted in Pollock, 1989: 17)

Increasingly, women ceased to have access to conventional forms of training; some, for example, were excluded from the newly organised artists' workshops. The women who did succeed in becoming artists did so by taking advantage of special circumstances, usually birth either into the nobility or into families of painters in which the absence of sons or the availability of materials and free teaching gave daughters an entry to an artistic career that would otherwise have been far less accessible to them. In short, as artistic production shifted towards the production of originals, rather than tokens of the same type, the conditions for women's participation as artists became less favourable.

By the late seventeenth century, the craft-based training offered in artists' workshops was replaced by official academies as places of art education and public exhibition. While women were not initially wholly excluded from these influential and prestigious bodies, they faced increasing difficulties in securing membership during the eighteenth and nineteenth centuries. One of the main reasons for this exclusion was that women were not officially permitted to study human anatomy from the naked, live model. The consequences of this were immense; for almost three hundred years, from the Renaissance to the heyday of the academies in the nineteenth century, the naked human figure was the basis of the most highly regarded forms of painting and sculpture – what the academic theorists of art described as 'history painting'; women were thus denied the training to contribute on the same basis as men to what was the most highly valued genre of painting.

Their exclusion from the study of the naked body constrained many women to practise exclusively in the genres of portraiture, still-life and flowers, genres considered within the academic canon of art as less significant. By association, the women who practised in the so-called 'lesser' genres were themselves devalued, considered artists of 'lesser' talent. Moreover, they tended to exhibit as amateurs, or as teachers and governesses, rather than as professional artists. This contributed to the masculinisation of the emerging mystique of the artist as a gifted, especially creative individual.

The exclusion of women from the study of the naked figure can, in part, be explained in terms of the emergence of gendered notions of propriety in the late eighteenth and nineteenth centuries, which suggested that women's respectability would be compromised by their perusal of a naked body. It was also supported by the attempted confinement of middle-class women to the private and domestic sphere. However, as this chapter will go on to show, this exclusion was not simply the result of already established sexual divisions, including a male-dominated public sphere, but was itself a consequence of a visual regime structured by a distinction between high and popular culture within which relations of looking – who looks, and who is looked at – contributed to the specific organisation of those divisions.

Women struggled against their exclusion from the academies during the course of the nineteenth century; ironically but perhaps not coincidentally, however, their access to the full academic curriculum occurred precisely at the point when the hegemony of academic tradition was being successfully challenged by new 'avant-garde' theories and practices. Nevertheless, when avant-garde artists turned from academic theory and took up the hitherto less prestigious fields of portraiture, landscape and still-life, women could and did take part in radical movements in art based upon these areas of representation. By the late nineteenth century, Victorian historians of art could rightly record the persistent presence of women in the history of art and note their growing numbers and gradual progress in the face of problems such as institutional exclusion and lack of recognition. However, at the same time that there was an increase in the numbers of women artists working professionally, women artists were represented as different, distinct and separate on account of their sex. Women artists, treated as a homogenous group by virtue of their shared gender, were thus effectively placed in a different sphere from men. Art by women was subsumed into bourgeois notions of femininity and art historically relegated to a special category which was presented as distinct from mainstream cultural activity and public professionalism which both remained the preserve of men.

Moreover, not only were the relations of access to training and the status of artists gendered, in part, through the definition of the author-function in relation to notions of originality, so too were those of reception. At a general level, it has been argued that the privileging of sight above other senses within Western cultures is patriarchal; Luce Irigiray, for example, argues that,

> Investment in the look is not as privileged in women as in men. More than other senses, the eye objectifies and masters. It sets at a distance, and maintains a distance. In our culture the predominance of the look over smell, taste, touch and hearing has brought about an impoverishment

of bodily relations. The moment the look predominates, the body loses its materiality.

(Irigiray, quoted in Pollock, 1989: 50)

The discourse of art has had a particular role in the development and exploitation of this investment, as has been documented by feminist art historians (Parker and Pollock, 1981; Pollock, 1989; Nead, 1988). They have shown that the sign of 'Woman' was central to mid-nineteenth century visual representation; indeed, they suggest that this formation has been so powerful in its various manifestations that it is not recognised as representation at all. That is, the representational work of constructing an absolute category 'Woman' has been effaced; this regime of representation has naturalised woman as image, as object to be looked at, and, further, has had the effect of privileging the gendered technique of objectification as an apparently neutral principle of aesthetic interpretation.

However, the actual processes underpinning this tendency are in some ways less visible than in the case of the processes of exclusion and segregation documented so far: women were not, on the whole, prevented from participating in the reception of painting, although careful guidelines for viewing were clearly explicated by the institutions of art. What is significant, however, are the terms of their (limited) inclusion. It was not simply the exclusion of women from particular forms of production, but also the *terms of their acceptance* as part of the legitimate audience for painting which contributed to both the creation of hierarchies of genres within visual culture and definitions of femininity.

At a general level, it is argued that visual culture was a particularly important site for the development of gendered notions of sexual propriety in the nineteenth century, and that representations of female sexuality were central to the constitution of such values (Nead, 1988; Pollock, 1989). Indeed, Lynda Nead suggests that such representations were organised around a dichotomy between the virgin and the whore, between respectable femininity on the one hand, and the fallen woman, the adulteress and the prostitute on the other. However, she is at pains to point out that this dichotomy was not uniformly present across the visual media; rather, what might be shown in graphic art, that is, prints and illustrations intended for reproduction in periodicals and engravings, might not be shown in an exhibition oil painting. As she notes,

> the fact of the presence of adultery in the graphic media and its relative absence in paintings should not be misinterpreted; it does not suggest that we can look to periodicals and newspaper illustrations to discover a truer picture of Victorian morality, neither is it simply a matter of representation and absence of representation. Instead, it raises the whole issue of the ways in which particular kinds of images are circulated and consumed and the specific conditions which surround their production at any given moment.
>
> (Nead, 1988: 63)

She goes on to argue that it was precisely through the circumscribed representation and restricted circulation of images of deviant femininities, linked to the internalisation of a gender-conscious bourgeois public, that the English school of art was able to distinguish itself as a form of high culture. She thus suggests that the relationship between artistic and moral propriety was mutually enhancing; the internalisation of a deliberately constricted conception of a moral public contributed to the development of painting as a form of high culture specific to the bourgeoisie; this artistic form, in turn, contributed to the gendered definition of the division between public and private spheres.

However, Nead also suggests that visual culture was characterised by a particular tension which surfaced in the representation of the prostitute:

> The artist who wished to represent the modern prostitute in a painting intended for public exhibition had to negotiate two apparently contradictory sets of expectations. On the one hand there were the expectations of realism; according to this paradigm pictures were expected to provide a sufficiently realistic portrayal of contemporary issues and to offer a clear, moral lesson. And on the other hand there were the expectations of pleasure, of art as an escape from deformity and imperfection; within this model 'woman' plays a central role as a beautiful, classless object to be contemplated and enjoyed.
>
> (Nead, 1988: 181–2)

Indeed, she suggests that it was the tension between condemning the prostitute for her pleasure in her own display, and consuming the representation of the prostitute for pleasure which set visual culture apart from other discourses on prostitution, and, in part, structured the ambivalence characterising this form of high culture.

As Janet Wolff notes (1990), this ambivalence was absent from a number of other practices. Alternative show spaces were oriented towards a more exclusively male audience, and paintings hung in billiard rooms or in gentlemen's clubs were more *risqué* than those hung in family rooms and public exhibitions. Sexuality also appeared legitimately, although in a displaced form, through the device of the representation of the exotic. Paintings of harems, the sale of female slaves and other typical figures of Orientalism were often characterised by more explicit representations of the female body: for example, Salome's dance,

> could be used as a medium that illustrated what were perceived to be the Orient's qualities. It could portray female nudity, rich and sequestered interiors, jewels, hints of lesbianism, sexual languor and sexual violence; in brief, it encapsulated the painted East.
>
> (Kabbani, 1986: 69)

At the same time, the art (and literature) of a more explicit sexuality was circulated in the secret and illicit world of pornography, and the sexual practices of young middle-class men were facilitated by casual liaisons at musical halls and fairs, places which were barred to 'respectable' women.

When this sexuality was represented within a painting which was intended for public exhibition, however, as in the case of *Olympia* (1863), there was great controversy. Indeed, Griselda Pollock argues that it is precisely the twist in the relations of looking inscribed in the work which explains its significance in the emergence of modernism (1989). She notes that,

> In some of his writings T.J. Clark correctly discusses the meanings of the sign woman in the nineteenth century as oscillating between two poles of the *fille publique* (woman of the streets) and the *femme honnête* (the respectable married woman). But it would seem that the exhibition of *Olympia*

precisely confounds that social and ideological distance
between two imaginary poles and forces the one to confront
the other in that part of the public realm where ladies do go
– still within the frontiers of femininity.

(Pollock, 1989: 54)

T.J. Clark (1985) argues that Olympia's nakedness inscribes
her class and thus debunks the mythic classlessness of sex
epitomised in the conventional image of the courtesan.
(Similarly, he suggests that while the fashionably blasé barmaid
at *A Bar at the Folies-Bergère* (1881–2) evades a fixed identity as
either bourgeois or proletarian, she participates in a play around
class in such a way as to signify both the appeal and horror of
modernity.) Pollock extends this argument by suggesting that the
impact of the displacement of the mythical nude courtesan with
Olympia's nakedness can be understood in terms of the
introduction of

the spaces of modernity into a social territory of the
bourgeoisie, the Salon, where viewing such an image is
quite shocking *because* of the presence of wives, sisters and
daughters. The understanding of the shock depends upon
our restoration of the female spectator to her historical and
social space.

(Pollock, 1989: 54: my emphasis)

For Pollock, then, the move from 'nudity' to 'nakedness' is
achieved through not only the explicit representation of the
prostitute's look, signifying the exchange between a seller of a
woman's body and a client which had been confined to a part of
the public realm which had (or should have) been invisible to
ladies, but also the deliberate inclusion of women as intended
viewers.

Pollock explores the masculinity embedded in modernism
along two axes: that of space and that of the look. She argues that
the set of social processes indexed by the term modernity was
experienced spatially in terms of access to a city which was
increasingly spectacularised for a class and gender-specific gaze.
In this way Pollock points to a coincidence between the spaces of
modernity and the spaces of masculinity as they intersect in the
territory of sexual exchange and identifies the significance of the
male gaze to the experience of modern public life. Importantly,

however, she further argues that the *frisson* of modernism was dependent upon the public acceptance of the legitimacy of this gaze for women, and, in part at least, their adoption of this masculinised spectator position themselves.

Certainly, the use of the male gaze was not confined to the gallery: one of the key figures to embody the novel forms of public experience of modernity is the *flâneur* or impassive stroller, the man in the crowd who goes, in Benjamin's phrase, 'botanizing on the asphalt'. The *flâneur* symbolises the privileges or freedom to move about the public arenas of the city, observing but never interacting, consuming the sights through a controlling but rarely acknowledged gaze, directed as much at other people as at the goods for sale: 'The *flâneur* embodies the gaze of modernity which is both covetous and exotic' (Benjamin, 1970: 67). As Janet Wolff has argued (1990), though, the *flâneur* is an exclusively masculine figure who contributed to the reconstruction of the social spaces of the city identified by Pollock through the overlaying of the gendered doctrine of separate spheres on to the division of public and private. Moreover, as in the masculinist myths of visual modernism, it was not simply the equation of the public realm with the masculine that defined the *flâneur* but access to a sexual realm.

However, this sexual realm was itself undergoing change in ways which meant, among other things, that women were increasingly drawn into the public sphere. As Elizabeth Wilson argues (1991), women from all classes did participate, albeit in limited ways, in public, specifically urban, life during the nineteenth century. This participation included not only involvement in paid work by many working-class women, but also the chaperoned use of public spaces by middle-class women, including the frequenting of the dream palaces of consumption – department stores. Furthermore, the boundaries between the pure and the fallen woman were increasingly blurred by the second half of the nineteenth century. Indeed, according to Nead, a critical point was reached at the end of the 1860s: just at the moment when the contagious diseases legislation was being used to categorise street prostitution more rigidly than ever before, other distinctions between respectable and non-respectable women were disappearing.

Nead suggests that these fears crystallised around the notion of 'the girl of the period', who, while she belonged to the respectable classes *looked* like one of the *demi-monde*. She reports on a series of articles in *The Saturday Review* between 1867 and 1868 condemning such 'fast' young women. The culmination of this series was an article entitled 'The girl of the period'. Her account of this article is worth repeating at some length:

> The article began by reflecting with pride on English girls in the past, when they had been 'content to be what God and nature had made them' and had fulfilled their roles as wife, mother and housekeeper. This pattern had changed, however, girls neglected their duties and concentrated instead on cultivating their appearance; the girl of the period had become: 'a creature who dyes her hair and paints her face, whose sole idea of life is plenty of fun and luxury'. In other words, the girl of the period indulges in pleasure and display – those defining features of female deviancy. The article warned respectable young women against imitating the habits of the *demi-monde*:
>
> 'What the *demi-monde* does in frantic efforts to excite attention, she also does in imitation . . . and then wonders that men sometimes mistake her for her prototype. She has blunted the fine edges of feeling so much that she cannot understand why she should be condemned for an imitation of form which does not include imitation of fact; she cannot be made to see that modesty of appearance and virtue ought to be inseparable, and that no good girl can afford to appear bad, under penalty of receiving the contempt awarded to the bad.'
>
> (Nead, 1988: 180)

Significantly, it is the process of imitation which is seen to be at the root of this anxiety; the respectable young woman is warned against imitating the habits of the *demi-monde*, the prototype. This imitation disturbs the belief that form and content are always in harmony; the warning is clear: 'no good girl can afford to appear to be bad'.

More generally, what such an account suggests is that the scopic economy in which men look while (some categories of) women are to be looked at was unstable in the face of the practice of imitation (a type of reactivation carried out, it seems, by the object or cultural work itself); men's investment in the look was not secure once the objects of their gaze acquired a life of their own and put to use their own capacity for copying. In this context, modernist painting can be seen, not only as a celebration of creative masculine individualism, but as a discourse around the paradoxes and anxieties of masculinity in which an investment in the privilege of looking is at risk. The figure of the artist, always assumed to be masculine in the critical and economic practices around modernist art, hysterically and obsessionally figures, debases and dismembers the dematerialised body of 'Woman' as sign. At the same time, however, women, through the practices of imitation, not only disturb the previously harmonious relation between form and content, but also undermine the foundational relation between the prototype and its copies and, in doing so, become embodied simulations.

By comparison with visual culture, women's participation in print culture, both as producers and as readers, has always been relatively well developed (Lovell, 1983). This was, in part, a consequence of the links between print culture and commodification which were present from the first stages of its development, themselves a consequence of the capacity of print technology to produce multiple copies with great ease. These links meant that, as discussed in Chapter 5, participation in, for example, novelistic culture was a relatively low status activity during much of the eighteenth and nineteenth centuries, and women's involvement was not as rigidly prescribed as in the case of the visual art world. Nevertheless, it is possible to trace the ways in which the regulation of women's involvement, both in production and as part of the audience, was an integral part of the social organisation of the cultural technology of print, and helped to structure the distinction between high and popular culture in this field too, and, in turn, to see the ways in which that organisation contributed to the ongoing definition of femininity.

By the eighteenth century, for example, the period in which novelistic culture became relatively widespread, the development of a distinctive private sphere to which middle-class women were increasingly confined meant that they came to function as authorities in the domain of domesticity, sentimentality and romantic love (Davidoff and Hall, 1987). This was a double-edged phenomenon: it celebrated 'feminine values' in a way which reinforced the powerlessness of women. However, the view of writing which was predominant linked it to this feminine role. This had the effect of encouraging the expansion of women's writing; indeed, Terry Eagleton refers to a 'deep-seated "feminisation" of values throughout the eighteenth century which is closely allied with the emergence of the bourgeoisie' (1990: 14). At the same time, though, this feminisation of literature defined it as a special category supposedly outside the political arena, with an influence on the world as indirect as women's was supposed to be. Consequently, the access that literate women gained to the print culture developing in eighteenth-century England had mixed consequences for their representation in and by writing. For many of the very agents that were enabling, even actively promoting, women's partici-pation in print culture were also engaged in containing it through the normative construction of femininity in writing and reading.

This tendency was particularly evident in the production of first-person narratives during this period. Women were extensively implicated in these outpourings of subjectivity, as producers, objects and readers of literary discourse. Indeed, up to the end of the eighteenth century, women dominated novel production, and produced primarily first-person fiction which had a predominantly female readership. However, Jane Spencer's study, *The Rise of the Woman Novelist* (1989), suggests that the establishment of a 'respectable' position for women writers was only granted them in return for the display of a number of 'feminine' characteristics, including spontaneity of expression, and 'artlessness'. It has also been argued (Perry, quoted in Felski, 1989: 101) that the use of the confessional mode of the diary and letter, in which a form of intimate address and the patterns of everyday speech were coupled with an attention to realistic detail, was deemed necessary to create an appearance of feminine authenticity; this appearance was confirmed through the ways in which the distinction between fact and fiction was often blurred for the reader of the epistolary fiction of this period.

Nevertheless, despite the limitations of such expectations, it has been argued that they made possible a public expression of feminine subjectivity. Rita Felski (1989), for example, suggests that the confessional genre of writing presupposed an audience of sympathetic readers, a public community which empathised and identified with the individual's articulation of feeling. Felski concludes that this literary subculture encouraged, even intended, what she calls a 'naive' reading, in which the text was integrated into the everyday life of its readers. However, this potentially solidary relationship between woman writer and woman reader, in which notions of the self were explored in relation to a (limited, but still collective) female community, was ultimately overtaken by other developments within the emerging novelistic culture.

For example, Kathryn Shevelow's analysis (1989) of the periodical literature of the eighteenth century shows an opposing, and ultimately more successful, way in which the construction of femininity in writing helped to encode a form of feminine identity that defined a rather more subordinate place for women in print culture. Her argument is developed through an analysis of the terms through which the early periodical collected, influenced and was influenced by, its audience. She suggests that, through its quotidian engagement with its audience and its historical situation as a 'new' form, the early periodical formulated a literary persona in relation to an audience which, as a self-reflective body of readers, did not exist prior to its organisation by the periodical. As the periodical developed, it was constantly engaged in negotiating this relationship to its audience, a relationship variously composed of a mixture of consumer-oriented solicitousness, a fabricated audience complicity in textual production, and an assumption of authority to prescribe readers' behaviour, all of which both made use of, and contributed to the development of, notions of appropriate gender identity for women.

More specifically, early periodicals were characterised by an address explicitly directed to women; perhaps not surprisingly this was conflated with an interest in issues of love, marriage, women's education and conduct. What Shevelow shows is that this address made use of representations of women as writers (of letters to the magazines) to characterise and to naturalise boundaries to feminine reading in particular and, by extension, to feminine conduct more generally. So, for example, the illusion of the publication of readers' letters allowed the *Tatler* to construct a rhetorical frame through which the conceit of audience correspondence with the journal's persona became a crucial component of the periodical's systematic attempts to reform the manners and morals of its readers: 'the *Tatler*'s display of female subjectivity emerged in a prescriptive way that rewrote the woman subject as exemplary of feminine conduct' (Shevelow, 1989: 106). The periodical thus defined itself as a distinct cultural form through the way in which it not only brought readers into engagement with selected representations of women, but also, through a form of transvestite ventriloquism, implicated them in processes of writing and reading which themselves were gendered, thus exerting a normative force on definitions of feminine duties and subjectivity. A significant component of these definitions was the naturalisation of associations between femininity and domesticity and the private world of emotions.

However, it is with the emergence of the novel as a form of high culture that the centrality of the discourses of gender to literary reproduction is most clearly revealed. Gaye Tuchman and Nina Fortin's analysis (1989) of the publishing industry during the late eighteenth and nineteenth centuries, for example, shows how the privileging of the realist novel above other kinds of writing was closely tied in with its masculinisation. They summarise the turn-around in the status of the novel thus:

> Before 1840 the British cultural élite accorded little prestige to the writing of novels, and most English novelists were women. By the turn of the twentieth century 'men of letters' acclaimed novels as a form of great literature, and most critically successful novelists were men.
>
> (Tuchman and Fortin, 1989: 1)

They explain this change by looking at the ways in which, during the course of the nineteenth century, male literary critics and novelists used their control of major literary institutions to transform the novel into a high culture form and, simultaneously, a male preserve.

Tuchman and Fortin's analysis is organised in terms of a number of periods in the novel's evolution over the course of the nineteenth century. They suggest that until 1840 the novel was a lowly genre, a status linked to its association with women, both as authors and as readers, and its concern with the theme of love. Poetry and essays, in contrast, were high status and associated with élite men. 1840–1879 is seen as a period of invasion; while most novelists were still probably women, men began to value the novel as a cultural form. This re-evaluation of the novel's status was linked to a number of changes in the organisation of literary production. Until this time publishers had been able to draw on a large pool of authors, most of whom were seen as potentially replaceable, and were thus not in a position to challenge the standard contracts offered to them. One reason that the author's position in relation to the publisher was relatively weak was that it was seen as reprehensible to write for money; and the distinction that was made between hacks and hobbyists undermined attempts by authors to improve their financial position. However, by the mid-century authors began to acquire greater bargaining strength.

This increasing strength was reflected in and reinforced by changes in the standard conditions of contracts. According to Tuchman and Fortin, there were six main kinds of contracts in the nineteenth century: subscription (up to 200 people underwriting the costs of publishing a book in return for a copy); commission (with the author assuming responsibility for costs and taking all the risk); profit-sharing; outright purchase of copyright for a lump sum; purchase of copyright for a limited and specified period of time (a lease) or for a specified number of copies; and payment of royalty. The popularity of each kind of contract changed during the course of the century; by the 1840s, for example, publishers rarely issued contracts involving either subscription or commission. While commissioning meant that the author took all the risk, if the book was a success the author could take his/her plates to another publisher for further editions, so publishers did not stand to benefit from its long-term success. In contrast, purchase of copyright, which became increasingly popular, facilitated not only the publisher's ability to benefit from the sustained success of a novel, but also the possibility of issuing a book in several formats (this was particularly important in the mid-nineteenth century because of the possibility of serialisation in monthly magazines). One contract for several books was also used to tie an especially successful or promising author to a firm. Royalty payments were used to cement this tie; their introduction meant that authors benefited directly from every copy sold, often at a better rate than authors on the half-profits system. In this way, changes in contract, in which copyright and royalty became more important, both helped to secure the conditions for the operation of the author-function and contributed to the success of long-term publishing strategies (Bourdieu, 1977).

It was also during this period that the activities of the

publishers' readers became more important. Readers had been used as early as 1799 to advise on the selection of manuscripts for publication. Initially readers were drawn from the ranks of the publishing trade; they were viewed as extensions of their employers, and their qualifications were that they were familiar with both their employers' tastes and 'the problems involved in the making and selling of books' (Tuchman and Fortin, 1989: 61). However, by the mid-century readers were often authors themselves, apparently employed to get the library reader's response. However, it seems likely that they assessed books on the basis of their employers' past preferences and the standards they shared with others in élite literary networks. They then gave *their notion* of what a typical library reader's response might be; according to Tuchman and Fortin they thus 'stood between authors and audience' (1989: 67). What is significant here is not so much that the relationship between the author and the audience was mediated by the publisher's reader – it had never been direct in any case – but that this mediation was now shaped by the ways in which some authors were able to judge others. In this way, peer evaluation came to rival that of past successes in the market in its importance for the author.

Nevertheless, in the late 1860s and 1870s, aspiring women writers still dominated fiction submissions and women still had a higher fiction acceptance rate than men. However, 1880–1899 is seen as a turning point by Tuchman and Fortin; in this period of redefinition, men of letters, including critics and publishers' readers, actively redefined the nature of a good novel and a great author. Literary criticism had become a source of income by this time; this financial reward was linked to a growth in the authority of the critic: indeed, Tuchman and Fortin argue that, by this time,

> The imprimatur of certain critics associated with particular circles revolving around élite literary journals indicated which novels were good literature and identified those who read these novels as participants in high culture. It also limited the ability of people outside those circles to claim cultural distinction simply because they read books – or even wrote them.
>
> (Tuchman and Fortin, 1989: 69)

Men's control of non-fiction was central to this process of

reputation-making; through that control men who were associated with élite publishers and periodicals were able to define good fiction. They privileged a new form of realism (a serious fictionalised depiction of plausible actions of socially and psychologically individuated characters in a stratified society), which was associated with 'manly' literature, and was, in part, defined in contradistinction to the improbabilities of earlier romances, most of them by women. They thus differentiated the literary from the popular novel through the use of a gendered hierarchy of form. Both men and women submitted more fiction during this period, but the rate at which men submitted fiction increased much more than that of women. In addition, relative to their rate of submission, men's acceptance rate increased and women's decreased.

This differential success is additionally linked by Tuchman and Fortin to the centralisation of cultural production in London and the increasingly important role of cultural brokers and entrepreneurs. They suggest that men were able to make better use of family contacts and school ties by converting them into literary opportunities. Such contacts provided a route into social and intellectual networks from which it was possible to gain employment on the many new journals, newspapers and magazines started during the second half of the nineteenth century. When women did attempt to make use of such contacts in this way, they faced practical constraints. For example, when Mrs Gaskell wanted to visit London in 1849 to see her publisher and to meet people in the literary world, she had to find another woman to travel with her as a chaperone, since her husband could not leave his work in Manchester, and it would not have been seen as proper for her to visit London alone (Wolff, 1990: 25). Men were also more likely than women to strike up personal friendships with their editors and publishers; such a friend would often introduce the author to potential sponsors, and was likely to give his work better promotion than that of other authors. Ellen Moers sums up the contrasting opportunities facing men and women writers during the nineteenth century:

> Male writers have always been able to study their craft in university or coffee-house, group themselves into movements or coteries, search out predecessors for guidance or patronage, collaborate or fight with their

contemporaries. But women through most of the nineteenth century were barred from the universities, isolated in their own homes, chaperoned in travel, painfully restricted in friendship. The personal give-and-take of the literary life was closed to them.

(Moers, 1977: 64)

Moreover, there were also some attempts to institutionalise these circles of contacts as a kind of social capital (Bourdieu, 1989; Moi, 1991): for example, during the late 1880s writers organised the Society of Authors to work collectively towards better terms in the standard contract for novels and better protection against American publishers' ongoing infringement of British copyrights. Women were initially excluded from the Society, although they were later admitted in a piecemeal way. In general, women writers were by now being paid less than men even for novels that sold as well and, within the confines of the critical double standard, were as well received.

Tuchman and Fortin suggest that 1901–1917 was the period which saw the sustained institutionalisation of men's dominance of the literary field: men's submission of fiction declined, but had a higher acceptance rate. Men's hold on the novel, particularly the high culture novel, coalesced, and its place at the top of the hierarchy of literary genres was secured. Tuchman and Fortin conclude that men 'had successfully invaded'; at the same time, 'men of letters' ceased in the main to be gentlemanly dilettantes, and formed a new class of professional writers. They thus conclude, on the basis of their research, that there were three inter-related processes through which a male invasion and transformation of novelistic culture were achieved: an increasing acceptance of the right of authors to control the conditions of their work and so to claim the status of professionals – a central aspect of this being secured through the use of copyright in contracts; the devaluation of novels by women by a cultural élite; and the definition of the novel as a high cultural form by a stress on particular types of realism. In short, the gendered transformation of literary reproduction both contributed to and was determined by support for the author-function; the operation of this function was, in turn, related to broader changes within the public sphere and the formation of a national culture.

This conclusion confirms the argument put forward by Terry Lovell (1987), who suggests that, at the beginning of the nineteenth century, doubts about the novel centred around three of its characteristics: its commercialisation; its feminisation; and the dominance of non-realist 'escapist' forms. She suggests that as the century progressed the situation of the novel changed significantly on all three counts (although she argues that this happened somewhat earlier than Tuchman and Fortin imply). Firstly, although the novel remained a commodity, the manner of its production and distribution – organised, in part, through the author-function – foregrounded its literary claims, and masked its relationship to commerce (for a discussion of this see Chapter 5). Secondly, although women continued to play a major part as consumers of fiction, and a substantial one as producers, the production of quality fiction became a male-dominated profession. Thirdly, a restoration of the novel's literary credentials was marked by a decided shift back towards the dominance of a realist aesthetic (Lovell, 1987: 73–4).

Significantly, Lovell also suggests that by the 1840s women were writing novels which addressed men as well as women, and the novel-reading public included a higher proportion of men than had been the case in the earlier period. Indeed, she argues that it was the shift in the gender of the addressee that may explain the fact that, while women were writing proportionately fewer novels than they had been, proportionately more of them were successful in the long term as literature. She thus suggests that a condition of literary canonisation may have been not so much that the author must be male, as that the work must be addressed to men and read by them, and not addressed exclusively, or even primarily, to women. However, while novels were increasingly required to address men, their actual readership continued to be largely female, and it is the consequences of this contradictory relation between internalised and actual audience which, it will be argued, characterise contemporary culture more generally.

The argument put forward so far, however, is that the transformation in the status and evaluation of the novel which occurred during the course of the second half of the nineteenth century was achieved through a refiguring of the gendered definition of the public and private spheres, and a reordering of the relations between them. This transformation in modes of literary reproduction was not simply a consequence of broader social and political changes, but was itself constitutive of such changes through the ways in which the cultural technology of print defined masculinity and femininity. That is, the continuing process of the 'separation of spheres' of male and female, public and private, was shaped by cultural institutions and practices. An important aspect of this was the way in which the rights to ownership, exploitation and use of literary property were differentially available to male and female authors. As noted above, this was linked to the gendered institutionalisation of the profession of writing in which the use of copyright helped to secure the rise of the male novelist. But inter-related to this was the way in which the notion of the audience which was internalised in literary reproduction was masculinised during the course of the century; that is, while the novel was assumed to be a public good, access (in the broadest sense) to rights of use was differentially structured in terms of gender and thus contributed to the formation of a male-dominated public sphere.

All this is not to suggest that the novel did not also challenge accepted representations of masculinity and femininity. Rather, it is to argue that 'Woman' was a central problem for the nineteenth-century novel as it was for the visual arts, a figure to which it ceaselessly returned, both as subject of the text, *and as a condition of its functioning as a cultural practice*. As Andreas Huyssen has so acutely noted, Flaubert was attributed his status as the father of literary modernism on the basis of 'an aesthetic based on the uncompromising repudiation of what Emma Bovary loved to read' (1986b: 189). Indeed, just as in the case of visual modernism, feminist scholars have argued that literary modernism can be seen as the surfacing of a 'battle of the sexes' (Gilbert and Gubar, 1988): from this perspective, the masculinist and misogynist current within the trajectory of modernism can be seen as a defensive response to late nineteenth-century feminist struggles and the increasing participation and visibility of women in the activities of the public sphere.

This battle can, for example, be seen in the struggle for 'freedom' of artistic expression, the emphasis placed on creative autonomy, the mystique attached to the author or artist (the Romantic figure of the author as genius acquired all the more defensive rhetorical force in the context of the growing number of writers for the mass market, doing superficially the same kind of work, from whom he must be distinguished), the prominence accorded to literary trials, including, for example, that concerning the alleged obscenity of *Lady Chatterley's Lover*, and the significance attached to the issue of censorship more generally. This struggle can be seen as part of the antagonistic potential inherent in the very idea of the avant-garde, in which aggression is directed against not only what is perceived as the dominant tradition in art, but also against the inhibitions of the bourgeois public. While women writers were an important part of this avant-garde, much of this aggression was also (and perhaps especially) targeted at women, not only symbolically, within the text, but also as writers and readers. The heroic individualism of the male author often went hand in hand with the exclusion of women authors from the literary enterprise, and was dependent upon the denial of the feminine, both within the text and as an appropriate context of reception.

More generally, there is now a wide range of work which suggests that the representation of sexual difference, specifically 'Woman' as sign, was both the object and the condition of many modernist cultural forms and practices (Pollock, 1989; Gilbert and Gubar, 1988; de Lauretis, 1987; Krauss, 1988). This argument has been reformulated here in terms of a consideration of the ways in which sexual difference functioned as a condition of cultural reproduction through both an intensification and institutionalisation of the gendered myth of originality associated with the author-function and a problematisation of the position of women in the audience for high cultural practices. However, struggles over the significance attached to the gendered composition of the internalised audience were not limited to high cultural practices; on the contrary, the rise of modernism was paralleled by what has been described as a feminisation of mass culture in which women – as producers and consumers – were held responsible for the debasement of taste and the sentimentalisation of culture. As Andreas Huyssen remarks,

> the political, psychological and aesthetic discourse around the turn of the century consistently and obsessively genders mass culture and the masses as feminine, while high culture, whether traditional or modern, clearly remains the privileged realm of male activities.
>
> (Huyssen, 1986b: 191)

There were numerous dimensions to this process of feminisation: 'from the obsessively argued inferiority of woman as artist . . . to the association of women with mass culture . . . to the identification of woman with the masses as political threat' (Huyssen, 1986: 194).

However, while it is obviously correct that one of the hidden subjects of the mass culture debate was precisely 'the masses' – their political and cultural aspirations, their struggles and their pacification via cultural institutions – the argument which suggests that the imputed femininity of the masses was merely metaphorical ignores the ways in which femininity in and of itself (also) posed a threat to cultural and political hierarchies. Conversely, it also ignores the ways in which the denigration of mass culture as feminine through, in particular, its association with standardisation (replication unlimited by originality), artifice and passivity contributed to the restructuring of notions of femininity, the changing boundaries between public and private, and the reconstitution of the category 'woman'. Similarly, while the imputed femininity of mass culture can be seen as a necessary contrast against which the increasingly obsessive masculinity of high culture was defined, such a contrast is misleading in that it masks the ways in which it was struggles over the implications of the imposition of a masculine internalised audience on to an actual female audience which, in part, defined both high and mass culture.

What is clear, however, is that the commercial exploitation of the technical capability for mass replication, associated with the newer technologies of culture, made possible a greater range of contexts of reception from which it became increasingly difficult to exclude women or even effectively regulate the conditions of their participation. Indeed, in some cases, the commercial development of these technologies meant that women were explicitly targeted as part of the mass audience-as-market; this tendency is evident in, for example, the growth of popular cultural forms aimed primarily at women, such as women's magazines (Winship, 1987), romantic fiction (Radway, 1987; Modleski, 1982) and the targeting of women for specific genres of film in the cinema. Maria LaPlace (1987), for example, offers an analysis of the 'Woman's Film' as the embodiment of many of the criteria believed (by producers) to be particularly desirable by the female audience:

Based on the results [of market research], a set of criteria was developed for attracting women to the movies; it was concluded that women favoured female stars over male, serious dramas, love stories, and musicals. Furthermore, women were said to want 'good character development', and stories with 'human interest'. In one sense, the woman's film can be viewed as the attempt to cover as much of this territory as possible.

(LaPlace, 1987: 138)

Indeed, it has been argued that the cinema spectator was, in general terms, envisaged as female:

In the 1920s, theatre managers' trade journals described the motion picture not only as a temple of a secular religion, but as an environment designed to stimulate the adoration of the female spectator in particular. A 1927 article in *Theater Management*, for example, stressed the importance of women as the primary component and motivators of film attendance and argued that both the appeal of the film and the theatre must be geared to pleasing women's sensibilities.

(Allen, 1980: 486)

Similarly, the targeting of a female audience was clearly important in the organisation and development of other mass media, such as broadcasting. Lynn Spigel's (1990) analysis of popular magazines in the period of television's introduction in the US suggests, for example, that they provided a set of discursive rules for thinking about and watching television in ways which attempted to domesticate and feminise the medium.

However, as many recent accounts of modern cultural technologies suggest, many popular cultural forms are simultaneously defined by the related processes of the objectification of women within the text and the attempted masculinisation of the viewing or reading audience (Berger, 1973; Mulvey, 1989). In other words, the female audience is continually defined in relation to a male internalised audience, whose perceived responses provide the normative framework against which women's actual responses are evaluated. These accounts thus suggest that the targeting of women as a key market for popular cultural production has been partially cross-cut by the internalisation of a masculine audience; so, for example, Laura Mulvey points to what she calls a certain 'masculinization' of spectatorship (1989).

It has been argued that one effect of this is the inculcation of a split subjectivity in the female members of the audience; John Berger, for example, suggests that women are encouraged to 'do to themselves what men do to them. They survey, like men, their own subjectivity' (1973: 63). What Berger fails to comment on is the way in which this process, while present to a limited extent in previous cultural practices, has only become widespread within the later stages of modern cultural reproduction. In relation to women's magazines, for example, there is no doubt that women are the intended audience, yet, as Janice Winship argues (1987), there has, over the post-war period, been a shift towards a more explicitly sexualised and glamorous representation of women. Arguably, such images address women primarily in terms of their (potential) relation to men; that is, they require women to self-objectify. Similarly, Mary Ann Doane suggests that the cinematic image has taken 'on the aspect of the trap [for the woman] whereby her subjectivity becomes synonymous with her objectification' (1989a: 31–2). The implication of such analyses is that, through the encouragement of self-objectifying techniques, modern cultural technologies are facilitating a novel, technically mediated organisation of the individual and social body of women. As Jane Gaines writes, women,

> early become practised in presentational postures, learning, in the age of mechanical reproduction, to carry the mirror's eye within the mind, as though one might at any moment be photographed. And this is a sense a woman in Western culture has learned, not only from feeling the constant surveillance of her public self, but also from studying the publicity images of other women ... in the pages of fashion magazines – *Elle, Seventeen, Vogue, Jackie,* and *Mademoiselle.*
>
> (Gaines, 1990b: 4)

This organisation has uncertain implications for feminine identities. On the one hand, it can be seen to contribute to femininity as a non-subjectivity, a non-being (MacKinnon, 1987); on the other hand, it contributes to the emergence of cyborg, hybrid or mosaic identities (Haraway, 1991). The conflicting possibilities of such technologies of gender can be seen, for example, in the ways in which the adoption of this self-objectifying identity by the female audience can be seen to have both helped to determine, and been shaped by, the development of a form of the institution of heterosexuality (Rich, 1980) in which the continual and public availability of (all classes of) women as objects of a male gaze has been increasingly encouraged. The contradictory and contested ways in which the female audience was constituted as both object and subject of the gaze can be seen as part of the process by which a distinctively modern organisation of the institution of heterosexuality was brought into being. Such representations have not been wholly effective: many writers (Bowlby, 1985; Winship, 1987; Partington, 1991; Stacey, forthcoming; and see Chapter 9)) have looked at women's contradictory and resistant appropriations of such representations. Yet other writers have documented the diverse ways in which, as part of this form of institutionalised heterosexuality, women have been encouraged to consider themselves as objects for the surveillance of others (MacKinnon, 1987); further, it can be argued that the 'democratisation' of fashion and the spectacularisation of leisure clearly provided conditions which were conducive to the more or less successful imposition of such processes of representation on women.

However, further complexity is added to the contradictory inclusion of women as part of the audience for popular culture when it is seen in relation to ongoing shifts in the gendered organisation of consumption, an increasingly important activity for women during the twentieth century. As the processes of commodification developed and there was an intensification in the volume, and a diversification in the range and types, of goods and services sold, it was women, and not men, who were chiefly responsible for purchasing them. As many writers have observed,

> the machine age transformed the home from the place of production into the place of consumption, radically changing the role of the patriarchal family, and therefore the position of women in it, electing them as managers of consumption.
>
> (Muscio, 1989: 122)

In this way, cultural and domestic technologies converged, within the more general process of mobile privatisation, to structure the home as a site of what Janice Winship has called the 'work of femininity' (1987).

In addition to the responsibility of purchasing commodities (first, upper- and middle-class, and then all), women were involved in the beautifying of their homes and themselves with 'luxury' products. In these and other ways, then, consumption was more and more closely linked to femininity. Rachel Bowlby writes that,

> On both counts – women's purchasing responsibilities and the availability of some of them for extra incursions into luxury – it follows that the organised effort of 'producers' to sell to 'consumers' would, to a large measure, take the form of a masculine appeal to women.
>
> . . . the making of willing consumers readily fitted with the available ideological paradigm of seduction of women by men, in which women would be addressed as yielding objects to the powerful male subject forming and informing them of their desires.
>
> (1985: 19–20)

Bowlby further notes that the display of commodities as spectacles offering the female shopper pleasure in looking, contemplation and the fantasy transformation of the self and her surroundings through consumption directly prefigured the pleasures which were to be offered to the female spectator in the cinematic context:

> The transformation of merchandise into a spectacle . . . suggests an analogy with an industry that developed fifty years after the first department stores: the cinema. In this case, the pleasure of looking, *just* looking, is itself the commodity for which money is paid.
>
> (Bowlby, 1985: 6)

Similarly, the cinema screen has been seen to reproduce a 'display window . . . occupied by marvellous mannequins' (Eckert, 1978: 4) in which goods are on view to the audience as objects of desire. At the same time, the gendered connections between looking, desiring and buying were intensified within the cinema industry by a number of strategies, including sumptuous design of the interiors of cinema theatres, tie-ins between the cinema and the fashion and cosmetics industries, and the building of cinema theatres near shopping areas.

By the mid-twentieth century, then, woman was both the object and audience of popular cultural reproduction, just as she was both the object and market for consumerism and other domestic technologies of reproduction. Moreover, not only were domestic and cultural technologies employed to similar effect, but, in addition, they were mutually enhancing. The woman who must purchase in order to increase her own status as valued object became the prototypical consumer of modern culture, and, conversely, the consumer whose desires were in a continual state of agitation was the ideal recipient of popular culture. At other levels too, consumer culture and popular culture reinforced each other: on the one hand, the women making up an audience were available for commodification for sale as a market to the consumer industries; on the other hand, the market of female consumers was addressed in ways which prepared them to act as an audience for the forms of popular culture associated with modern cultural technologies.

As with the case of the links between cultural and sexual technologies, however, this process of reinforcement did not and does not result in complete overlap. This is, in part, a result of the continuation and elaboration of the practices of imitation associated earlier with the 'girl of the period' in a context in which the activities of the audience are seen to have increasing importance.[1] In relation to cinema, for example, it has been argued that the location of the possibilities of spectatorship, within the problematic of sexual difference, means that, for 'the female spectator there is a certain overpresence of the image – she *is* the image. . . . the female look demands a becoming' (Doane, 1991: 22). This process of becoming, or doubling of representation, involving a blurring of the opposition between production and reception, has been understood as a feminine masquerade in which women flaunt their femininity in order to hold it at a distance (see Modleski, 1986a; Butler, 1990): masquerade can 'manufacture a distance from the image, to generate a problematic within which the image is manipulable, producible and readable by the women' (Doane, 1991: 32).

More generally, feminine imitation or mimicry has been theorised as a playful repetition in which women resubmit themselves to a masculine discourse so as to show that they remain 'elsewhere':

To play with mimesis is thus, for a woman, to try to recover the place of her exploitation by discourse, without allowing herself simply to be reduced to it. It means to resubmit herself – inasmuch as she is on the side of 'perceptible', of 'matter' – to 'ideas', in particular to ideas about herself, that are elaborated in/by masculine logic, but so as to make 'visible', by an effect of playful repetition, what was supposed to remain invisible: the cover-up of a possible operation of the feminine in language. It also means to 'unveil' the fact that, if women are such good mimics, it is because they are not simply reabsorbed into this function.

(Irigiray, 1985: 76)

It is thus possible to argue that, as a result of the increasing importance of audience activities, the dynamic of representation of sexual difference which structures popular culture is not 'Woman' as sign but femininity as (dis)simulation, a mask for a non-identity, a bodily resubmission to 'ideas about herself'. Doane writes, 'Masquerade . . . involves a realignment of femininity, the recovery, or more accurately, simulation of the missing gap or distance. To masquerade is to manufacture a lack in the form of a certain distance between oneself and one's image' (1991: 26). From this perspective, the indeterminable identity of femininity is the moment at which the representational construct of 'Woman' and the experience of women (as variously identified and subject to multiple determinations) come together (Russo, 1986); as such, it is a key site of the contested convergence between cultural and social reproduction.

As Jean Grimshaw[2] has recently pointed out, it is necessary to consider the conditions under which mimicry, parody or simulation is effective, or, indeed, even possible; she suggests that housework, for example, is an activity whose socially structured repetitiveness undermines the potential subversiveness of parody. Indeed, Joan Riviere, the first to theorise the concept of masquerade (her essay was first published in 1929), does not see it as affirmative play, but as an anxiety-riden compensatory gesture, a position which is potentially disturbing and uncomfortable for women. Indeed, she suggests it is commonly seen as socially inappropriate behaviour. As Doane notes in her discussion of Riviere, this invocation of social propriety is not merely moralistic, but an important recognition that masquerade is a charade in power, and, as such, is circumscribed by the constraints imposed on women who make a spectacle out of themselves (also see Russo, 1986). Nevertheless, the emergence of feminist and other oppositional counter-cultural spaces since the 1960s has exercised an important influence upon the changing relationship between culture, politics and identity (Felski, 1989). From this point of view, the importance of feminism does not lie so much in the development of uniquely 'feminine' or 'subversive' styles of art, but rather in its effectivity in creating a relatively widespread and influential politicisation of processes of reception affecting the reactivation of both avant-garde and popular works[3] and its challenging of the distinction between the personal and the political.

To conclude then, it was argued in the first half of this chapter that the elevation of high culture above popular culture was secured, in the cases of both the visual arts and literature, through the gendered use of the author-function. That is, this function was implemented in such a way as effectively to exclude women from participation in production; furthermore, it was associated with the internalisation of a normative masculine audience and the denial of a feminine context of reception. Paradoxically, however, this internalisation highlighted the significance of representations of 'Woman' as sign within high culture. This significance can be related to the internalisation of the audience as a self-reflexive public discussed in Chapter 5. It was suggested there that this internalisation contributed to the development of an aesthetic personality which involved a continual problematisation of the self and its relation to the real. The masculinisation of this audience outlined here suggests that 'Woman' as sign became an increasingly important site for this problematisation in both literature and the visual arts since she was the figure of the 'other' through which a masculine self could most easily and endlessly be problematised.

Representations of women have also been central to popular culture, but for rather different reasons and in rather different ways. In many cases such representations should be understood in the context of the explicit targeting of women as an audience and the increasing importance attached to the practices of reception within contemporary cultural reproduction. While this address has been integral to the development of popular culture, women's inclusion was partially cross-cut by an attempted masculinisation of the audience's activity, including a require-ment for the female viewer to adopt a self-objectifying response. In this respect at least then, the attempted masculinisation of the internalised audience is common to both high and popular culture. Significantly, however, the effectivity of this inclusion must be seen as partial, perhaps especially so among the audience for popular culture. This audience may have been defined in relation to the (historically changing) patriarchal categorisation of 'woman', yet the actual members of the audience, despite their inclusion in self-objectifying terms, are active participants in the (dis)simulation of femininity. Their practices of reactivation are never finally contained, and consequently have the potential to subvert the current convergence between cultural and social (specifically sexual and domestic) reproduction. Moreover, the commercial impetus behind the development of the technologies of replication continually undermines the cultural limits which have conventionally been placed on women's ability to participate in this mode of reproduction. The resulting tendency towards the feminisation of the audience can be seen to have precipitated a crisis in the cultural forms which link cultural and social reproduction, a topic which will be considered, somewhat speculatively, in the next and final chapter.

NOTES

1 'Politics, parody and identity', a paper given at the conference 'Feminist Theory. An International Debate', Glasgow, 1991 in which Grimshaw discussed Judith Butler's *Gender Trouble* (1990).
2 It is interesting to note here the description of popular culture by Leslie Fiedler, in his famous article, 'The middle against both ends', as 'a product of the same impulse which has made available the sort of ready-made clothing which aims at destroying the possibility of knowing a lady by her dress' (in B. Rosenberg and D. Manning White (eds) *Mass Culture: The Popular Arts in America*, New York: The Free Press, 1957: 539).
3 At the same time, however, such a counter-cultural space or, perhaps more accurately, set of overlapping communities is itself, as an oppositional discursive space, conditioned by and dependent upon existent cultural technologies. And, as Huyssen points out, 'it has always been men rather than women who have had real control over the productions of mass culture' (1986b: 205).

9

SIMULATION, GENDER AND CONTEMPORARY CULTURE

At the heart of the arguments presented so far has been an investigation of the changing organisation of cultural reproduction. Two related dimensions of reproduction have formed the twin axes of analysis: the capacity for copying at the moment of production, and the relation between production and reception. While much of this book has been concerned with an historical investigation of the social organisation of these two dimensions, this chapter will, after a very brief review of their key phases, consider, somewhat speculatively, their contemporary significance for cultural values.

Raymond Williams' categorisation of the means of cultural production provided the initial basis for an investigation of the first dimension. The technical capacity for the production of separable cultural goods – that is, goods which are potentially spatially and temporally independent of the context of their production – and in particular techniques of mass or multiple copying, were argued to have created radically new possibilities for cultural reproduction. Such possibilities were seen to have been realised within a general mode of replication in contradistinction to an earlier mode of repetition. A particular concern for cultural producers within the later mode is the management of innovation; the most recent phase of this was described in terms of the emergence of branding. At its simplest, branding refers to the process by which the cultural work is designed to function as its own advertisement, or, to put this another way, is designed to create an audience for itself.[1]

It has been argued that, through the regime of rights associated with trademark, this audience and its reception activities, are, subject to the strength of the brand, made available for exchange, either as audiences for other cultural works, or as users for other kinds of goods. Trademark was thus identified as the legal principle which is coming to organise the exchange of cultural works by defining the terms under which brands are protected and exploited as intellectual property both within and outside the culture industry. As such, it is a mechanism by which cultural reproduction is being brought into line with social, specifically economic, reproduction. The extent and significance of such a convergence have been the subject of some debate; a consideration of the second dimension of reproduction may shed some light on the issues that this debate raises.

The second dimension, that is, the relation between production and reception, was also seen to have acquired a new significance with the emergence of modern technologies of culture as a consequence of the 'deep contradiction' between production and reception associated with their implementation (Williams, 1981; Thompson, 1990). Of particular importance here is the way in which the internalisation of (some notion of) the audience has been achieved as part of the development of particular means of communication; particular concern has thus been paid to the ways in which, in Ien Ang's terms, cultural institutions 'desperately seek the audience' (1991). However, their conceptions of the behaviour of audiences should not be confused with reception as it occurs in actual recipients, which has been described here in terms of reactivation. The internalised audience has thus been understood here as a discursive construct, a moving resultant of the power-laden ways in which the actual audience is known, rather than as a description of how the audience for cultural works actually makes use of them. In this respect, then, this analysis makes use of a concept of technologies of culture as not simply the means of cultural production but as a set of techniques of knowledge-power (Foucault, 1980).

The argument put forward was that the technical capability of mechanical production facilitated a radical transformation in the structure of cultural reception: it meant that the concept of the audience internalised was abstract, that is, it was made radically uncertain, detached from traditional contexts, and concentrated in masses (Radnoti, 1986). It was further suggested that it was precisely this (potential) abstractness of the audience that 'liberated' the cultural producer, not in a heroic sense, but as a result of the unpredictability of the orientation of the audience, and in this sense helped to secure the terms of the autonomy of the cultural field. However, it was also argued that the commercial and political manipulation of the production of cultural goods had the effect of containing this unpredictability; this was achieved through the internalisation of limited, that is, unified and controlled, conceptions of the audience. It was further suggested that the study of the processes of internalisation of the audience allows an exploration of the links between the cultural and social, specifically political, reproduction. The gendered dimensions of this process of internalisation was, for example, seen to have contributed to the changing constitution of 'women' as a social category.

The latest phase in this process of internalisation was described in terms of virtual inclusion. This term refers to the simulation of the presence of an audience in cultural works themselves, and takes a variety of forms, ranging from those in which members of the audience are actually present, such as quiz and talk shows and phone-ins, through the use of their recorded presence, including letters' pages, canned laughter and opinion polls, to those forms in which the audience is, literally, a structuring absence, such as 'interactive' computer programmes and karaoke.[2] Many of these forms are visible in a single text, such as, for example, the television programme *That's Life*, which employs a range of such techniques, including the use of: letters and photographs from audience members; recorded interviews with members of the public 'on the street'; audience votes to 'choose' series' presenters; and the setting-up of public service campaigns which require audience participation.

Virtual inclusion can be seen as an attempt to predetermine not only the composition but also the activity of the audience. Audience 'participation' is constrained by the ways in which the cultural work presumes certain kinds of response: Bruce Forsyth pushes an audience member to stand on a cross on the ground for the right angle for the camera; Cilla Black presides over a romantic *Opportunity Knocks*; and Kilroy-Silk goads members of his selected audience to confront each other in polarised debates. The simulation of audience participation is multi-levelled in such programmes: in the case of *Blind Date*, for example, contestants compete for the favour of the 'live' audience, whose own, carefully stoked, response is an integral part of the success of such programmes, and thus helps to determine the marketability of the programme's broadcast audience to advertisers. Yet virtual inclusion is not actual incorporation: each level of internalisation is not absolute. The contradictions in this process, in particular those related to the simulation of femininity, can be seen to limit the effectivity of branding within the contemporary culture industry, and thus offset the convergence between cultural and social reproduction.

Throughout this book there has been an emphasis on struggles between participants in particular regimes of rights, and this latest regime is currently the subject of multiple conflicts, many of which are focused on the moment of reception and what is seen, in the latest phase of mobile privatisation, as the eradication of public life for everyone (Haraway, 1991). Some analysts of contemporary culture suggest that the new emphasis on the moment of reception can be understood in the context of the rise of a new fragment of the middle class, that is, the service classes which are currently seeking to assert their authority through the elaboration of a novel relation to cultural reception characterised by play, parody and reflexivity (Featherstone, 1991; Lash and Urry, 1987; Bourdieu, 1984). But, as was suggested in the last chapter, such forms of identity can be seen not only in terms of intra-class relations, but also in terms of an attempt to anchor masculine identity in the face of the radical instability introduced by the threat of the pervasive feminisation of the audience for cultural reproduction.

The case of Camp is illustrative of the competing processes at work here. In her 'Notes on Camp' (1987), Susan Sontag argued that play figured prominently in the elevation of style over content and aesthetics over morality which was evident in this movement's opposition to modernist taste. One dimension of this understanding of play relates to the ways in which things were taken in a *double* sense, so that the intended, 'serious' meaning of an object or action was subverted at another level of meaning. A second dimension, however, concerns an openness to the *multiple* possibilities of fun inherent in the style or manner in which something was done; in this case, Camp was a mode of 'enjoyment, appreciation – not judgement' (1987: 291). The notion of play in Camp thus both ordered the internalisation of a split audience, in which one audience's knowledge of another, less knowing audience, was inscribed in the text itself, and thus provided a new basis for the judgement of taste, and yet simultaneously contributed to a sense of play which was totally opposed to judgement – the sheer enjoyment of experience, of the senses, the emotions. Thus, while the prominence of some aspects of Camp can be related to the success of the cultural project of the service classes, this account obscures the contradictory links between Camp and femininity.[3]

More generally, what Alice Jardine (1985) has called gynesis, a valorisation of the feminine or 'Woman', has been seen to be central to Camp and other postmodern subcultures while Lyotard (1984) argues that the creation of the androgyne is one of the major goals of a society organised around the continual circulation of exchange objects. However, the politics of this 'post-gender' world (Haraway, 1991) are not certain; as Creed notes, 'this postmodern fascination with the androgyne and the "neuter" subject may indicate a desire *not* to address problems associated with the specificities of the oppressive gender roles of patriarchal society, particularly those constructed for women' (1987: 66). Indeed, Jardine argues that gynesis, as written by men, could well prove to be a 'new ruse of reason'; that is, it is not confined to a positive re-evaluation of the possibilities of femininity, but also comprises forms of hostility to the feminine. Craig Owens (1983), for example, points to aggressive symptoms of man's 'recent loss of mastery' or cultural authority in the visual arts including a multiplicity of signs of mastery, a mourning of loss and images of phallic women.

Lynne Joyrich's analysis of television (1990) provides a parallel example of such aggression in the domain of popular culture. She suggests that contemporary television is marked by a violent hypermasculinity, an excess of 'maleness', indicative of the tensions associated with the threat of feminisation. She points at attempts to gain the status of 'quality' television by producing texts that can function under the name of the author, and the attempted creation of 'proper' spectator distance through the mimicry of cinematic conventions, as well as 'the obsessive remarking of the masculinity of certain thematics' (1990: 166). *Miami Vice* is seen as a prime example of the last tactic; she writes,

> *Miami Vice*'s central dilemma revolves around the identity of 'V/vice' and the possibility of differentiating between the cops and the crooks, the men and their roles. Clearly at

stake here is a question of masculinity in which all stable distinctions have dissolved, in which the feminized object of the look and trouble of the text constitute a position shared by everyone.

(Joyrich, 1990: 167)

She suggests that such dilemmas are resolved through both the neutralisation or absence of women and the return of the dream of male bonding played out in all its violent excess and contradiction. Sport media events, video games, heavy-metal music, and the focus on the male body in the films of Stallone and Schwarzenegger,[4] provide obvious other examples of similarly ambivalent responses to the threat of a feminised world.[5]

Similarly, feminist interpretations of a number of recent films (sometimes taken as emblematic of an apparently gender-neutral postmodern culture), such as *Videodrome* and *Blade Runner*, suggest that the feminised merger of cultural technology and body has been anticipated with anxiety as well as pleasure. In *Videodrome*, the protagonist, Max Renn is literally transformed into a VCR through the effect of a video signal deployed by a malevolent conspiratorial organisation. His body is extended, mutated, endowed with the new organs required by a televisual culture; videos act as a kind of prosthetic device, a technological extension of the human body. Max Renn thus becomes – to cite Baudrillard – 'a pure screen, a switching center for all the networks of influence' (1983a: 133). However, as Doane points out, this is represented as a gendered process:

> *Videodrome* specifies contemporary cultural experience as a mass of technologically produced images and sounds which penetrate and transform the body. The film clearly represents its protagonist's feminisation by the television discourse and his consequent vulnerability to a kind of rape by pulsating video cassettes and furthermore elaborates an intricate thematics linking the opposition hardware/software to that between masculinity and femininity.
>
> (Doane, 1989b: 212)

In this fantasy, the breakdown of the subject and the object is achieved literally; mind, body and technology are on intimate terms, allowing the possibility of unlimited replication, copying and simulation, but it is a horrifying and deadly experience for its male protagonist. Similarly, Doane argues, in *Blade Runner* the horrific effects attributed to technologies of reproduction, cultural and biological, indicate anxieties about the apparent excesses of the maternal in a feminised contemporary culture characterised by replication.

Indeed, it can be argued more generally that the female body is the contested site of a convergence between not only social and cultural, but also biological and cultural reproduction. Donna Haraway (1991), for example, suggests that the technical organisation of the reproduction of nature, specifically human life, and the technical organisation of culture and imagination display similar tendencies in which the (human) organism is constituted as a problem of coding, and both biology (molecular genetics, ecology, sociobiological evolutionary theory and immunobiology) and culture (telecommunications technology, computer design, database construction and management) are types of cryptography. Yet she also believes that while cyborgs are products of a global system of the informatics of domination, they are also dynamic, mobile and programmable; that is, they offer opportunities that haven't yet been calculated, perhaps particularly for women. She suggests, for example, that there are 'great riches for feminists in explicitly embracing the possibilities inherent in the breakdown of clean distinctions between organism and machine and similar distinctions structuring the Western self' (Haraway, 1991: 174).

Other feminist writers suggest that technology is always the tool of a phallocentrically designed project, but, as noted in the last chapter, argue that contemporary forms of simulated feminine identity constitute a radical disturbance or interruption in the logic of this system of communication.

This interpretation of reactivating practices such as mimicry, masquerade, and the living out of cyborg imagery as acts of alternativity stands in contrast to that proposed by Baudrillard who, while stating the belief that 'Reproduction is diabolical in its very essence; it makes something fundamental vacillate' (1983a: 153), explicitly argues against those theorists who,

> would like to make a new source of revolutionary energy (in particular in its sexual and desire version). They would like to . . . reinstate it in its very banality, as historical negativity. Exaltations of micro-desires, small differences, unconscious

practices, anonymous marginalities ... and to transfer it back to political reason.

(Baudrillard, quoted in Joyrich, 1990: 160)

For Baudrillard, this transfer is impossible: he insists upon the anonymity of the feminised masses who are neither subject nor object. But for many feminist analysts, women are simultaneously object and subject, simulacra not signs, already living the cyborg myth, and such acts do not require translation: they are already political.

Such writers stress the particularistic, diverse and unpredictable meanings made by members of the social audience; not indeterminate but variously, and always specifically, determinate. Judith Butler writes,

> The critical task for feminism is not to establish a point of view outside of constructed identities; that conceit is the construction of an epistemological model that would disavow its own cultural location and, hence, promote itself as a global subject, a position that deploys precisely the imperialist strategies that feminism ought to criticize. The critical task is, rather, to locate strategies of subversive repetition enabled by those constructions, to affirm the local possibilities of intervention through participating in precisely those practices of repetition that constitute identity and, therefore, present the immanent possibility of contesting them.

(Butler, 1991: 147)

For her and many other feminists, the practices of reactivation do not inevitably result in the consolidation of gender identities but sometimes in their displacement, (dis)simulation and remobilisation.

This debate can be reformulated in the terms employed elsewhere in this book, including that of rights, property and value. For Baudrillard (1988), use value cannot undermine exchange value, or offer an alternative to it: rather use value ensures exchange value and underwrites its centrality; it is its alibi. For him, as for trademark law, the internal contradictions of contemporary reproduction can only be exposed through over-use, by the implosion of meaning created by the unthinking engulfment of everything by the feminised masses. His analysis thus colludes with the institutionalised knowledge of the audi-

214

ence in which the masses are a totalised but unknowable category of object-others. What has been suggested here is that the alibi of use value is not always reliable (Willis, 1991); that it cannot always be contained as property. Indeed, Irigiray argues that the very notion of property, and hence possession of something which can be constituted as other, is antithetical to women. 'Nearness, however, is not foreign to woman, a nearness so close that any identification of one or the other, and therefore any form of property is impossible' (1985: 31). Similarly, Spivak suggests that use value is unstable: it 'is both outside and inside the system of value-determination' (1987: 162). Such discontinuous theories of value allow use value or reactivation to act as a 'deconstructive lever' and make it capable of putting 'the entire textual chain of value into question' (1987: 162). Virtual inclusion is not actual incorporation; replication can be uncoupled from reproduction.

NOTES

1 In advertising, the function of a brand is to produce an audience which will act as a market for the product that is the object of the campaign over a substantial length of time.

2 Karaoke – that is, special recordings that have had the vocals removed – make up almost a third of new recordings issued in Japan. The latest karaoke equipment can shift the music up or down four semitones to accommodate the singer's range, as well as disguise wobbly, cracking voices. The equipment is currently being merged with musical instrument and audio technologies (*The Economist*, 21 December 1991).

3 A study of the links between homosexuality and Camp is provided by Jon Savage's analysis of British pop culture (1990): he shows how homosexual subcultures have informed and, on occasion, dominated virtually every pop-style since the mid-1950s and never more so than in the Camp styles associated with the mid-1980s.

4 Male stars are paid much more than female stars – usually twice or even three times as much – and their careers as stars tend to last far longer:

> Much of what sells big in the movie business are outsized, fantasy, action pictures and I think that men have a difficult time going to see women in these roles. Male stars get paid more than female stars because men will go out to see men, and women will go out to see men, and men have a difficult time going out to see women.
>
> (Joe Roth, chair of Twentieth Century Fox,
> quoted in Kent, 1991: 93)

5 Brabara Creed writes,

> Figures such as Sylvester Stallone and Arnold Schwarzenegger
> (once described by an Australian critic as 'a condom stuffed
> with walnuts') could only be described as 'performing the
> masculine'. Both actors often resemble an anthropo-
> morphised phallus, a phallus with muscles, if you like.
> (Parodies of a lost ideal or menacing images of an android
> future?) They are simulacra of an exaggerated masculinity,
> the original completely lost to sight, a casualty of the failure of
> the paternal signifier and the current crisis in master
> narratives.
>
> (Creed, 1987: 65)

Such an analysis seems to owe something to Lacan who argues that
'the fact that femininity takes refuge in this mask . . . has the strange
consequence that, in the human being, virile display itself appears as
feminine' (quoted in Doane, 1991: 34).

BIBLIOGRAPHY

Abercrombie, N. (1990) 'The publishing industry', unpublished paper.
—— (1991) 'The privilege of the producer', in R. Keat and N. Abercrombie (eds) *Enterprise Culture*, London and New York: Routledge.
Adorno, T. (1975) 'Culture industry reconsidered', *New German Critique*, 6, 12: 12–19.
—— (1976) *Introduction to the Sociology of Music*, New York: Continuum.
—— (1991) *The Culture Industry: Selected Essays on Mass Culture*, London and New York: Routledge.
Adorno, T. and Horkheimer, M. (1982) *Dialectic of Enlightenment*, New York: Continuum.
Aglietta, M. (1979) *A Theory of Capitalist Regulation: The US Experience*, trans. D. Fernbach, London: New Left Review.
Allen, J. (1980) 'The film viewer as consumer', *Quarterly Review of Film Studies*, 5, 4: 481–99.
Amin, A. and Robins, K. (1990) 'The re-emergence of regional economies? The mythical geography of flexible accumulation', *Society and Space*, 8, 1: 7–34.
Anderson, B. (1990) 'Apprehensions of time', in T. Bennett (ed.) *Popular Fiction: Technology, Ideology, Production, Reading*, London and New York: Routledge.
—— (1991) *Imagined Communities*, London: Verso.
Ang, I. (1991) *Desperately Seeking the Audience*, London and New York: Routledge.
Arditti, R., Duelli Klein, R. and Minden, S. (eds) (1984) *Test-tube Women: What Future for Motherhood?*, London: Pandora.
Arriaga, P. (1985) 'Toward a critique of the information economy', *Media, Culture and Society*, 7, 3: 271–96.
Auty, M. and Roddick, N. (eds) (1985) *British Cinema Now*, London: British Film Institute.
Barron, I. and Currow, R. (1979) *The Future with Microelectronics*, London: Frances Pinter.
Barwise, P. and Ehrenberg, A. (1988) *Television and its Audience*, London: Sage.
Bataille, G. (1982) *Story of the Eye*, trans. J. Neugroschel, Harmondsworth: Penguin.

217

Baudrillard, J. (1983a) *Simulations*, New York: Semiotext(e).

—— (1983b) 'The ecstasy of communication' in H. Foster (ed.) *The Anti-Aesthetic: Essays on Postmodern Culture*, San Fransisco: Bay Press.

—— (1988) *Selected Writings*, Cambridge: Polity Press.

—— (1990) *Revenge of the Crystal: Selected Writings on the Modern Object and its Destiny, 1968–1983*, trans. P. Foss and J. Pefanis, London: Pluto.

Becker, H. (1982) *Art Worlds*, Berkeley: University of California Press.

Bell, D. (1974) *The Coming of the Post Industrial Society*, Harmondsworth: Penguin.

Benjamin, A. (ed.) (1991) *The Problems of Modernity: Adorno and Benjamin*, London and New York: Routledge.

Benjamin, W. (1970) *Illuminations*, London: Fontana.

Bennett, S. (1982) 'Revolutions in thought: serial publication and the mass market for reading', in J. Shattock and M. Wolff (eds) *The Victorian Periodical Press: Samplings and Soundings*, Leicester: Leicester University Press.

Bennett, T. (1990) *Outside Literature*, London and New York: Routledge.

—— (ed.) (1990) *Popular Fiction:Technology, Ideology, Production, Reading*, London and New York: Routledge.

—— (1992) 'Putting policy into cultural studies', in L. Grossberg *et al.*, (eds) *Cultural Studies*, London and New York: Routledge.

Bennett, T., Mercer, C. and Woollacott, J. (eds) (1986) *Popular Culture and Social Relations*, Milton Keynes: Open University Press.

Berger, J. (1973) *Ways of Seeing*, London: BBC Books.

Berland, J. (1992) 'Angels dancing: cultural technologies and the production of space', in L. Grossberg *et al.* (eds) *Cultural Studies*, London and New York: Routledge.

Bianchini, F. (1987) 'GLC R.I.P. Cultural policies in London, 1981–1986', *New Formations*, 1: 103–18.

Bordwell, D. Staiger, J. and Thompson, K. (1985) *The Classical Hollywood Cinema: Film Style and Mode of Production to 1960*, New York: Columbia University Press.

Bourdieu, P. (1977) 'La production de la croyance: contribution à une économie des biens symboliques', *Actes de la Recherche en Sciences Sociales*, February.

—— (1984) *Distinction: A Social Critique of the Judgement of Taste*, trans. R. Nice, Cambridge, Mass.: Harvard University Press.

—— (1989) *La Noblesse D'Etat: Grandes Ecoles et Esprit de Corps*, Paris: Minuit.

Bowlby, R. (1985) *Just Looking: Consumer Culture in Dreiser, Gissing and Zola*, London: Methuen.

Brewster, B. (1975/6) 'Brecht and the film industry', *Screen*, 16, 4: 16–31.

Buck, L. and Dodd, P. (1991) *Relative Values or What's Art Worth,?* London: BBC Books.

Bürger, P. (1984) *Theory of the Avant Garde*, trans. M. Shaw, Manchester: Manchester University Press.

Burns, T. (1979) *The BBC: Public Institution and Private World*, London: Macmillan.

Butler, J. (1990) *Gender Trouble*, New York and London, Routledge.

Campbell, C. (1989) *The Romantic Ethic and the Spirit of Modern Consumerism*, Oxford: Basil Blackwell.

Cardiff, D. and Scannell, P. (1981) *The Historical Development of Popular Culture in Britain*, 2, U203, Milton Keynes: Open University Press.

—— (1986) ' "Good luck workers!" Class, politics and entertainment in wartime broadcasting', in T. Bennett *et al.* (eds) *Popular Culture and Social Relations*, Milton Keynes: Open University Press.

—— (1991) *A Social History of British Broadcasting. Vol. 1: 1922–1939: Serving the Nation*, Oxford: Basil Blackwell.

Carey, J. (1989) *Communication as Culture: Essays on Media and Society*, Boston: Unwin Hyman.

Castells, M. (1983) *The City and the Grass Roots: A Cross-cultural Theory of Urban Social Movements*, London: Edward Arnold.

—— (1989) *The Informational City: Information Technology, Economic Restructuring and Urban-regional Process*, Oxford: Basil Blackwell.

Centre for Contemporary Cultural Studies (1982a) *Making Histories: Studies in History-Writing and Politics*, London: Hutchinson.

—— (1982b) *The Empire Strikes Back: Race and Racism in 70s Britain*, London: Hutchinson.

Chartier, R. (ed.) (1989) *The Culture of Print: Power and the Uses of Print in Early Modern Europe*, trans. L.G. Cochrane, Cambridge: Polity Press.

Christopherson, S. and Storper, M. (1986) 'The city as studio, the world as back lot: the impact of vertical disintegration on the location of the motion picture industry', *Environment and Planning D: Society and Space*, 4, 3: 305–21.

Clark, C. (1986) *Publishing Agreements: A Book of Precedents*, London: Allen and Unwin.

Clark, T.J. (1980) 'Preliminaries to a possible treatment of "Olympia", in 1865', *Screen*, 21, 1: 18–41.

—— (1985) *The Painting of Modern Life: Paris in the Art of Manet and His Followers*, London: Thames and Hudson.

Clayton, S. and Curling, J. (1979) 'On authorship', *Screen*, 20, 1: 35–63.

Collins, R. (1986) 'Wall-to-wall "Dallas"? The US–UK trade in television', *Screen*, 27, 3–4: 66–78.

Collins, R. *et al.*, (eds) (1986) *Media, Culture and Society. A Critical Reader*, London: Sage.

Connell, I. (1983) 'Commercial broadcasting and the British Left', *Screen*, 24, 4: 70–80.

Coser, L.A. Kadushin, C. and Powell, W.W. (1982) *Books: The Culture and Commerce of Publishing*, New York: Basic Books.

Crane, D. (1987) *The Transformation of the Avant-Garde: The New York Art World, 1940–1985*, Chicago: University of Chicago Press.

Creed, B. (1987) 'From here to modernity: feminism and postmodernism', *Screen*, 28, 2: 47–67.

Curran, J. (1986) 'The impact of advertising on the British mass media', in R. Collins *et al.* (eds) *Media, Culture and Society. A Critical Reader*, London: Sage.

Curran, J. and Seaton, J. (1985) *Power Without Responsibility. The Press and Broadcasting in Britain*, London: Methuen.

Curran, J. Gurevitch, M. and Woollacott, T. (1977) *Mass Communication and Society*, London: Edward Arnold.

Curran, J. Smith, A. and Wingate, P. (eds) (1987) *Impacts and Influences. Essays in Media Power in the Twentieth Century*, London: Methuen.

Davidoff, L. and Hall, C. (1987) *Family Fortunes: Men and Women of the English Middle Class*, London: Hutchinson.

Debord, G. (1977) *Society of the Spectacle*, Detroit: Black and Red.

De Certeau, M. (1988) *The Practice of Everyday Life*, trans. S. Rendall, Berkeley: University of California Press.

De Lauretis, T. (1987) *Technologies of Gender: Essays on Theory, Film and Fiction*, Basingstoke: Macmillan.

DiMaggio, P. (1977) 'Market structure, the creative process, and popular culture: toward an organizational reinterpretation of mass-culture theory', *Journal of Popular Culture*, 11, 2: 436–52.

DiMaggio, P. and Useem, M. (1978) 'Cultural property and public policy', *Social Research*, 45, 2: 356–89.

Doane, M.A. (1989a) 'The economy of desire: the commodity form in/of women', *Quarterly Review of Film and Video*, 11: 23–33.

—— (1989b) '*Commentary*: Cyborgs, origins and subjectivity', in E. Weed (ed.) *Coming to Terms*, London and New York: Routledge.

—— (1990a) 'Information, crisis, catastrophe', in P. Mellencamp (ed.) *Logics of Television: Essays in Cultural Criticism*, London: British Film Institute.

—— (1990b) 'Technophilia: technology, representation and the feminine', in M. Jacobus *et al.*, (eds) *Body Politics: Women and the Discourse of Science*, London and New York, Routledge.

—— (1991) *Femmes Fatales: Feminism, Film Studies and Psychoanalysis*, London and New York: Routledge.

Dudovitz, R.L. (1990) *The Myth of Superwoman: Women's Bestsellers in France and the United States*, London and New York: Routledge.

Dunn, R. (1991) 'Postmodernism: populism, mass culture and avant-garde', *Theory, Culture and Society*, 8: 111–35.

Dyer, R. (1979) *Stars*, London: British Film Institute.

Eagleton, T. (1990) *The Ideology of the Aesthetic*, Oxford: Basil Blackwell.

Eberts, J. and Ilott, T. (1990) *My Indecision is Final: The Rise and Fall of Goldcrest Films*, London: Faber and Faber.

Eckert, C. (1978) 'The Carole Lombard in Macy's window', *Quarterly Review of Film Studies*, 3, 1: 1–21.

Eco, U. (1979) *The Role of the Reader*, Bloomington: Indiana University Press.

—— (1985) 'Innovation and repetition: between modern and post-modern aesthetics', *Daedalus*, 114, 4: 161–84.

Edelman, B. (1979) *Ownership of the Image: Elements for a Marxist Theory of Law*, trans. E. Kingdom, London: Routledge & Kegan Paul.

—— (1987) 'The character and his double', in L. Appignanesi (ed.) *The Real Me: Postmodernism and the Question of Identity*, London: ICA.

Eisenstein, E.L. (1979) *The Printing Press as an Agent of Change: Communications and Cultural Transformations in Early-Modern Europe*, Vol. 1, Cambridge: Cambridge University Press.

Elliott, P. (1977) 'Media organisation and occupations: an overview', in J. Curran *et al.*, (eds) *Mass Communication and Society*, London: Edward Arnold.

—— (1986) 'Intellectuals, the "information society" and the disappearance of the public sphere', in R. Collins *et al.* (eds) *Media, Culture and Society. A Critical Reader*, London: Sage.

Ellis, J. (1982) *Visible Fictions. Cinema, Television, Video*, London and New York: Routledge.

—— (1986) 'Broadcasting and the state: Britain and the experience of Channel 4', *Screen*, 27, 3–4: 6–24.

Ewen, S. (1977) *Captains of Consciousness. Advertising and the Social Roots of the Consumer Culture*, New York: McGraw Hill.

Ewen, S. and Ewen, E. (1982) *Channels of Desire. Mass Images and the Shaping of American Consciousness*, New York: McGraw Hill.

Faulkner, R.R. and Anderson, A.B. (1987) 'Short-term projects and emergent careers: evidence from Hollywood', *American Journal of Sociology*, 92, 4: 879–909.

Featherstone, M. (1991) *Consumer Culture and Postmodernism*, London: Sage.

Fekete, J. (1988) 'Vampire value, infinitive art and literary theory: a topographic meditation', in J. Fekete (ed.) *Life After Postmodernism. Essays on Value and Culture*, London: Macmillan.

Felski, R. (1989) *Beyond Feminist Aesthetics: Feminist Literature and Social Change*, Cambridge, Mass.: Harvard University Press.

Feltes, N. (1982) 'The moment of *Pickwick*, or the production of a commodity text', in P. Humm, P. Stigant and P. Widdowson (eds) *Popular Fictions: Essays in Literature and History*, London: Methuen.

Feuer, J. Kerr, P. and Vahimagi, T. (1984) *MTM: Quality Television*, London: British Film Institute.

Finnegan, R. Salaman, G. and Thompson, K. (eds) (1987) *Information Technology: Social Issues. A Reader*, London: Hodder and Stoughton.

Flint, M.F. (1985) *A User's Guide to Copyright*, London: Butterworth.

Foster, H. (ed.) (1987) *Discussions in Contemporary Culture. Number One*, Seattle: Bay Press.

Foucault, M. (1979) 'What is an author?', *Screen*, 20, 1: 13–33.

—— (1980) *Power/Knowledge: Selected Interviews and Other Writings, 1972–1977*, New York: Pantheon Books.

Franklin, S. (1990) 'Deconstructing "desperateness": popular media representations of infertility', in M. McNeil, I. Varcoe and S. Yearley (eds) *The New Reproductive Technologies*, London: Macmillan.

Franklin, S. Lury, C. and Stacey, J. (eds) (1991) *Off-Centre: Feminism and Cultural Studies*, London: HarperCollins Academic.

Frith, S. (1978) *The Sociology of Rock*, London: Constable.

—— (1983) *Sound Effects: The Sociology of Rock*, London: Constable.

—— (1988) *Music for Pleasure. Essays in the Sociology of Pop*, Cambridge: Polity Press.

Frow, J. (1988) 'Repetition and limitation: computer software and copyright law', *Screen*, 29, 1: 4–20.

Gaines, J. (1990a) 'Superman and the protective strength of the trademark', in P. Mellencamp (ed.) *Logics of Television: Essays in Cultural Criticism*, London, British Film Institute.

—— (1990b) 'Introduction: fabricating the female body', in C. Herzog and J. Gaines (eds) *Fabrications: Costume and the Female Body*, London and New York: Routledge.

Garnham, N. (1979) 'Contribution to a political economy of mass-communication', *Media, Culture and Society*, 1: 123–46.

—— (1983) 'Public service versus the market', *Screen*, 24, 1: 6–27.

—— (1985) 'Telecommunications policy in the UK', *Media, Culture and Society*, 7, 1: 7–29.

—— (1990) *Capitalism and Communication: Global Culture and the Ownership of the Image*, London: Sage.

Giddens, A. (1990) *The Consequences of Modernity*, Cambridge: Polity Press.

Gilbert, S. and Gubar, S. (1988) *No Man's Land: The Place of the Woman Writer in the Twentieth Century*, New York: Yale University Press.

Golding, P. Murdock, G. and Schlesinger, P. (eds) (1986) *Communicating Politics. Mass Communications and the Political Process*, Leicester: Leicester University Press.

Gomery, D. (1986) 'Vertical integration, horizontal regulation: the growth of Rupert Murdoch's US media empire', *Screen*, 27, 3–4: 78–86.

Granovetter, M. (1985) 'Economic action and social structure: the problem of embeddedness', *American Journal of Sociology*, 91, 3: 481–510.

Grossberg, L. Nelson, C. and Treichler, P. (eds) (1992) *Cultural Studies*, London and New York: Routledge.

Habermas, J. (1989) *The Structural Transformation of the Public Sphere: An Inquiry into a Category of Bourgeois Society*, trans. T. Burger with F. Lawrence, Cambridge: Polity Press.

Hall, S. (1986) 'Popular culture and the state', in T. Bennett *et al.* (eds) *Popular Culture and Social Relations*, Milton Keynes: Open University Press.

—— (1987) 'Minimal selves', in L. Appignanesi (ed.) *The Real Me: Postmodernism and the Question of Identity*, London: ICA.

Hall, S. and Jefferson, T. (eds) (1976) *Resistance Through Rituals: Youth Subcultures in Postwar Britain*, London: Hutchinson.

Haraway, D. (1991) *Simians, Cyborgs and Women: The Reinvention of Nature*, London: Free Association Books.

Harvey, D. (1989) *The Condition of Postmodernity: An Enquiry Into the Origins of Cultural Change*, Oxford: Basil Blackwell.

Haug, W.F. (1986) *Critique of Commodity Aesthetics: Appearance, Sexuality and Advertising in Capitalist Society*, trans. R. Bock, Cambridge: Polity Press.

Heath, S. (1982) *The Sexual Fix*, London: Macmillan.

—— (1990) 'On screen, in frame: film and ideology', in T. Bennett (ed.) *Popular Fiction: Technology, Ideology, Production, Reading*, London and New York: Routledge.

Hebdige, D. (1988) *Hiding in the Light: On Images and Things*, London and New York: Routledge.

Heller, A. and Feher, F. (eds) (1986) *Reconstructing Aesthetics: Writings of the Budapest School*, Oxford: Basil Blackwell.

Hepworth, M. and Robins, K. (1988) 'Whose information society? A view from the periphery', *Media, Culture and Society*, 10, 3: 323–43.

Hirsch, F. (1976) *The Social Limits to Growth*, Cambridge, Mass.: Harvard University Press.

Hirsch, P.M. (1972) 'Processing fads and fashions: an organisation-set analysis of cultural industry systems', *American Journal of Sociology*, 77, 4: 639–59.

—— (1978) 'Production and distribution roles among cultural organisations: on the division of labour across intellectual disciplines', *Social Research*, 45, 2: 315–30.

Hirst, P. and Kingdom, E. (1979/80) 'On Edelman's *Ownership of the Image*', 20, 3–4: 135–41.

Hood, S. (1967) *A Survey of Television*, London: Heinemann.

Hunter, I. (1992) 'Aesthetics and cultural studies', in L. Grossberg *et al.*, (eds) *Cultural Studies*, London and New York: Routledge.

Huyssen, A. (1986a) *After the Great Divide. Modernism, Mass Culture and Postmodernism*, London: Macmillan.

—— (1986b) 'Mass culture as Woman: modernism's other', in T. Modleski (ed.) *Studies in Entertainment. Critical Approaches to Mass Culture*, Bloomington and Indianapolis: Indiana University Press.

Innis, H.A. (1950) *Empire and Communications*, Oxford: Oxford University Press.

—— (1951) *The Bias of Communication*, Toronto: University of Toronto Press.

Irigiray, L. (1985) *This Sex Which Is Not One*, translated by C. Porter and C. Burke, Ithaca: Cornell University Press.

Jacobus, M. Fox Keller, E. and Shuttleworth, S. (eds) (1990) *Body Politics: Women and the Discourses of Science*, London and New York: Routledge.

James, L. (1973) *Fiction for the Working Man*, Harmondsworth: Penguin.

Jameson, F. (1984) 'Postmodernism, or the cultural logic of late capitalism', *New Left Review*, 146: 55–92.

Jardine, A. (1985) *Gynesis: Configurations of Women and Modernity*, Ithaca and London: Cornell University Press.

Jhally, S. (1982) *The Codes of Advertising. Fetishism and the Political Economy of Meaning in the Consumer Society*, London: Frances Pinter.

Johnson, R. (1983) 'What is cultural studies anyway?', Stencilled Paper, no. 74, Centre for Contemporary Cultural Studies, University of Birmingham.

Joyrich, L. (1990) 'Critical and textual hypermasculinity', in P. Mellencamp (ed.) *Logics of Television: Essays in Cultural Criticism*, London, British Film Institute.

Kabbani, R. (1986) *Europe's Myths of Orient: Devise and Rule*, London: Pandora.

Kaplan, E.A. (1987) *Rocking Around the Clock. Music, Television, Postmodernism and Consumer Culture*, London: Methuen.

Kent, N. (1991) *Naked Hollywood: Money, Power and the Movies*, London: BBC Books.

Kermode, K. (1991) Review of *In Bed with Madonna*, Vox, August: 102.

Kerr, P. (ed.) (1986) *The Hollywood Film Industry*, London: Routlege & Kegan Paul.

King, B. (1985) 'Articulating stardom', *Screen*, 26, 5: 27–50.

Krauss, R. (1988) *The Originality of the Avant-Garde and Other Modernist Myths*, Cambridge, Mass.: MIT.

Kroker, A. and Cook, D. (1986) *The Postmodern Scene: Excremental Culture and Hyper-Aesthetics*, New York: St Martin's Press.

Lacan, J. 'The meaning of the phallus', in J. Mitchell and J. Rose (eds) *Feminine Sexuality and the Ecole Freudienne*, New York: Norton.

Lange, D. (1982) 'Recognizing the public domain', *Law and Contemporary Problems*, 44, 4: 147–78.

LaPlace, M. (1987) 'Producing and consuming the woman's film: discursive struggle in *Now Voyager*', in C. Gledhill (ed.) *Home is Where the Heart Is: Studies in Melodrama and the Woman's Film*, London: British Film Institute.

Laqueur, T. (1976) 'The cultural origins of popular literacy in England, 1500–1858', *Oxford Review of Education*, 2, 3: 255–75.

Lash, S. (1990) *Sociology of Postmodernism*, London and New York: Routledge.

Lash, S. and Friedman, J. (eds) (1992) *Modernity and Identity*, Oxford: Basil Blackwell.

Lash, S. and Urry, J. (1987) *The End of Organised Capitalism*, London: Polity Press.

Lash, S., Abercrombie, N., Lury, C. and Shapiro, D. (1990) 'Flexible specialization in the culture industries', unpublished paper.

Leiss, W., Kline, S. and Jhally, S. (1986) *Social Communication in Advertising: Persons, Products and Images of Well-Being*, London: Methuen.

Lewis, J. (1990) *Art, Culture and Enterprise: The Politics of Art and the Cultural Industries*, London and New York: Routledge.

Locksley, G. (1986) 'Information technology and capitalist development', *Capital and Class*, 27: 81–107.

Lovell, T. (1983) 'Writing like a woman: a question of politics', in Barker, F., Hulme, P., Iverson, M. and Loxley, D. (eds) *The Politics of Theory*, Colchester: University of Essex.

—— (1987) *Consuming Fiction*, London: Verso.

Lunn, E. (1985) *Marxism and Modernism: An Historical Study of Lukacs, Brecht, Benjamin and Adorno*, London: Verso.

Lury, C. (1990) 'The advertising industry', unpublished paper.

Lury, K. (1990) 'Madonna and the three 'P's: parody, postmodernism and pleasure', unpublished paper.

Lusted, D. (1991) 'The glut of the personality', in C. Gledhill (ed.) *Stardom: Industry of Desire*, London and New York: Routledge.

Lyotard, J-F. (1984) *The Postmodern Condition: A Report on Knowledge*, Manchester: Manchester University Press.

McCabe, C. (1986) *High Theory/Low Culture. Analysing Popular Television and Film*, Manchester: Manchester University Press.

McCabe, C. and Stewart, O. (eds) (1986) *The BBC and Public Service Broadcasting*, Manchester: Manchester University Press.

MacKinnon, C. (1987) *Feminism Unmodified: Discourse of Life and Law*, Cambridge, Mass.: Harvard University Press.

McQuail, D. (1989) *Mass Communication Theory: An Introduction*, London: Sage.

Martin, B. (1981) *A Sociology of Contemporary Cultural Change*, Oxford: Basil Blackwell.

Mattelard, A. (1979) *Multinational Corporations and the Control of Culture*, Brighton: Harvester Press.

Mattelard, A. Delcourt, X. and Mattelard, M. (1984) *International Image Markets: In Search of an Alternative Perspective*, London: Comedia.

Mellencamp, P. (ed.) (1990a) *Logics of Television: Essays in Cultural Criticism*, London: British Film Institute.

—— (1990b) 'TV time and catastrophe, or *Beyond the Pleasure Principle* of television', in P. Mellencamp (ed.) *Logics of Television: Essays in Cultural Criticism*, London: British Film Institute.

Melody, W.H. (1987) 'Telecommunications policy directions for the technology and information services', in R. Finnegan *et al.* (eds) *Information Technology: Social Issues. A Reader*, London: Hodder and Stoughton.

Miege, B. (1979) 'The cultural commodity', *Media, Culture and Society*, 1, 3: 297–311.

—— (1987) 'The logics at work in the new cultural industries', *Media, Culture and Society*, 9, 3: 273–89.

—— (1989) *The Capitalization of Cultural Production*, New York: International General.

Modleski, T. (1982) *Loving with a Vengeance: Mass-produced Fantasies for Women*, London and New York: Routledge.

—— (1986a) 'Femininity as mas(s)querade: a feminist approach to mass culture', in C. McCabe and O. Stewart (eds) (1986) *The BBC and Public Service Broadcasting*, Manchester: Manchester University Press

—— (ed) (1986b) *Studies in Entertainment. Critical Approaches to Mass Culture*, Bloomington and Indianapolis: Indiana University Press.

Moers, E. (1977) *Literary Women*, London: W.H. Allen.

Moi, T. (1991) 'Appropriating Bourdieu: feminist theory and Pierre Bourdieu's sociology of culture', *New Literary History*, 22, 4: 1017–51.

Morse, M. (1985) 'Talk, talk, talk', *Screen*, 26, 2: 2–15.

—— (1990) 'An ontology of everyday distraction: the freeway, the mall and television', in P. Mellencamp (ed.) *Logics of Television: Essays in Cultural Criticism*, London: British Film Institute.

Mulgan, G.J. (1991) *Communication and Control: Networks and the New Economies of Communication*, Cambridge: Polity Press.

Mulvey, L. (1975) 'Visual pleasure and narrative cinema', *Screen*, 3, 16: 6–18.

—— (1989) *Visual and Other Pleasures*, London: Macmillan.

Murdock, G. (1980) 'Authorship and organisation', *Screen Education*, 35: 19–34.

Murdock, G. and Golding, P. (1982) 'Large corporations and the control of communications industries', in M. Gurevitch *et al.* (eds) *Culture, Society and the Media*, London and New York: Routledge.

Muscio, G. (1989) 'Mass images of consumption', *Quarterly Review of Film and Video*, 11: 121–5.

Myers, K. (1986) *Understains: The Sense and Seduction of Advertising*, London: Comedia.

Nead, L. (1988) *Myths of Sexuality: Representations of Women in Victorian Britain*, Oxford: Basil Blackwell.

Nelson, C. and Grossberg, L. (eds) (1988) *Marxism and the Interpretation of Culture*, London: Macmillan.

Nicholls, B. (1988) 'The work of culture in the age of cybernetic systems', *Screen*, 29, 1: 22–48.

Nicholson, L.J. (ed.) (1990) *Feminism/Postmodernism*, London and New York: Routledge.

Novek, E., Sinha, N. and Gandy, O. (1991) 'The value of your name', *Media, Culture and Society*, 12, 4: 525–43.

Ong, W. (1982) *Orality and Literacy: The Technologizing of the Word*, London: Methuen.

Owens, C. (1983) 'The discourses of others: feminists and post-modernism', in H. Foster (ed.) *The Anti-Aesthetic: Essays in Postmodern Culture*, San Francisco: Bay Press.

Oyama, S. (1985) *The Ontogeny of Information: Developmental Systems and Evolution*, Cambridge: Cambridge University Press.

Parker, R. and Pollock, G. (1981) *Old Mistresses: Women, Art and Ideology*, London: Routlege & Kegan Paul.

—— (eds) (1987) *Framing Feminism: Art and the Women's Movement 1970 – 1985*, London: Pandora.

Partington, A. (1991) 'Melodrama's gendered audience', in S. Franklin, C. Lury and J. Stacey (eds) (1991) *Off-Centre: Feminism and Cultural Studies*, London: Harper Collins Academic.

Peterson, R.A. and Berger, D.G. (1975) 'Cycles in symbol production: the case of popular music', *American Sociological Review*, 40: 158–73.

Piore, M. and Sabel, C. (1984) *The Second Industrial Divide*, New York: Basic Books.

Pollock, G. (1989) *Vision and Difference: Femininity, Feminism and the Histories of Art*, London and New York: Routledge.

Porter, V. (1979/80) 'Film copyright and Edelman's theory of law', *Screen*, 20, 3–4: 141–7.

—— (1983) 'The context of creativity: Ealing Studios and Hammer Films', in J. Curran and V. Porter (eds) *British Cinema History*, London: Weidenfeld.

—— (1989) 'The re-regulation of television: pluralism, constitutionality and the free market in the USA, West Germany, France and the UK', *Media, Culture and Society*, 11, 1: 5–27.

Punter, D. (1986) *Introduction to Cultural Studies*, London: Longman.

Radnoti, S. (1986) 'Mass culture', trans. F. Feher, in A. Heller and F. Feher (eds) *Reconstructing Aesthetics: Writings of the Budapest School*, Oxford: Basil Blackwell.

Radway, J. (1987) *Reading the Romance: Women, Patriarchy and Popular Literature*, London: Verso.

—— (1992) 'Mail-order culture and its critics: the Book-of-the-Month Club, commodification and consumption, and the problem of cultural authority', in L. Grossberg *et al.* (eds) *Cultural Studies*, London and New York: Routledge.

Rich, A. (1980) 'Compulsory heterosexuality and lesbian existence', *Signs: Journal of Women in Culture and Society*, 5, 4: 631–60.

Riley, D. (1988) *Am I That Name?: Feminism and the Category of 'Women' in History*, London: Macmillan.

Riviere, J. (1929) 'Womanliness as masquerade', *The International Journal of Psychoanalysis*, 10; reprinted in H.M. Ruitenbeek (1966) (ed.) *Psychoanalysis and Female Sexuality*, New Haven: College and University Press.

Robins, K. and Webster, W. (1986) 'Broadcasting politics – communications and consumption', *Screen*, 27, 3–4: 30–46.

—— (1987) 'Dangers of information technology and responsibilities of education', in R. Finnegan *et al.* (eds) *Information Technology: Social Issues. A Reader*, London: Hodder and Stoughton.

Rodden, J. (1989) *The Politics of Reputation: The Making and Claiming of 'St George' Orwell*, Oxford: Oxford University Press.

Rojek, C. (1985) *Capitalism and Leisure Theory*, London and New York: Routledge.

Russo, J. (1986) 'Female grotesques: carnival and theory', in T. de Lauretis (ed.) *Feminist Studies/Critical Studies*, Basingstoke and London: Macmillan.

Said, E.W. (1985) *Orientalism*, London: Penguin.

Saunders, D. (1988) 'Copyright and the legal relations of literature', *New Formations*, 4: 125–43.

Savage, J. (1990) 'Tainted love: the influence of male homosexuality and sexual divergence on pop music and culture since the war', in A. Tomlinson (ed.) *Consumption, Identity and Style: Marketing, Meanings and the Packaging of Pleasure*, London and New York: Routledge.

Scannell, P. (1986) '*Radio Times*: the temporal arrangements of broadcasting in the modern world', paper presented to International Television Studios Conference, London.

Scott, A. (1988) *New Industrial Spaces*, London: Pion.

Sepstrup, P. (1989) 'Implications of current developments in West European broadcasting', *Media, Culture and Society*, 11, 1: 29–54.

Shapiro, D. (1990) 'The television industry', unpublished paper.

Shapiro, D. Abercrombie, N. Lash, S. and Lury, C. (1992) 'London's culture industries: a case of vertical disintegration', in H. Ernste (ed.) *Regional Development and Contemporary Industrial Response: Extending Flexible Specialisation*, London: Belhaven Press.

Shevelow, K. (1989) *Women and Print Culture: The Construction of Femininity in the Early Periodical*, London and New York: Routledge.

Silverstone, R. Hirsch, E. and Morley, D. (1990) 'Information and communication technologies and the moral economy of the household', CRICT Discussion Paper, Brunel University.

Simmel, G. (1990) *The Philosophy of Money*, D. Frisby (ed.) London and New York: Routledge.

Sinclair, J. (1987) *Images Incorporated: Advertising as Industry and Ideology*, Beckenham: Croom Helm.

Slater, D. (1987) 'On the wings of the sign: commodity culture and social practice', *Media, Culture and Society*, 9, 4: 457–80.

Smith, A. (1972) *The Politics of Information: Problems of Policy in Modern Media*, London: Macmillan.

—— (1976) *The Shadow in the Cave: The Broadcaster, the Audience and the State*, London: Quartet Books.

—— (1987) 'Telecommunications and the fading of the industrial age: information and the post-industrial economy', in J. Curran *et al.* (eds) *Impacts and Influences. Essays in Media Power in the Twentieth Century*, London: Methuen.

Smythe, D. (1982) *Dependency Road: Communications, Capitalism, Consciousness and Canada*, New Jersey: Ablex.

Sola Pool, I. de (1987) 'Electronics take command', in R. Finnegan *et al.* (eds) Finnegan *et al.*, (eds) *Information Technology: Social Issues. A Reader*, London: Hodder and Stoughton.

Sontag, S. (1987) *Against Interpretation and Other Essays*, London: André Deutsch.

Spallone, P. and Steinberg, D. (eds) (1987) *Made to Order: The Myth of Reproductive and Genetic Progress*, New York: Pergamon.

Sparks, C. (1988) 'The popular press and political democracy', *Media, Culture and Society*, 10, 2: 209–23.

Spencer, J. (1989) *The Rise of the Woman Novelist: From Aphra Behn to Jane Austen*, Oxford: Basil Blackwell.

Spigel, L. (1990) 'Television in the family circle: the popular reception of a new medium', in P. Mellencamp (ed.) *Logics of Television: Essays in Cultural Criticism*, London: British Film Institute.

Spivak, G. (1987) *In Other Worlds*, London: Methuen.

Stacey, J. (forthcoming) *Stargazing: Hollywood Cinema and Female Spectatorship in 1940s and 1950s Britain*, London and New York: Routledge.

Stanworth, M. (ed.) (1987) *Reproductive Technologies: Gender, Motherhood and Medicine*, Cambridge: Polity Press.

Stinchcombe, A.L. (1959) 'Bureaucratic and craft administration: a comparative study', *Administrative Science Quarterly*, 4: 168–87.

Suleiman, S. Rubin (1990) *Subversive Intent: Gender, Politics and the Avant-Garde*, Cambridge, Mass.: Harvard University Press.

Sutherland, J.A. (1978) *Fiction and the Fiction Industry*, London: University of London.

Taylor, C. (1989) *Sources of the Self: The Making of the Modern Identity*, Cambridge: Cambridge University Press.

Thompson, J.B. (1990) *Ideology and Modern Culture: Critical Social Theory in the Era of Mass Communication*, Cambridge: Polity Press.

Timpanaro, S. (1980) *On Materialism*, trans. L. Garner, London: Verso.

Touraine, A. (1971) *The Post Industrial Society: Tomorrow's Social History*, London: Random.

Tuchman, G. (1982) 'Culture as resource: actions defining the Victorian novel', *Media, Culture and Society*, 4, 1: 3–18.

Tuchman, G. with Fortin, N.E. (1989) *Edging Women Out: Victorian Novelists, Publishers and Social Change*, London and New York: Routledge.

Tunstall, J. (1970) *Media Sociology: A Reader*, London: Constable.

—— (1983) *The Media in Britain*, London: Constable.

Turner, B.S. (ed.) (1990) *Theories of Modernity and Postmodernity*, London: Sage.

Turner, G. (1990) *British Cultural Studies: An Introduction*, Boston: Unwin Hyman.

Urry, J. (1990) *The Tourist Gaze*, London: Sage.

Veblen, T. (1925) *The Theory of the Leisure Class: An Economic Study of Institutions*, London: Allen and Unwin.

Viera, J.D. (1988) 'Images as property', in L. Gross, J.S. Katz and J. Ruby (eds) *Image Ethics. The Moral Rights of Subjects in Photographs, Film and Television*, New York: Oxford University Press.

Ward, K. (1989) *Mass Communications and the Modern World*, London: Macmillan.

Watt, I. (1957) *The Rise of the Novel: Studies in Defoe, Richardson and Fielding*, London: Chatto and Windus.

Weed, E. (ed.) (1989) *Coming to Terms*, London and New York: Routledge.

Wernick, A. (1991) *Promotional Culture: Advertising, Ideology and Symbolic Expression*, London: Sage.

Widdowson, I. (1982) *Re-reading English*, London: Methuen.

White, H. and White, C. (1965) *Canvasses and Careers*, New York: John Wiley.

Williams, R. (1974) *Television: Technology and Cultural Form*, London: Fontana/Collins.

—— (1980) *Problems in Materialism and Culture*, London: Verso.

—— (1981) *Culture*, Glasgow: Fontana.

—— (1984) *The Long Revolution*, Harmondsworth: Penguin.

—— (1985a) *Culture and Society, 1780–1950*, Harmondsworth: Penguin.

—— (1985b) *Towards 2000*, Harmondsworth: Penguin.

—— (1989) 'Culture is ordinary', *The Guardian*, 3 February.

Williamson, O. (1987) *The Economic Institutions of Capitalism*, New York: Free Press.

Willis, S. (1991) *A Primer for Daily Life*, London and New York: Routledge.

Wilson, E. (1991) *The Sphinx in the City*, London: Virago Press.

Winship, J. (1987) *Inside Women's Magazines*, London: Pandora.

Wolff, J. (1983) *Aesthetics and the Sociology of Art*, London: Allen and Unwin.

—— (1985) 'The invisible *flâneuse*: women and the literature of modernity', *Theory, Culture and Society*, 2, 3: 37–46.

—— (1990) *Feminine Sentences: Essays on Women and Culture*, Cambridge: Polity Press.

Wolff, J. and Seed, J. (eds) (1988) *The Culture of Capital: Art, Power and the Nineteenth Century Middle Class*, Manchester: Manchester University Press.

Women's Studies Group, Centre for Contemporary Cultural Studies (1978) *Women Take Issue: Aspects of Women's Subordination*, London: Hutchinson.

Zukin, S. (1988) *Loft Living: Culture and Capital in Urban Change*, London: Radius.

NAME INDEX

SUBJECT INDEX